belonged to

received 1917

Karen Gusler

small
voices

OTHER BOOKS

By Josef and Dorothy Berger

DIARY OF AMERICA

By Josef Berger

POPPO

BOWLEG BILL

CAPE COD PILOT

IN GREAT WATERS

small voices

by
Josef & Dorothy
Berger

PAUL S. ERIKSSON, INC.
New York

© Copyright 1966 by Josef & Dorothy Berger.
All rights reserved. No part of this book may
be reproduced in any form without permission
of the Publisher, Paul S. Eriksson, Inc., 119
West 57th Street, New York, N.Y. 10019.
Published simultaneously in the Dominion of
Canada by Fitzhenry & Whiteside, Ltd., On-
tario. Library of Congress Catalog Card Number 66-26648. Designed by Arouni. Manu-
factured in the United States of America by
The Haddon Craftsmen, Inc., Scranton, Pa.

To
Melanie Morris

Preface

"Gosh! What d'ya want to keep a diary for?" He picked up a windfall from under the apple tree and shied it at a listening squirrel. "What d'ya put in it?"

"Whatever I like," she said. "You're in it."

"Who, me?" He shook his head. These women! "Well, I know one thing—I'll never keep a diary."

"Why not? It's fun. Try it and you'll see."

"Nope. Too many things I don't want anybody to know."

"But you don't have to let anybody see it, so I don't see why you say that."

From the worldliness of twelve years he smiled down at her. " 'Cause part of my life is secret and the rest of it's nothing."

Maybe he has a point there. But sometimes secrets need to be told, even if only to one's self. Getting them off to a diary is safer—if they are secrets—than trusting somebody else. After all, who is Dear Diary?

So reasoned Anne Frank, whom we are saving for another anthology, to do with the diaries of teen-agers. In her diary Anne wrote, "I hope I shall be able to confide in you completely, as I have never been able to do in anyone before, and I hope you will be a great support and comfort to me." Along with heartbreak, Anne's diary brought "great support and comfort" to a sick world, something she had never dreamed of doing. Among the hazards of keeping a diary—and the delights of reading one—is the revelation of so very much more than its creator intends.

After examining the output of many hundreds of diarists, young and old, we knew we wanted to put together a book of the secrets of children, for others to share as we have. Early on, we knew it in our hearts. It took a few more years to get it through our heads.

Here we have the uninstructed exercise of a child's free will. Few writings of children come out that way. Mostly they are school compositions, assigned; or thank-you notes or other obligatory letters; or show-off stuff—the first two and a half pages of great novels—everything but the spontaneous confiding of a young mind, unmotivated except to spill itself. This is rare. We think it is worth trying to get our hands on.

For kindnesses that have helped to make this book possible, we owe thanks to more parents, educators, editors, and children than we can mention. In this, as in past works, we were given much necessary assistance by public libraries and those who work in them, historical societies and special manuscript collections in many cities of this country and Great Britain. For their most valuable advice and encouragement we are grateful to Prof. Saul Benison, Department of History, Graduate Faculties, Brandeis University, and Miss Judith Shapiro.

Josef and Dorothy Berger

Brooklyn Heights
June 20, 1966

Contents

TABLE OF CONTENTS

TABLE OF CONTENTS

TABLE OF CONTENTS

In the wildwood a shudder
To the touch of the breeze,
A choir of small voices
Among gray trees,
This frail fresh murmur,
The breathing of grass,
This roll of pebbles
As breakers pass,
This sleepy sighing,
This plaintive ado,
This anthem pulsing
While soft falls the dew—
Is it the crying
Of me and you?

—Paul Verlaine

small
voices

"I feel different from everybody."

Anaïs Nin
[Age 11]

Many persons who attain greatness have kept diaries, but not many diaries can be called great. One, now coming to light, clearly bears the stamp. When the first volume of the diary of Anaïs Nin was published in the spring of 1966, the praises of the critics bore out the judgment of a small group of leading writers who had read parts of it in manuscript and had been talking about it for years as one of the major personal chronicles to come out of our time. "One of the most remarkable journals in the history of letters," wrote one reviewer, and another: "A great book, a new and beautiful kind, shining a strange light on literature itself." Novelist Henry Miller, who describes Anaïs Nin as "a luminous being," believes her diary "will take its place beside the revelations of St. Augustine, Petronius, Abelard, Rousseau and Proust."

Miller's esteem of Miss Nin's work—in addition to the diary she has written eleven novels and a collection of short stories—is shared by such perceptive minds as Edmund Wilson, William Carlos Williams and Tennessee Williams. These works, says Mr. Wilson, "mix a sometimes exquisite poetry with a homely realistic observation." As Anaïs Nin describes her own writing, the theme is "the quest of self through the intricate maze of modern confusions," and this search also runs through her diary.

Anaïs Nin was born in Paris. "At the age of eleven I decided to become a creative writer—that is, one who makes his own laws and forms—and I will confess that in my first novel, written at that age, I followed my painfully and carefully printed name with: 'Member of the French Academy.'"

Also when she was eleven, her world fell apart when her father, Joaquin Nin, a Spanish composer of music, deserted his family. His wife took their three children to America. Anaïs worshiped her father. Now in the helplessness of childhood to withstand the full impact of such a blow, she clung to the adored image. Coming over on the boat she began her diary as a way of addressing her thoughts to him and of sustaining the hope within herself that somehow, some day, they would reach him and bring him back to her. In America, time couldn't steal the image from her. Two years later she was writing, "In my eyes my father has the beauty, the proud and magnificent beauty of my dreams." And again—to him—"There is an emptiness, a void in our life which only you could fulfill."

At 13 she was trying hard to explain the mystery of herself. "Is there anyone who will understand me? I do not understand myself. Time does nothing to my com-

panions in school. For me each day is a novelty, and it seems to me that my character changes every day. Even if I wear the same dress, it seems to me that I am not the same girl . . . My dear Diary, it is Anaïs who is speaking to you, and not someone who thinks as everybody should think. Dear Diary, pity me, but listen to me."

At 15 she was exceptionally beautiful. She quit school to work as a fashion mannequin and artist's model. For two years she supported her mother and two brothers. She became a professional dancer, but had to give it up because of ill health. She studied psychiatry, then went back to her first love, the writing of fiction.

But throughout that time she faithfully kept her diary. It grew on her with the years. In the drama of her life it became an intrusive alter ego, an understudy that refused to keep its place and at times broke onstage with her. When friends would tell her she was spending too much time on it, she would agree that it was "my hashish, my opium pipe," and sometimes she would turn upon it as a living thing, accusingly, and write in it, "You have hampered me as an artist."

Nevertheless, she took it with her everywhere, writing, writing, in the realization that for her, this was the way of capturing "the air of truth which cannot be imparted if it is not in the first casting." In a recent lecture before a writers' conference she said, "It is important to keep a notebook. First because it puts you at ease with writing. It is informal. Then, because the keeping of notes becomes a discipline, like sketching for the artist. It was while keeping notebooks that I discovered how to capture the living moment."

The first published installment of the diary of Anaïs Nin, covering the four years 1931-1934, is a small part of the 150 manuscript volumes that make up the record to date. It does not include the following entries which she made as a child and which, up to now, have never been published in book form.

November 19, [*age 11*] I write here many things I never tell anyone. Today when I opened a book at hazard, I read: "Life is only a sad reality." Is it true? Perhaps! I have never discussed this. Today I want to know, and even though my diary is dumb, I will ask: Is it true? Oh, if anyone asked me this on my dark, sad days when I was thinking of father—oh, I would certainly say yes, but that is all. Certainly I have not suffered yet—I am only eleven, and I cannot say; I must wait longer before I can answer this question.

Though my curiosity is not satisfied, I resign myself to talk about other things. When I see a beggar, I want to be rich, merely to help him. I ask myself, how is it possible there should be beggars with so many rich men on earth? Only it is true, many rich men don't give. If I could only give, give! With this idea I gathered all my toys to give to the chapel.

I don't know what is wrong with me. I confess, that question—is life only a sad reality?—occupies my mind. Silly idea! No doubt I have many silly notions, many crazy ones. I know. I admit it. Just the same—I want to know.

January 11. I work hard at school, but that does not prevent me from doing what I prefer to do.

I have written a story, <u>Poor Little</u> One. I only love either very gay or very sad things. I hate school, and everything about this new life in this big city. Mother asked me why. Why? Why? Because I love silence, and here it is always noisy; because everything here is somber, shut in, severe, and I love gay landscapes. I love to see the sky, to admire the beauty of nature, and here the houses are so tall, so tall one does not see anything. If you do catch a little corner of the sky, it is neither blue nor pink nor quite white—no, it is a black sky, heavy, lugubrious, soiled by the pride and vanity of modern men and women.

I say this because I hate the modern. I would have loved to live in the first century, in Ancient Rome; I would have loved to live in the time of great castles and gracious ladies; I would have loved the time of Charlotte Corday, when any woman could become a heroine.

I must recognize that I am crazy, but since my diary is destined to be that of a mad woman, I cannot write reasonable things in it! And they would not be my thoughts.

February 3 How beautiful it is now! It has snowed for days, so hard that all the streets and houses are white in spite of the furious work of human beings to take it all away. Even the sky has taken part in this feast of pure color, and now I love it. But it will last so little, because the snow is being chased away, and the sky will be in mourning again. Everybody pushes it away except the children.

In the classroom, we open the windows when the teacher has her back turned, and we run and fight to catch the snowdrops, and when one of us catches one you see a face blossom into a beautiful smile. I had caught several when the teacher, jealous of our joy, rolled angry eyes, and closed the window. Then all the children went back to their desks, but more determined than ever to come back to the snow some time. I am going to dream about snow and birds, which I love so much.

February 27. I must tell about a singular dream I had last night. I found myself in a grand salon, carpeted in dark gray. I was seated on a small chair which smelled of pine. Then a fine lady dressed in black velvet and wearing a belt of diamonds or something sparkling rushed towards a grand piano on which she played a long, sad melody. It made me sad. Then she stopped, went to a big easel, took a brush, and began to paint. She painted a somber woods, with a pale blue sky in the distance. In one minute she was through. Then she advanced towards a big desk, and taking up a pen and a big book, her big eyes looking at me and then at the sky, she began to write. She wrote pages and pages. I could see they were big and beautiful poems, full of charm, tenderness and sweetness. I could not read them but I feel sure they were beautiful. Then she closed the book, laid down the pen, and came silently towards me. And then I heard this word: Choose.

Oh, how much I hesitated! First I remembered the beautiful melody, then I suddenly turned towards the easel—it was so beautiful—and with a paintbrush I could describe the sweet and charming landscapes, all the beauty of nature. But suddenly I turned towards the big desk, loaded with books. An invisible force led me towards that corner. Involuntarily I seized the pen. Then the lady, smiling, came to me and gave me a big book, saying, "Write. I will guide you." Without any difficulty I wrote things which I think were beautiful. Pointing to a corner where men with venerable beards, as well as queens and pretty ladies were writing without pause, the lady said, "Your place is there."

As soon as the lady was gone, I softly put down the book. I went towards the piano. I wanted to try it. First my fingers went very well. I liked what I was playing. But suddenly I had to stop. I did not know any more. Then, looking at the piano, sadly I thought: I cannot. Then I tried to paint again. My landscape was already pretty, but I stopped and saw that big smudges spoiled the whole thing, and then I said, "Adieu, I don't want this."

Then I took up the pen again, and I began to write without stopping.

My dream was very long, but it seems so strange, I want to tell it so as to be able to reread it. Mother is calling me. I wish I could dream this way again.

May 12. I would like that nobody should ever know me. I would like to live isolated and alone. I envy the lives of those souls who can feel such peace, such sweetness in solitude. In one of my stories I uncover the sweetness of this solitude which everybody fears. Why? Because they are sick, and blind.

There is one thing which troubles me. I feel different from everybody. I notice no child in my class of my age thinks as I do. They are all alike, they are in accord. I

9

know their thoughts, their ambitions. And I make comparisons. I am altogether different. Instead of being like brothers to me, they are strangers. My desires, my dreams, my ambitions, my opinions, are different. Why am I not like everybody?

Glancing over this notebook, I said to myself, "Yes, these are my thoughts, but they are contrary. Am I what is called an eccentric, an "original" as the French say? Must I be looked upon by the world as a curiosity? Certainly I do not seek to contradict what people think, and still, when I reread these pages, I think my feelings are contrary to what is called happiness. When I reread these pages I like to be able to say, "This is a special story. Does it matter if no one understands? Am I writing for the world? No. My language is unknown. What a joy it will be if I am overlooked! Then my treasures will belong to me alone. When I die I will burn these pages and my thoughts scribbled here will live only in eternity with the one who expressed them!"

But of course, if someone should understand, if someone should hear this contradictory language, these novel impressions, I would be very happy indeed.

Mother has visitors. I have opened the window to breathe the night air. The young face of Miguel appears in my mind, and he seems to look at me with sympathy. I begin to think about him. I remember the first moment when my aunt introduced us. He leaned down and took my hand with a smile. He said to my aunt, "She is pretty." He seemed sincere. It is the first time anyone has said this of me in my presence. What is this passion which moves me? I remember the words of a song: "Fly, fly, young girls, away from love!"

I got 93½ at school. But Pauline got 94, and even if I am a foreigner, that is not good enough.

"I am tired of only me to play with."

Mary Scarborough Paxson

[1872-1948]

Even with an older sister, Mary Paxson, at eight years, found herself wishing at times that she had "a twin sister just my age." With only two years between them, Mary and Maggie did many things together. But Maggie wasn't always around, and besides, there are some things—like letting a little mouse out of a trap when nobody is looking—that eights don't tell tens. But what a pity that this "twin" hiding in the blank pages of a notebook didn't demand that Mary continue writing through the nearly three-score and ten years of her life that remained, instead of dropping it, as she did, after three years.

The Paxsons came from England to Pennsylvania in

11

*1682, the same year that William Penn did. Mary's fa-
ther, like Paxsons before him, was a Quaker. He was an
astute dealer in real estate and postmaster of the town of
Carversville.*

*Mary lived to be 76. She never married, nor, when she
was "grone up," did she carry out a promise to "make
books like Louisa Alcott does," nor take up any other
career. But another kind of promise, left unstated in the
diary but sparkling in every line of it, was fulfilled. Mrs.
Paul Niemeyer, librarian of the Bucks County Historical
Society, tells us, "The people with whom I have talked
who knew her all describe her as a charming gentle-
woman."*

We could gave guessed that.

January 15, 1880. i got laughed at in school today and i
dident like it, the teacher asked me what is the smallest
fur berring annimal and i said a catterpiller and i ought
to say a mouse and i dont care a catterpiller is littler than
a mouse and it has fur on it.

January 16. mama says I mustent forget to make cappital
eyes when I mean me.

February 7. Maggie and I went to the librerry and we got
little women to read, we love the books that Louisa Alcott makes. when I am grone up I am going to make
books like Louisa Alcott does.

February 21. I am eight years old today. mama gave me
a book and that is the most I got, Maggie gave me a
bottle of colone and papa gave me a little pocket book
with 25 cents in it, that is the most money I ever had all
at once before.

March 21. I let a little mouse out of the trap today, nobody saw me do it.

June 18. Maggie and I went fishing today and we got our feet soking wet, we dident catch any fish only one bull frog and we dident know what to do with it. so we cut the line, and it was an awful wicked thing to do to let it go with the fish hook fast in its stummick. we were afraid to take it off of the hook. Maggie said it was my bull frog because I caught it and I said it was her bull frog because she told me to dangel the worm in front of it.

October 7. It is Maggie's birthday and she is ten years old and she is fat and I am lean.

October 15. I had to wipe dishes for our girl tonight, Mama says its the only way to learn how and I dont care if I dont learn how.

December 25. It is Christmas and its another holliday that dident come on a school day. They dont any hollidays ever come any more only on Saturdays and Sundays and they are hollidays anyway.

February 1, 1881. I like all my lessons but mental arithmetic. I like my dolls only I havent any real nice ones any more. I have only five and there is something the matter with all of them. I want a new one terribly bad but Mama says I must be patient, thats what you have to wait for til your Mothers and your Fathers get ready.

February 14. Today is valentine day, I dont know why but it is, and Maggie got a valentine and so did I. Maggie's has two burds and they look as if they are going to bite each other. Mine has two hearts and a stick run through them to keep them together like the bucher fixes schewers in meat.

February 21 and I am nine years old today it is my Birthday thats why, and tomorrow is George Washingtons Birthday only he is not living and I am. He died of laryngittis and I have had it twice and never died yet.

March 1. I have had a sore throat so stayed home from school. I want Maggie to come home. I am tired of only me to play with. I made some poetry today and it is beautiful I think and so does Mama think so too, here it is

> *Little Robin Red-breast*
> *Sing away with glee*
> *Go and build your nest*
> *Away up in a tree,*
> *Then hatch your eggs of blue*
> *Up in your nest so high*
> *And soon your babies new*
> *Will learn how to fly.*

March 4. Here are some words I must fix right, isn't, can't, evry.

Papa says Garfield our new president is to be ennagurated today, he gets it done in Washington where he has to live because he was made a president thats why.

Beths eyes fell in her head today and now I can't play with her ever again. I do want a doll so bad with real hair and shoes and stockings. Anna and Meg and Jo look bad but I just can't play with Beth without eyes.

April 30. Papa gave me a new doll because I worked a puzzle he said I couldent work that's why. It has wax hair and painted shoes. I do want a baby with real hair and real shoes but Ime very glad to have this one. I named her Eleanor after nobody.

June 11. Maggie is going to be a doctor when she is grone up and I am going to keep house and sew and cook but not wipe dishes.

August 28. We made bows and arrows and the first thing I did when I shot my arrows was to brake a window pane, because my arrow went the wrong way. Mama says its the safest to shoot right up in the air and thats just what I was doing when the window got smashed.

September 12. There was a arora bory alice tonight.

February 25. Maggie and I went to the store today and got candies. Mine was a red soljier toy candy and so was Maggies and I named mine Ben Shaw, he was my Uncle and Maggie named hers Abrum Linkum and he was shot too like President Garfield was, and we had to change the names of our candy men because I didn't want to eat my Uncle and Maggie didn't want to eat Mr. Abrum Linkum so she named her soljier Jefferson Davis and I named mine Benny Dick Arnuld, two men that ought to be eat and we ate them up heads first.

October 19. I wish I had a twin sister just my age.

March 2, 1884. I haven't any more pages because I tore them out because I needed paper once and I guess I won't write any more diarys. Goodbye.

"I hope God heard it in spite of all the noise."

"Dirk Van Der Heide"

[*Born 1929*]

He was a sturdy Dutch boy with straight taffy-colored hair that fell over his forehead, mild blue eyes, and a smile that quickly lit up his rather solemn face. He had been keeping a diary for three years. One afternoon in his room in a suburban home near Rotterdam he chewed at a pencil and read over as much as he had done of a composition about Erasmus. He wasn't satisfied, didn't think his teacher would be either, and fretted because it was due tomorrow.

Tomorrow never came—not the taken-for-granted tomorrow of a boy whose only cares were homework and the normal unreasonableness of parents and the nuisance of a tagalong little sister. On the night of May 9, 1940, that kind of world ended. Five straight days of blitzkrieg turned the city into a bombed-out shambles.

Few diarists are historians trained to the conscious

task of picking out what seems meaningful in the day-to-day spinning of a chaotic world. But diaries are the first draft of history. He who keeps one slips into a debt to his time, a sense of the need for a written record when something big is doing. Come hell or high water—both of which came to Rotterdam—his pen races on. Perhaps that is why the American publishing house that got hold of this diary only a few months after the dreadful days it describes rushed it into print with the comment, "It remained for a boy of twelve to make the most moving document that has come out of the horror of modern war. Only the mind of a boy could record events in the purity of their immediate impact."

Dirk van der Heide was not his real name. All names in the book were changed to conceal the identity of his father and other relatives from the Nazi army that had overrun Holland. A quarter of a century later, we tried to learn who "Dirk" was and what had become of him since he was brought to America. Nothing remained in the files of the publisher, and the editor in charge of the book had died. We wrote to half a dozen organizations in Holland. We tried to locate the translator and other persons, however remotely connected, who might know something. Our search yielded nothing. But the diary from which these excerpts are taken is, we think, yield enough.

May 10, 1940. Something terrible happened last night. War began! Before daylight I woke up. I could hear explosions and people were shouting and running under our windows. Mother rushed in, in her dressing gown,

17

and told me to put on my coat and come quickly. Father had Keetje in his arms. We hurried across the street to the Baron's and went down into his air-raid shelter. There were great flames shooting into the sky, and beams from the searchlights, and the sirens were going very loud. Voices on the radio sounded strange and terribly excited.

Father put Keetje into Mother's arms and went away. A few minutes later he came back, dressed and carrying a gas mask and knapsack. He kissed Mother and Keetje and me very hard and then hurried out. Mother said, "I must go to the hospital." She promised to come back as soon as she could.

In a little while the bombs began to fall. I held Keetje's hand and she squeezed mine until it hurt. Once the cellar seemed to rock back and forth, and the Baron said, "That was close." The radio said 1,500 people had been killed in Rotterdam since 3 A.M. The bombing we thought lasted hours was over in 27 minutes.

Tonight it started again. Mother came home on a bicycle. She looked tired and white-faced.

May 11. The worst air raid of all has just come. About half the houses on our street are gone. Mevrouw Hartog broke down and yelled and got everyone nervous. I think she almost went crazy. Heintje Klaes was killed when he went out to look. We put our fingers in our ears but it didn't help much.

The fire wagons are working outside now and half the people in the shelter have gone out, including Uncle Pieter. I went out for a while and they were taking dead people out of the bombed houses. Uncle Pieter sent me back.

There is a strange smell in the air like burnt meat and a strange yellow light from the incendiary bombs. Three men were killed trying to move away a bomb that hadn't gone off. One was our postmaster and I loved him very much. It is awful to watch the people standing by their wrecked houses. They don't do much. Our house wasn't hit but the street in front of it is just a great big hole and the cobblestones are thrown up on our lawn. It doesn't look as if there ever was a street there. Mother is going to be surprised when she sees it.

Twelve people on our street were killed and I knew every one of them but I knew Heintje Klaes best. Mevrouw Klaes has been crying. Some people prayed all the time and some sang the national anthem and some just sat and stared. Jan Klaes is Mevrouw Klaes's other son and he is fighting somewhere as my father is.

I said a prayer for Father and I hope God heard it in spite of all the noise. Uncle Pieter has gone off to the hospital to find Mother. It is getting late and I think he is worried. But I know he will find her.

Poor little Keetje doesn't know what is happening. I think I do, and it is worse than anything I ever heard about and worse than the worst fight in the cinema. The ambulances coming and going, and so many dead people, make it hard for me not to cry. I did cry some while the bombing was going on, but there were so many other little children there that I don't think anyone noticed me.

Later. Uncle Pieter came back. He didn't find Mother because she is dead. I can't believe it but I know Uncle Pieter wouldn't lie. We aren't going to tell Keetje yet.

The ambulances are still screaming. I can't sleep or write any more now or anything.

May 12. I can't believe Mother is dead and that we will never see her again. Mother was killed when the hospital was bombed. I cried almost all night and I am ashamed of what I did in front of everybody. After Uncle Pieter told me about Mother getting killed I tried to run away from him. I tried to get out into the street to fight the Germans. I don't know everything I did. I think I was crazy. I was all right until the bombs started to fall around midnight and then I couldn't stand it. I know I yelled and kicked and bit Uncle Pieter in the hand, but I don't know why. I think I was crazy.

We are in Dordrecht now. It has been a terrible day. Dordrecht is only a few miles from our home. Usually it takes a half-hour. It took us six hours to get here in Uncle Pieter's car. We left home at ten o'clock this morning. I almost cried again, and Keetje did because Mother didn't come to say goodby. Our house never looked prettier than when we drove away, in spite of the smashed windows. I hope we don't have to stay away long.

The road out of Rotterdam was full of people going south to get away from the bombing. There were all kinds of people, rich and poor, walking and riding. Some of the children were being carried and some were pushed along in baby carriages piled up with food and blankets and things like that.

About three o'clock some German planes came over. Five of them dived down toward the road. We thought they were falling, but they shot at us with machine guns. We all got under the car. Other people threw themselves on the ground and into roadside ditches. Soldiers tried to shoot the pilots. The planes kept going back and forth above us, very low and loud, and then suddenly they went south.

There was great confusion after they left. A young woman sat by the roadside in front of us, holding her head and groaning. There was blood coming out of her head and a hole in the side. It made me sick. About fifty people were wounded and many were killed. All the way down the road we saw wounded people and people just lying still in the road. It was awful. Many children were crying.

After many more hours of driving they reached the Dutch seaport at Vlissingen. Uncle Pieter, described by the boy as "rich," managed to get passage on the steamer to Harwich, England. From there he took the children by rail to London.

May 15. Uncle Pieter has just come back with terrible news. Holland has surrendered to the Germans. It is all in the papers. Uncle Pieter is almost crying. I wonder where Father is. I wonder how the Baron and all our friends are. There was a dreadful bombing in Rotterdam today. The English newspaper says one-third of the city was destroyed.

July 3. We are on the boat now. We sailed yesterday, some time after dark, for America. It was hard to leave Uncle Pieter. He kissed us many times and hugged us very hard. Uncle Klaas will meet us in New York.

September 28. I have not written in my dairy for so long

—not since I got to America. Uncle Klaas and Aunt Helen met us. Aunt Helen is an American with long red fingernails and a very pretty face. When we got through customs we drove to Uncle Klaas's apartment. The streets were very exciting. I remember particularly when we crossed one and Uncle Klaas said, "This is Broadway." But sometimes when airplanes go over I want to run and hide.

"... *the awful sweetness of walking with God*"

Esther Edwards

[1732-1755]

Two hundred years ago the Reverend Jonathan Edwards of Northampton, Massachusetts, was known far and wide for scaring the members of his congregation half to death—so much so that some of them wondered if the tortures of hell could really be much worse than writhing through a two-hour sermon once a week from the Reverend Mr. Edwards. "The God that holds you over the pit—much as one holds a spider or some loath-

some insect over a fire—abhors you and is dreadfully provoked! He looks upon you as worthy of nothing but to be cast into the flames! You are ten thousand times as abominable in His eyes as the most hateful serpent is in ours! And yet, it is nothing but His hand that holds you from falling into the fire every moment . . ."

Nine-year-old Esther Edwards was not particularly frightened. She dutifully loved the God of her "honored father", and she loved him too. She also tolerated his shortcomings with a humor befitting one far beyond her years. As this diary suggests, the quaint little miss who was one day to become the mother of Aaron Burr had a mind of her own and knew how to speak it—even if it took "large words."

Northampton, Massachusetts, *February 13, 1741.* This is my ninth birthday, and Mrs. Edwards, my mother, has had me stitch these sundry sheets of paper into a book to make me a journal.

January 9, 1742. Mrs. Edwards was 33 years old today. That seems very old. I wonder if I shall live to be thirty-three. [She died when she was 23.] Mrs. Edwards seemed very serious all the day long; as if she were inwardly praying, "Lord, so teach me to number my days that I may apply my heart unto wisdom." Indeed, this she said to us girls when we were trying to practice some birthday frolics on her. And when she came from her devotions her face actually shone, as though, like Moses, she had come down from the Mount. I do not think we girls ever will be so saintly as our mother is. At any rate, we do not begin so. I do not know as I want to be.

February 13. Have just come tripping upstairs from morning worship and the song of the service still follows me. I have been thinking what a singing family the Edwards family is. Mother's voice we have heard in psalms and hymns and spiritual songs ever since our early babyhood. She sang us on our pilgrim way when we were in our cradles. And to all the house her voice is always uplifting like the lark's, as though her soul were mounting up to heaven's shining gate on wings of song. If father ever gets low-spirited from his "humors", as he calls them, her voice is to him like medicine, as David's harp was to King Saul. And when she once begins, there is Sarah and Jerusha and myself, like the ascending heights of an organ, ready to unite in making a joyful noise to the Lord, all over the house, so that our home is more like an aviary than the dwelling of a Colonial parson.

My mother says my journal thus far is rather stilted and mature for me; though everything in the family is mature.

March 6. Have just been caring for my mocking-bird, who is now rewarding me with song. The cat was lurking in the hall and I have just driven her away with a broom with which I have been sweeping the living-room. Though down by the fireside, at twilight, she is my favorite too. And even father, sometimes, while with us after supper, seems to enjoy her purring as he strokes her in his lap. Though I doubt if she has much divinity about her unless it is in her sparks of electricity when she is rubbed the wrong way.

May 1. I have just come back from a wonderful ride with

my honored father, Mr. Edwards, through the spring
woods. He usually rides alone. But today he said he had
something he wanted to show me. The forests between
our house and the full-banked river were very beautiful.
The wild cherry and the dogwood were in full bloom.
The squirrels were leaping from tree to tree, and the
birds were making a various melody. Though father is
usually taciturn or preoccupied—my mother will call
these large words—even when he takes one of us children with him, today he discoursed to me of the awful
sweetness of walking with God in Nature. He seems to
feel God in the woods, the sky, and the grand sweep of
the river which winds so majestically through the woody
silences here.

When we reached the "Indian's Well" I slid off and
brought a birchbark cup of crystal water for father to
drink. But not before I had given myself a great surprise.
For, having put on my mother's hat in sport, the first
reflection in the dark water seemed to be the face of my
mother instead of my own!

June, 1743. My mother has just come into the house with
a bunch of sweet peas and put them on the stand where
my honored father is shaving, though his beard is very
slight. We have abundance of flowers and a vegetable
garden which is early and thrifty. My honored father, of
course, has not time to give attention to the garden, and
so Mrs. Edwards looks after everything there. Almost
before the snow has left the hills, she has it plowed and
spaded by Rose's husband, who does all the hard work
there. She is our colored cook. We hire her services from

one of the prominent people in Father's parish, who owns both her and her husband. That word "owns" sounds strange about people!

Ten years later Esther married President Aaron Burr of Princeton University. She had two children, girl and boy. When her son, who was also named Aaron, was two years old she wrote in her diary:

September 2, 1757. Aaron is a little, dirty, noisy boy, very different from his sister Sally. He begins to talk a little, is very sly, mischievous, and has more sprightliness than Sally. I must say he is handsomer, but not so good-tempered. He is very resolute and requires a good govern to bring him to terms.

Had she herself lived longer, perhaps little Aaron would have been given the kind of "govern" he needed, and American history would have been different. But that same year his father died, and eight months later so did Esther. Aaron Burr grew up to be handsome, "sprightly" and resolute, a man of tremendous personal charm. He was one of the most brilliant young lawyers in America, with hopes of some day becoming President. But the "sly and mischievous" streak persisted too, and in time shadowed his life. His chief troubles began with the famous duel in which he shot and killed his rival in politics, Alexander Hamilton. This wrecked his career. Soon afterwards he was accused of engineering a plot to overthrow the government. President Jefferson had him brought to trial, but the charge was never proved. To this day the argument goes on among students of American history as to whether Aaron Burr was innocent or guilty of high treason.

"In speling I got 100%"

Emily Wortis

[Born 1938]

Emily was seven years old when her grandfather gave her a blank book and asked her to keep a diary. Her father is a well known psychiatrist living in the Brooklyn Heights section of New York. Her mother is a social worker. They decided not to give her any help with the diary—in fact not even to read it unless she gave them permission. She didn't, in so many words; but now and then she would leave it on the hall table, where they would be sure to see it, open at a certain page.

Emily is grown up now, married, has a little daughter, and teaches English at Northwestern University.

October 2, 1945. Sadiday. Today I vomited.

Sunday. The first thing I did was, well I heard a cat's voice do you no we have one? by the way lests go on with our diary I climed down 3 flights of stairs and when I open the door there was a big black cat not ours boy was I mad.

Thursday. Today was assembly in school we saw two plays and slides they were boring. When we came bak our class was being varnished. In the afternoon Joel was supposed to take a seat but he said he wud like to set by me what a day

Saturday. It is Navy day and we went up on a roof and had a perfect view we saw the president and manny other things

Monday. Today four 5 A girls came in our class and three 8 B girls came and two 6 A boys came in. And everyone new me becose I am the president of the class in speling I got 100%.

Saturday, November 5. I played with my pepperdolls.

Sunday. I have skeeped 7 days so it will be very long. Saturday was the Movie Festival for children it was not very good. I was the critic and I said wat I thot. I dont rember any more but Ill try to think abot it and if I rember any more Ill tell you tomoro oh now I rember we went to Shelter Island well nows time for bed good night

Monday. Grandpa and grama came over and Willa came over and Flossie and Amy and Michael and David and Edith came over, and Daddy showed evry slide we have and was very cute about it.

28

Tuesday, December 4. I cant keep track of all the days so maybe I shouldn't right evryday because I have home work and music lessons and guitar lessons and Brownies and manny other things.

January 10, 1946. Wensday. When I came home I rang the bell Daddy ancerd he hid behind the door but I fond him. Goodby. Emily Wortis.

"I did have joy feels all over."

Opal Whiteley
[Born 1897]

In her sixth year Opal was living with the Whiteleys in an Oregon lumber camp. They called her Opal Whiteley. Before that she had lived in far-away places and had been taught many things a child of a poor northwest woodsman could not be expected to know. She had heard wonderful stories about nature, history, myths of antiquity. Then, suddenly there were no more stories. She had been much loved and suddenly there was no more love. How it happened, Opal couldn't tell. Waves . . . a wild

29

sea . . . "we were in the water" . . . a woman's face, disappearing. That much she seemed to remember, fleetingly. And from that time on she spoke of her "angel mother" and "angel father."

The Whiteleys insisted she was their child. While nobody but Opal bothered to contradict them, still it was puzzling. How could she be a Whiteley—this little one who spoke English in such a curious idiom, completely her own, and who, when she couldn't hit on the right word or phrase, resorted time and again to French, a language the Whiteleys had never known? Where had she picked up all those names of old-world nobility? Or that astonishing familiarity with the classics?

And there were other mysteries. The child was given to running off alone in the woods. Too much of the time her eyes were on the blue hills beyond. She talked to trees, befriended animals—not only barnyard pets but wild ones, wood rats, toads, even yellow jackets. She gave them names like Felix Mendelssohn the mouse and Lars Porsena of Clusium the crow. And the tame things followed her about and the wild ones came to her and nestled up to her as if they had forgotten to be wild.

When questions were put to the Whiteleys, they would repeat flatly that Opal was their child. But only that; to further inquiry they were silent.

The child grew up, and then something took place that raised the questions all over again—not in the northwest woods, but in New York, London, Paris, Calcutta. The event was the publication of Opal Whiteley's childhood diary in the Atlantic Monthly *magazine.*

It wasn't an every-century occurrence for the Atlantic
*to give over its very grownup pages to the work of a six-
year-old. But before its readers finished the first page of
the diary they were no longer surprised. This was not the
work of a six-year-old; it was the tumbling, dancing,
sparkling outpouring of one of the most joyous minds
ever to express itself at any age. It was one long haunting
love song of a lover of earth in rhythms no singer had
ever used before, a token of return for the love of every
fern and flower, every velvety little thing that lived and
scurried through the woods.*

*Like everything else about Opal, the story of her diary
is difficult to believe and impossible to disprove. It begins
with her first year in Oregon. In her sprawling print she
covered every scrap of paper she could find in the house
or beg from the neighbors. When Opal was twelve years
old a foster-sister, in a sudden fit of anger, tore the manuscript into little pieces. But Opal collected them—
literally hundreds—packed them up and hid them away.*

*In September, 1919—she was 22 then—she sat in the
Boston office of one of the foremost editors of his time,
Ellery Sedgwick of the* Atlantic Monthly. *She had brought
in a manuscript, a book about nature. Sedgwick wasn't
interested. What did interest him was the personality of
the author and the answers she gave when he began to
question her about herself. Had she, by any chance, ever
kept a diary?*

*On hearing about her childhood jottings, Sedgwick
telegraphed to Los Angeles, where the fragments were
stored. They were shipped to Boston. Opal was taken*

into the home of Sedgwick's mother-in-law, and there, for the next several months, she worked at putting the torn bits of paper together. They were pasted on sheets, transcribed, and edited. The only changes were corrections of spelling and a necessary minimum of punctuation.

With what emerged, Sedgwick was enchanted. So were critics and readers by the thousands who followed the tiny adventures of Opal serially in the Atlantic or later in book form. "One of the most striking human documents of the times," said the New York World. The London Daily Telegraph: "Every true lover of children will read it spellbound." The London Times: " . . . the most complete picture of a child's inner life that can be imagined." Letters poured in from around the world, many over famous signatures. A few readers were bewildered or skeptical. No one could deny the diary was a marvelous piece of writing. But how could a little child have done it?

There might have been more doubters had Ellery Sedgwick not been known as a man of integrity and an extremely knowledgeable editor; had he not examined the manuscript at first hand and closely watched its restoration; and had he not declared, "I have no doubt that the original diary of Opal Whiteley is entirely genuine. I took endless pains to establish her story."

But the best answer to any doubt, we think, is the diary itself. How could a little child have written it? How could anyone but a little child have written it!

Another question could not be answered so easily. Who was Opal Whiteley? Opal had an answer, but it only *drew around her a deeper fog. Her real name, she said, was Francoise Marie de Bourbon-Orleans, and she was a princess, the daughter of Henri, Prince of Orleans, an explorer who died in Saigon in 1901; and a great-great granddaughter of Louis Philippe, last of the Bourbon kings of France. On her mother's side, she said, she was related to Her Royal Highness the Maharana of Udaipur, India.*

The claims, of course, were put down to childish fancy. But Opal stuck to her story. How did she know? Because one of her foster-grandmothers had told her she was not a Whiteley and then had revealed her real parentage. Her story was not shrugged off by everybody. In fact, the very persons who might have known most about it acted as if they were inclined to take it very seriously indeed. The mother of the late Prince Henri —Opal's paternal grandmother if the story was true— was living in London and invited Opal to visit her, and then paid for a trip to India so that Opal could meet the relatives she claimed there. Opal was accepted into the royal house of Udaipur and stayed there ten months. She had a letter on stationery of the Maharana which greeted her as "my dear daughter."

Since these disclosures were made, magazine articles and books have been published about Opal Whiteley and who she was—or wasn't. Enough remains both of certainty and doubt to justify the prediction that the mystery will never be cleared up.

In this book, what matters is not how well-born Opal Whiteley may have been, or how unwell-born, but how very well indeed she could write at the age of six. And of that, which is the greatest mystery of all, we have no doubt whatever.

Today the folks are gone away from the house we do live in. I sit on our steps and I do print. I like it—this house we do live in being at the edge of the near woods. So many little people do live in the near woods. I do have conversations with them. Back of the house are some nice wood rats. The most lovely of them all is Thomas Chatterton Jupiter Zeus. By the woodshed is a brook. It goes singing on. Its joy song does sing in my heart. Under the house live some mice. I give them bread scraps to eat. Under the steps lives a toad. He and I—we are friends. I call him Lucian Horace Ovid Virgil.

Between the ranch house and the house we live in is the singing creek where the willows grow. We have conversations. And there I do dabble my toes beside the willows. I feel the feels of gladness they do feel.

Near unto the road, long ways between the brooks, are ranch houses. I have not knowing of the people that do dwell in them. But I do know some of their cows and horses and pigs. They are friendly folk. Around the ranch houses are fields. When the mowers cut down the grain they also cut down the cornflowers that grow in the fields. I follow along after and I do pick them up. Of some of them I make a guirlande. I do put it around the neck of William Shakespeare. He does have appreciations. As we go walking down the lane I do talk to him about the one he is named for. And he does have understanding. He is such a beautiful gray horse and his ways are the ways of gentleness. Too, he does have likings like the likings I have for the hills that are beyond the fields and where the trails and tall fir trees like the wonderful ones that do grow by the road.

The other road does lead to the upper logging camps. It goes only a little way from the ranch house and it comes to a riviere. Long time ago this road did have a longing to go across the riviere. Some wise people did have understandings and they did build it a bridge for it to go across on. It went across the bridge and it goes on and on between the hills—the hills where dwell the talking fir trees. By its side goes the railroad track. Its appears are not so nice as the appears of the road, and it has got only a squeaky voice. But this railroad track does have shining rails. They stretch away and away like a silver ribbon that came from the moon in the night. I go a-walking on these rails. I get off when I do hear the approaches of the donkey engine.

Thomas Chatterton Jupiter Zeus [the wood rat] has been waiting in my sunbonnet a long time. He wants to go on explores. Too, Brave Horatius [shepherd dog] and Isaiah [plain dog] are having longings in their eyes. And I hear Peter Paul Rubens [pig] squealing in the pen. Now I go. We go on explores.

While I was taking water in the jug to the men in the field, from her sewing basket Lars Porsena of Clusium [crow] took the mamma's thimble and she didn't have it and she couldn't find it. She sent me to watch out for it in the house and in the yard and everywhere. I know how Lars Porsena of Clusium has a fondness for collecting things of bright colors; so I ran to his hiding-place in the old oak tree. There I found the mamma's thimble. But she said the pet crow's having taken it was as though I had taken it because he was my property. So I got a spanking with the hazel switches that grow near unto our back steps. Inside me I couldn't help feeling she ought to have given me thanks for finding the thimble.

Afterwards I made little vases out of clay. I put them in the oven to bake. The mamma found my vases of clay. She threw them out the window. When I went to pick them up they were broken. I felt sad inside. I went out to talk things over with Michelangelo Sanzio Raphael. He is that most tall fir tree that grows just back of the barn. I scooted up the barn door. From there I climbed on to the lower part of the barn roof. I walked up a ways. Up there I took a long look at the world about. One gets such a good wide view of the world from a barn roof. After, I looked looks in four straight ways and four corner ways. I said a little prayer. I always say a little prayer before I jump off the barn into the arms of Michelangelo Sanzio Raphael, because that jump is quite a long jump. Today when I did jump I did land right proper in that fir tree. It is such a comfort to nestle up to Michelangelo Sanzio Raphael when one is in trouble. He has an understanding soul.

After I talked with him and listened unto his voice I slipped down out of his arms. I intended to slip into the barn corral but I slid off the wrong limb in the wrong way. I landed in the pig-pen on top of Aphrodite, the mother pig. She gave a peculiar grunt. It was not like those grunts she gives when she is comfortable.

I felt I ought to do something to make up to her for

having come into her home out of the arms of Michelangelo Sanzio Raphael instead of calling on her in the proper way. I decided a good way to make it up to her would be to pull down the rail fence in that place where the pig-pen is weak, and take her for a walk. I went to the woodshed. I got a piece of clothesline rope. While I was making a halter for the mother pig, I took my Sunday-best hair ribbon—the blue ribbon the Uncle Henry gave to me. I made a bow on that halter. I put the bow just over her ears. That gave her the proper look. When the mamma saw us go walking by, she took the bow from off the pig. She put that bow in the trunk. Me she put under the bed.

By and by—some long time it was—she took me from under the bed and gave me a spanking. After she did it she sent me to the ranch house to get milk for the baby. I walked slow through the oak grove, looking for caterpillars. I found nine. Then I went to the pig-pen. The chore boy was fixing back the rails I had pulled down. His temper was quite warm. He was saying prayer words in a very quick way. I went not near unto him. I slipped around near Michelangelo Sanzio Raphael. I peeked in between the fence rails. Aphrodite was again in the pigpen. She was snoozing, so I tiptoed over to the rain barrel by the barn. I raise mosquitoes in the rain barrel for my pet bats. Aristotle eats more mosquitoes than Plato and Pliny eat.

Just as I was going to knock on the back door for the milk, I heard a voice on the front porch. It was the voice of a person who has an understanding soul. I hurried around to the front porch. There was Sadie McKinzie with a basket on her arm. She beamed a smile at me. I went over and nestled up against her blue gingham apron with cross stitches on it. The freckles on Sadie Mc-Kinzie's wrinkled face are as many as the stars in the Milky Way, and she is awful old—going on forty. Her hands are all brown and cracked like the dried-up mud puddles by the roadside in July, and she has an understanding soul. She always has bandages ready in her pantry when some of my pets get hurt. There are cookies in her cooky jar when I don't get home for meals, and she allows me to stake out earthworm claims in her backyard.

She walked along beside me when I took the milk home. When she came near the lane she took from her basket wrapping-papers and gave them to me to print upon. Then she kissed me goodbye upon the cheek and went her way to her home.

After the mamma had switched me for not getting back sooner with the milk she told me to fix the milk for the baby. I sit here on the doorstep printing this. The baby is in bed asleep. The mamma and the rest of the folks is gone to the ranch house. When they went away she said for me to stay in the doorway to see that nothing comes to carry the baby away.

By the step is Brave Horatius. At my feet is Thomas Chatterton Jupiter Zeus. I hear songs—lullaby songs of the trees. The back part of me feels a little sore but I am happy listening to the twilight music of God's good world. I'm real glad I'm alive.

Today I do sit here at my desk while the children are out for play at recess time. I sit here and I do print. I cannot have goings to talk with the trees that I do mostly have talks with at recess time. I cannot have goings down to the riviere across the road. I sit here in my seat. Teacher says I must stay in all this whole recess time.

It was after our reading lesson this morning. Then it was teacher did call my name. I stood up real quick. I did have thinks it would be nice to get a smile from her like the smile she did smile upon Lola. And teacher did ask me eight things at once. She did ask me what is a pig and a mouse and a baby deer and a duck and a turkey and a fish and a colt and a blackbird. And I did say in a real quick way, "A pig is a cochon and a mouse is a mulot and a baby deer is a daine and a duck is a canard and a turkey is a dindon and a fish is a poisson and a colt is a poulain and a blackbird is a merle. And after each one I did say, teacher did shake her head and say, "It is not," and I did say, "It is." When I was all through she did say, "You have them all wrong. You have not told what they are. They are not what you said they are." And when she said that I did just say, "They are—they are—they are."

Teacher said, "Opal, you sit down." So I did. But when I sat down I said, "A pig is a cochon, a mouse is a mulot . . ." Teacher says, "Opal, for that you are going to stay in next recess and both recess times tomorrow and the next day and the next day." Then she did look at all the school and she did say as how my not getting to go out for recess times would be an egg sam pull for all the other children in our school.

They are out at play. It is a most long recess, but I do

know a pig is a cochon and a mouse is a mulot . . . So I
do know for Angel Father always did call them so. He
knows. He knows what things are. Sometimes I do have
lonesome feels. This is a most long recess.

Today the grandpa dug potatoes in the field. Too, the
chore boy did dig. I followed along after. My work was
to pick up the potatoes they got out of the ground. Some
of them were very plump. Some of them were not big.
All of them wore brown dresses. Potatoes are very interesting folks. To some piles I did stop to give geology
lectures, and some I did tell about the caterpillars going
to hiver sleep in silken cradles and some in woolen go.
And all the time I was picking up potatoes I did have
conversations with them. I did tell about my hospital at
St. Germain-en-Laye in the near woods and about all the
folks that were in it and that are in it, and how much
prayers and songs and menthol helps them to have well
feels. And to some other potatoes I did talk about my
friends, about the talks that William Shakespeare and I
do have together and about Elizabeth Barrett Browning
[cow] and the poetry in her tracks. And one I did
tell about the new ribbon Aphrodite [mother pig]
has to wear and how she does have a fondness for chocolate creams. I did tell of the little bell that Peter Paul
Rubens [plain pig] does wear to cathedral service [at
her own "cathedral" in the near woods, not far from her
"hospital"]. I did tell how Louis II, le Grand Conde, is a
mouse of gentle ways and how he does have likings to
ride in my sleeve.

Too, I did have thinks of the potatoes and all their

growing days there in the ground and all the things they did hear. Earth-voices are glad voices and earth-songs come up from the ground through the plants. And in their flowering, and in the days before these are come, they do tell the earth-songs to the wind. And the wind in her goings does whisper them to folks to print for other folks so other folks do have knowing of earth-songs.

I have thinks these potatoes growing here did have knowings of star-songs. I have kept watch in the field at night and I have seen the stars look kindness down upon them and I have walked between the rows of potatoes and I have watched the star-gleams on their leaves. And I have heard the wind ask of them the star-songs the star-gleams did tell in shadows on their leaves. And as the wind did go walking in the field, talking to the earth-voices there, I did follow her down the rows. I did have feels of her presence near. And her goings made ripples on my nightgown. Thomas Chatterton Jupiter Zeus did cuddle more close in my arms and Brave Horatius followed after.

When a little way I was gone from the door, I did look looks about. I saw brown leaves and brown birds. Brown leaves were erable leaves and chene leaves, and the brown birds were wrens. And all their ways were hurry ways. I did turn about and I did go in a hurry way to a root in the near woods. I so went to get my little candle. Then I did go to the Jardin des Tuileries. Often it is I do go there near unto the near woods. Many days after I was here come, I did go to look for Jardin des Tuileries. I found it not. Sadie McKinzie did say there is none such here. Then, being needs for it and it being not, I did have it so. And in it I have put statues of hiver and all the others, and here I do plant plants and little trees. And every little tree that I did plant, it was for someone that was. And on their borning days I do hold services by the trees I have so planted for them.

Today I did go in quick steps to the tree I have planted for Louis Philippe, roi de France, for this is the day of his borning in 1773. I did have prayers. Then I did light my little candle. Seventy-six big candles Angel Father did so light for him, but so I cannot do, for only one little candle I have.

Afterwards I did have thinks about Thomas Chatterton Jupiter Zeus—about his nose, it feels. I went in the way that does go to the hospital. That dear pet rat's nose is getting well. Some way he got his nose too near that trap they set for rats in the barn. Of course when I found him that morning I let him right out of the trap. He has a ward all to himself in the hospital. For breakfast he has some of my oatmeal. For dinner he has some of my dinner. And for supper I carry to him corn in a jar lid. Sadie McKinzie, who has on her face many freckles, and a kind heart, gives me enough menthol to put on his nose seven times a day. And he is growing better. And today, when I was come to the hospital, I took him in my arms. He did cuddle up.

Too, he gave his cheese squeak. That made me have lonesome feels. I can't carry cheese to him any more out of the house we live in. I can't because, when the mamma learned that I was carrying cheese to Thomas Chatterton Jupiter Zeus she said to me while she did apply a kindling to the back part of me, "Don't you dare carry any more cheese out to that rat." But I do carry him into the kitchen to the cheese. I let him sniff long sniffs at it. Then I push his nose back and I cut from the big piece of cheese delicate slices for Thomas Chatterton Jupiter Zeus. This I do when the mamma isn't at home.

Today I did go to the house of Sadie McKinzie. I did go that way so that she might have knowings of the nose-improvements of Thomas Chatterton Jupiter Zeus. When I was most come here he did squeak more of his cheese squeaks. It was hard, having hearing of him and not having cheese for him. I could hardly keep from crying. He is a most lovely wood rat, and all his ways are ways of gentleness. And he is just like the mamma's baby; when he squeaks he does have expects to get what he squeaks for.

I did cuddle him up more close in my arms. And he had not squeaks again for some little time. It was when I was talking to Sadie McKinzie he did give his squeaks. He began and went on and did continue so. I just couldn't keep from crying. His cheese-longings are like my longings for Angel Mother and Angel Father. He did just crawl up and put his nose against my curls. The things I was going to say did go in a swallow down my throat.

Sadie McKinzie did wipe her hands on her blue gingham apron with cross-stitches on it. She did have askings what was the matter with Thomas Chatterton Jupiter Zeus. And I just said, "O Sadie McKinzie, it's his cheese squeak." And she said not a word, but she did go in a

43

quick way to her kitchen. She brought back a piece of cheese. It wasn't a little piece. It was a great big piece. There's enough in it for four breakfasts and six dinners. When Sadie McKinzie did give it to me for him, she did smooth back my curls and she did give me three kisses, one on each cheek and one on the nose. She smiled her smile upon us, and we were most happy, and we did go from her house to the cathedral in the near woods. There I did have a thank service for the goodness of God and the goodness of Sadie McKinzie and the piece of cheese that did bring peace to the lovely Thomas Chatterton Jupiter Zeus.

The man that wears gray neckties and is kind to mice—he and I, we do have knows the fairies walk often in these woods, and when I do have needs of more color pencils to make more prints with, I do write the fairies about it. I write to them a little letter on leaves of trees and I do put it in the moss box at the end of the old log. Then, after they do come walking in the woods and find the letter, they do bring the color pencils and they lay them in the moss box. I find them there and I am happy.

I went to look for the fairies today. I went to the near woods. I hid behind the trees and made little runs to the big logs. I walked along the logs and I went among the ferns. I did tiptoe among the ferns. I looked looks about. I did touch the fern fronds and I did have feels of their gentle movements. I came to a big root. I hid in it. I so did to wait waits for the fairies that come among the big trees.

While I did wait waits I did have thinks about that

letter I did write on the other day for more color pencils that I do have needs of to print with. I thought I would go to the moss box by the old log. I thought I would have goes there to see if the fairies yet did find my letter.

The letter—it was gone. Then I did have joy feels all over. The color pencils—they were come. There was a blue one and a green one and a yellow one. And there was a purple one and a brown one and a red one. I did look looks at them a long time. It was so. nice, the quick way the fairies did bring them.

While I was looking someone did come near the old root. It was my dear friend Peter Paul Rubens. I gave him four pats and showed him all the color pencils. Then I did start to go to the mill by the far woods. Peter Paul Rubens went with me and Brave Horatius came a-following after. All the way along I did feel glad feels and I had thinks how happy the man that wears gray neckties and is kind to mice would be when he did see how quick the fairies did answer my letter and bring the color pencils.

When we were come near the mill by the far woods it was near gray-light-time. The lumber men were on their home way. They did whistle as they did go. Two went side by side, and three came after. And one came after all. It was the man that wears gray neckties and is kind to mice. Brave Horatius made a quick run to meet him and I did follow after. I did have him guess what it was the fairies did bring me this time. He guessed a sugar lump for William Shakespeare every day next week. I told him it wasn't a right guess. He guessed some more. But he couldn't guess right, so I showed them all to him. He was surprised. He said he was so surprised the fairies did bring them this soon. And he was so glad about it. He always is.

I am very happy.

The wind was calling. His calling was to the little wood folk and me. He did call more again. "Come, petite Francoise, go explores." He was in a rush. I raced. Brave Horatius ran. We played tag with the wind.

The wind does have many things to tell. He does toss back one's curls so he can whisper things in one's ear. Today he whispered little whispers about the cradles of moths-to-be that hang a-swinging on the bushes in the woods. I went around to see about it. I looked looks on many bushes. Some brown leaves were swinging from some bushes. No cradles I found.

By and by I came to a log. I climbed upon it. I so did this to to look more looks about. The wind did blow in a real quick way. He made music all around. I danced on the log. It is so much a big amount of joy to dance on a log when the wind does play the harps in the forest. Then I do dance on tiptoe. I wave greetings to the plant-bush folks that do dance all about.

Today a grand pine tree did wave its arms to me. And the bush branches patted my cheek in a friendly way. The wind again did blow back my curls. They clasp the fingers of the bush people most near. I did turn around to untangle them. It is most difficult to dance on tiptoe on a log where one's curls are in a tangle with the branches of a friendly bush that grows near unto the log and does make bows to one while the wind doth blow.

When I did turn to untangle my curls I saw a silken cradle in a hazel branch. I have thinks the wind did just tangle my curls so I would have seeing of that cradle. It was cream with a hazel leaf half-way around it. I put it to my ear and I did listen. It had a little voice. It was not a tone voice. It was a heart voice. While I did listen I did feel its feels. It has lovely ones.

I did hurry in the way that does lead to the house of the girl that has no seeing. I went so she too might know its feels and hear its heart voice. She does so like to feel things. She has seeing by feels.

Today, after she did feel the feels of the cream cradle she asked me what the trees were saying. And I led her in the way that does lead to that grand fir tree Good King Louis VI. And when we were come unto him I did touch his fingertips to her cheek. She liked that. Then we did stand near unto him and I told her of the trees in the night, of the things they tell to the shadows that wander through the woods. She said she didn't think she would like to be a shadow.

And just then she stubbed her toe. She did ask me what that was there near unto her foot. I told her it was a ville I did build there—the ville of St. Denis. I told her there was needs of it being near unto Good King Louis VI for he so loved it. So I builded it there where his branches shelter it and his kindness looks kind looks upon it. And I did tell her about his being on his way to St. Denis when he died. While I builded up again the corner of the abbey I did give explanations about how lovely it is to be a gray shadow walking along and touching the faces of people. Shadows do have such velvety fingers.

We went on to where dwell Alan of Bretagne and Etienne of Blois and Godefroi of Bouillon and Raymond of Toulouse. To each I led the girl who has no seeing and she was glad to know them all. They are grand trees.

As we went our way we did listen unto the voices. And I took all the hairpins that was in her hair out of it. I so did so the wind could blow it back and whisper things into her ears. Today near eventime I did lead the girl who has no seeing a little way into the forest where it was darkness and shadows were. I led her toward a shadow that was coming our way. It did touch her cheeks with its velvety fingers. And now she too does have liking for shadows. And her fear that was is gone.

I have been out in the field that is nearest unto the woods. I have been having talks with William Shakespeare. Today he is not working in the woods with the other horses. He is having a rest day. He was laying down near unto one of the altars I have builded for Saint Louis. He did lay there all the afternoon. Tiredness was upon him.

I gave his nose rubs, and his neck and ears too. And I did tell him poems and sing him songs. He has likes for me to so do. After I did sing him more, sleeps did come upon him. The breaths he did breathe while he was going to sleep, they were such long breaths. And I gave unto him more pats on the nose and pats on the neck. We are chums, William Shakespeare and me. This evening I will come again to wake him. I'll come just before suppertime so he may go in with the other horses to eat his supper in the barn.

I did. Sleeps was yet upon him. He looked so tired lying there. I went up to pet his front leg but it was stiff. I petted him on the nose and his nose it was so cold. I called him but he did not answer. I said, "William Shakespeare, don't you hear me calling?" But he did not answer.

I have thinks he is having a long rest so he will have ready feels to pull the heavy poles tomorrow. I now go goes to tell the man that wears gray neckties and is kind to mice about William Shakespeare having all this rest day and how he has sleeps in the field. Thomas Chatterton Jupiter Zeus is going goes with me. We will wait on the stump by the path he does follow when he comes home from work at eventime.

We are come back. The man that wears gray neckties and is kind to mice did go with us to see William Shakespeare having his long sleep there in the field by the altar of Saint Louis.

Now I do have understanding. My dear William Shakespeare will no more have wakeups again. Rob Ryder cannot give him whippings no more. He has gone to a long sleep—a very long sleep. He just had goes because tired feels was upon him. I have so lonesome feels for him, but I am glad that Rob Ryder cannot whip him now no more.

I have covered him over with leaves. To find enough I went to the far end of the near woods. I gathered them in my apron. Sometimes I could hardly see my way because I could not keep from crying. I have such lonesome feels.

William Shakespeare did have an understanding soul. And I have knows his soul will not have forgets of the willows by the singing creek. Often I will leave a message there on a leaf for him. I have thinks his soul is not far gone away. There are little blue fleurs ablooming where he did lay him down to sleep.

"I discovered all the particulars of this machine."

Richard Barrett
[Born 1813]

It is possible that eight-year-old Richard Barrett's mechanical interests, along with his "lattin", kept him too busy to do much writing. Anyhow, after filling fewer than a dozen small pages, this British lad gave up keeping a diary, and little more is known of him than that he lived in London and was related to the famous diarist and novelist Fanny Burney. In Richard's day, early in the last century, only a small proportion of the houses in London had running water, and rarer still was the home equipped with a water closet. Richard's diary is kept today among a collection of treasured rarities in the New York Public Library.

1821. I got up   dressed   went down stairs at 11 minutes to ten of our Clock   35 minutes to fast   had breakfast went into the garden to get a stick for the frame of a drum. Bottle top impracticable so I went in and learnt my lattin and grumbled all the time   played till dinner was sulky made these verses

> *there was a very little boy*
> *he was his mothers only joy*
> *in every thing he took delight*
> *and very soon he learnt to fight*
> *then he nothing else did do*
> *but go and fight by to and to*
> *and when he came to be a man*
> *so fast you cant think how he ran*
> *and when with running he did die*
> *to Hel or Heaven he did fly*

I got up   rose   dressed   went to breakfast   learnt my lattin   was in a very good humor   broke the water closet   played
I worked   pretended to be asleep   Hetty came and said she would wake me by pulling my toes   I pretending to be dreaming and snoring began kicking and throwing my arms about   Hetty fought with feet and arms   I began kicking violently and kicked her head   Dressed, came down stairs and had breakfast, and went down to see the

plumber mending the water closet and discovered all the
particulars of this machine, and think if it was broken
again I could mend it.

today is 22 of December. got up went down dressed
in the nursery played at marbles in the kitchen with
Hetty went up stairs and when Pappa came down pretended to be learning my lesson

*This, we are sorry to say, is the end of Richard Bar-
rett's diary. The reason we wish he had gone on with it
isn't to learn whether his "discovery" really would have
enabled him to mend the water closet if it were to break
down again, or even whether he may have tested his mas-
tery over "the particulars of this machine" by deliberately breaking it. What does make us wish for more is the
blythe candor that makes for the best diaries but is hard
for most of us to achieve when we write to ourselves.
Here, nipped in the bud, might have been another Pepys.*

"I do wish mother would talk to me."

Euphemia Mason Olcott

[1844-1922]

A desperate little girl, having nobody in the house to listen to her fears, or to reassure her, opened her heart day after day to the blank pages of a diary. That was more than a hundred years ago. After Euphemia Mason Olcott died, the family gave the diary into the safekeeping of the New York Historical Society. There it has lain, unpublished, and except by the librarian, perhaps unread, ever since. Euphemia lived to be nearly 78 years old. She never married.

I wish this journal to be private.

E. M. Olcott

Nyack [New York] *July 29, 1856.* It is now my twelfth birthday and I am going to try once more to keep a journal. God has spared my life another year but I fear I am not thankful enough to Him for it. I trust He will make me more so.

This evening we had a dance and some games and had a very pleasant time.

July 30. We went to a picnic today and had a delightful time. Miss Annie Tallman made us six kinds of cake and fresh biscuit and we had apples and pears and candy and ice-water. When we had finished the water the cows came into the woods and we got some fresh milk.

August 2. After breakfast Annie, Neely [her younger brother] and I took a long walk and then amused ourselves till dinner. We then played store till it was time to dress after which Annie and I took another walk. We have been dancing and playing till now. Nine o'clock. I'm going to bed.

August 10. I heard two very excellent sermons today.

September 14. Today was communion in our church. Oh, how hard it seemed to me to sit alone in the pew with Neely when so many went to commemorate the death of our Savior, and not to be allowed to join them. Dear Savior, make me thy child. May I grow in grace every day and set a good example to all my companions.

October 5. Last Wednesday Emma Thompson came back to school. I was very glad to see her for I love her dearly. I really trust she is one of God's own children from some conversations we have had together. We have commenced our little seasons of prayer and we enjoy them and find them very profitable. As I am not very well I will stop writing now.

October 19. Two weeks since I have written in my journal. I have heard two very good sermons today. One this morning, Dr. Chambers, and one this afternoon from Grandfather. This afternoon when Grandfather was speaking about Christ's love, it seemed to me as if I could not withhold myself from coming forward and professing my love to Him before the world. Oh, I hope mother will let me join at the December communion. I hope too that I may have a good opportunity to converse with her. I was at Katie's yesterday and we had a delightful talk and prayer together. I hope I do not lean too much on her but it seems as if I could not live without her.

November 15. Katie has just gone from here. She was here all day and we had a delightful talk. She tells me that she is often worried and perplexed with fears as to whether she is a true Christian or not. But oh, it seems to me as if she must be one. Besides the talk, we read the fourteenth chapter of John together and also prayed. I think it did us good; at least I am sure it did me. We have resolved to try to pray with true faith that the sermon we will hear tomorrow will be suited to us, and will encourage us to "look to Jesus as the author and furnisher of our faith"—God so help us to do. Amen. In reading we came to that verse, "If ye love me keep my commandments." It seems very strange to me. It seems impossible that I do not love Christ, who has done so much for me; yet I am sure I do not keep His commandments. Perhaps I do not love Him sincerely enough, for I give Him a very small proof of my love.

November 30. I heard a lovely sermon from Dr. DeWitt this morning. The text was, "I am a stranger." As mother says, "the very mood was heavenly." Oh, I have had so many doubts this week as to whether I am a Christian or not. I fear I ought not to have cherished a hope that I am one until I had more fully examined myself. Yet I did try to examine myself every night when I was going to bed. Oh! my mind has no rest. Two weeks from today will be Communion in Fourth Street Church. How I wish I was prepared to join the church. But yet, how very, very dreadful it would be if I were to join unworthily and so drink damnation to myself. Oh, Christ Jesus, will Thou not help me and send Thy Holy Spirit to guide me. How I love dear Katie! (And even now, after my good resolutions, I have been unkind to my brother Neilson and thereby grieved my Heavenly Father.) How much dear Katie helps me along in my Christian progress. What would I do without it.

December 5. Brooklyn. I have heard two beautiful sermons today from Dr. Bethune. I say beautiful, though I did not understand all of the one this morning. This P.M., however, I understood every word and I hope I shall never forget it. The text was, "It is a fearful thing to fall into the hands of the living God." One thing he said impressed me very much. It was, "The apostle Paul does not tell us when we sin against God that we are careless or negligent, but he says that we <u>trample on the Son of God</u>. Every one was moved to tears.

I enjoyed a delightful prayer and conversation with Meta this afternoon.

December 28. I cannot write much tonight as I have a very lame hand but I will try and do my best. I have been twice to church today. Heard two very good sermons.

Anna Suydam is in the city. Of course she is at Katie's. I try not to be jealous but it seems as if she loved Katie so much better than she did me. I have shed many tears about it but I have resolved to do so no longer. I know that Katie loves me and that is a comfort.

Old Mrs. Meyer is dying. Dr. Nielson is very feeble. It makes me feel very sad to see so many old friends dropping into the grave. What a blessing, though, to know that they all trust in Jesus. Oh, if *I* were to be called away, where would I go? To heaven or hell? Oh, what a momentous question! Soon it will be 1857. Oh, where will I be this time next year? Perhaps I will still be living but oh!—perhaps I shall be in eternity. Would to God I knew whether I was a Christian or not.

'Tis a point I long to know
Oft it causes anxious thought
Do I love the Lord or no?
Am I His or am I not?

January 4, 1857. Mrs. Meyer died on Tuesday, the 30th of December and was buried on the very last day of the year. The funeral services were very pleasant. All four of the ministers officiated.

Katie and Anna staid with me last Monday night and we enjoyed pleasant prayer and conversation together. Yet I could not help noticing in the morning the girls were impatient to go, as if my society was not agreeable. If Katie was to see this she would say I was foolish, but I really cannot help it. But I will write no more on this subject.

Uncle Isaac's little baby died yesterday. It was only three and a half months old. It must have suffered terribly for its chest was leeched and blistered.

January 11. I have heard two very good sermons today. Meta was here yesterday to spend the day.

January 14. Today Emma and I took dear Emma Leland down for the first time to pray. It was a very solemn time. Oh, I hope she is going to renounce the world and take up Christ and love and cling to Him and if I have been permitted to be in God's hand the instrument of leading her to do it, I feel as if I could not be half thankful enough.

February 3. I have heard very sad news today. Little Fanny Wyman is to appear on the stage at Burton's Theatre tonight. Oh, such a life as is before her! God preserve her from the snare into which she has fallen.

February 21. I can count in our family during the last two years seven deaths. Oh, what a warning it should be to me! Last night it seemed as if I heard a voice whispering warnings into my ear and telling me to prepare to die. Oh, I wish Katie, dear dear Katie were here to pray with me. By the way, speaking of her, she has felt so melancholy lately. She even doubted my love one day and she also told me that she sometimes feared and felt as if she was going to die soon. May God preserve her life.

February 22. I have heard two very good sermons today.

Yesterday afternoon I bought a little book named "Rules for Holy Living." It has questions in it for every day. The one for today is, "Am I <u>now</u> in the favor of God?" I have thought much about it and have so often found myself sinning and disobeying God's Holy law. Oh, it seems as if I could not be a Christian! Tomorrow if I live, I must have a talk with Katie. I am afraid I lean too much on her, but she has helped me so much! May God bless her.

March 1. Dr. DeWitt preached a most excellent sermon this afternoon. The sermon, I trust, did me much good. For several days I have had a great many doubts and fears. I felt that I was not a Christian and my sins weighed me down. I knew <u>how</u> to come to Christ, that I must come by faith and prayer, yet when I knelt down it seemed as if my sins rose up like a barrier or mountain between me and God, but today when dear Dr. DeWitt was preaching, a light seemed to burst on me and my Savior became very precious to me. Oh, if my peace only lasts! I wish Katie was here to talk and pray with me.

Next Sabbath is communion in our church. Oh, I wish—but it is wrong to wish that I could join, but Mother does not wish it as I am only 12, but oh!—it would be a great satisfaction and delight to sit down at my Master's table.

March 10. I was in Brooklyn from Saturday until this morning and had a very delightful time. I heard two splendid sermons from Dr. Bethune. He said that he thought <u>everyone</u> that felt a desire to join the church should be allowed to do so. Oh, after hearing such sermons I do wonder why <u>I</u> cannot be allowed to join. But I must be patient.

This has been an eventful day for our school. We voted for the May Queen, and Emma Thompson was chosen. She will, I think, make a very pretty queen. She has chosen for crowners Katie Brower and Lou Underhill, and for first maids of honor Maggie Hutton and me.

March 15. When I began my last birthday to keep a journal I hardly thought I would finish it. I have finished that book and commenced another. God only knows whether I will live to finish it. Oh!—I wonder if I am prepared to die. I wish I knew. I feel my sins more than I ever did in my life before. Seems to me that instead of progressing in grace as I ought to, I am worse and worse.

March 29. Father told me tonight "in confidence" that he was not happy, and when I asked him why, he said he "had many troubles and so many reasons" why he should be unhappy. I never felt before that I ought to pray for my parents, but I am going to begin now with God's help never to discontinue it.

April 12. Anna Suydam was in town from Wednesday till Friday. I spent one evening with her at Auntie Brower's, and they wanted me to stay all night, but father would not let me. This was a hard trial of my patience, as we had had no chance to talk on the subject that interests us both the most, but I tried to submit and I hope God helped me. It was especially hard just now, as little Julius has died lately and also Arthur Brown, and it would have been so pleasant for us three, Katie, Anna and I, to talk together about them. But I must not complain.

April 19. I have felt very desponding lately, and I cannot think I am a Christian. Oh, I do wish mother would sometimes talk and pray with me as she used to!

April 25. I think I never realized so fully that Christ has

60

endured all the trials that we have to endure. I wonder if He ever went to school, for it is there that I have the greatest trials to bear.

May 3. On Wednesday I went to see dear Anna Baldwin, determined, God helping me, to have a talk with her. When I went up the steps my heart beat so I could hardly stand, and I was dreadfully afraid she would not be home. But she was, and I had a delightful talk. She asked me if I had lately spoken to mother. I was sorry to be obliged to say no, for I want to talk to her very much, yet somehow I never can start it myself, and mother never does. I think if she knew how much I wanted to, she would.

October 4. Oh, I fear I am backsliding. I am growing, it seems to me, worse and worse every day. I do wish mother would talk to me sometimes—she has not done so since I was very small—if she would write me a little note occasionally, it would be better than it is now.

*"I asked Edward would he like to have children with me
and he acted odd."*

Maggie Owen

[Born 1896]

*Alone in the world was small, spunky Maggie Owen of
Roscommon, Ireland. She lived with her great-aunt Kate
Melody at Castle Rea. At thirteen she was sent to a con-
vent in Paris, and a few years later traveled alone to
America. Maggie married a United States Army officer,
had a son, and took to writing. The boy, Thomas Wadelton, liked to write too. At thirteen he turned out a very
funny little book entitled* My Mother Is a Violent
Woman.

*While living with her great-aunt at Castle Rea, Maggie
kept a diary.*

January 24, 1908. This is me birthday, and I was given
this book for a present, and a gold sovereign along with

it, a prayer book also that I have too many of. I am twelve years of age.

[Undated, as are most of her entries.] Tonight is a beautiful night and moonlighted. I looked out the window for long in meditation. Aunt sent me here in punishment for losing me temper and getting me eye blacked in a fight. Tis hard to be a noble character when they pick on me. Aunt says I'm too big a girl to fight but I doubt if I'd got off with only one black eye had I been smaller.

Aunt says tis shamed she is because Vincent's mother sent over a note saying Vincent was on the broad of his back with the hurt I put on him and maybe he'll have the doctor to him. Twas Vincent gave me me the black eye. He sneaked up behind me with a cold pig's tail and dropped it down me back and away with him and I after him. I caught him up and licked the porrige out of him. I got the eye and me drawers were torn off me almost on a hedge. I larruped him well.

I took a long walk over the hill. Some lads cast stones at a poor dog and he tried to hide from them. I was going to strike them with a stick I had along with me but remembered I'm not to fight. So I spoke to them sweetly with reason. They stopped their casting stones at the dog and cast them at me.

February 1. Tis leap year. Leap year is when a lady can ask the hand of a gentleman in marriage without being forward. I used to think a knight in armor would ride up on a white horse and bear me off in marriage to an enchanted castle. No one wears armor these days.

I'd like to marry a tall handsome man that had jet

black hair and a kindly nature. He should have a mustache, no doubt, and they stylish, though I don't like the taste much. I don't think money special but I'd like him to be a landed gentleman and have a lake with white swans and a boat that I could sit in under a lace parasol and drag me hands in the water. Some lilies in it too.

There is a new boy in the town visiting his uncle. He is an English boy. His name is Edward. He wears golf breeches with tassels to them at the knees, and fancy stockings. He has skinny legs. He was long sick. It may well be twas the sickness made him skinny. His father is a British soldier in India. He is a fine boy but he talks funny. Bess [servant at Castle Rea] says he talks as if he'd a mouthful of buttermilk and she doesn't like him at all. I think him fine. His uncle brought him to call, and Aunt says he has beautiful manners. I am poor mannered. I slopped me tea on me good wool frock and was colded afterwards. Aunt says tis no wonder the British think us barberryians.

This was a long day. Before tea Edward came over with his uncle. We played at jackstraws. I like Edward fine. It may well be that I'll marry him, do his legs fill out. As he gets to the age of proper breeches they'll not show. I expect it may well be we could keep our secrets from each other.

Edward thinks it would be nice to be married to me but says I'll have to go to live in India as he's to be an army officer the like of his father. I am an adventurous child and would like to go off all the time. I would like to come back to visit with a long gowen I'd have to hold up when I got out of the kerrege, and with a fine silk petticoat that would rustle, and a veil. Wouldent I cut a dash just!

I asked Edward would he like to have some children with me and he acted odd.

Today I was off to Edward's for tea. His uncle is a full-fleshed man and gay. I've been there oft before but today was different because of Edward. I had on me green silk frock and Bess said for God's sake be careful, did I mess it she'd have the blame of it. She put wool drawers on me because me silk frock is thinner than the wool frock I wear, and she's fearsome of a cold for me as she'd be blamed for that also. I wished she hadent put the drawers on me. It dident feel so much the like of a party as they itched me. I bore the itching with Christian fortitude.

Edward took me for a long walk by the water before our tea and we talked of serious matters. Edward would like to marry me but he is a Protestand and I a Catholic and we cant see how it can be come over. Neither of us will budge an inch.

We had real China tea in great English cups, and the Major held his cup with both hands. I did it also and found it was easier to drink. I like Edward's uncle, a bachelor retired. He said, You're to be a beauty, Marget. Ged!—you are a beauty right now! I wish I knew what <u>Edward</u> thinks of me.

Today I rode alone with Crofty [Castle Rea stable-
man.] We met Edward and his uncle near to home and
they rode back along with us for tea. It was very exciting.

Two days running I've seen Edward. I think I have deep
love for Edward. I don't know have I or not, but there is
no one that would not laugh me down did I ask them.

I told Edward of the diary and he wanted to see it. I'll
show him the bits I think best and nothing about himself.
Edward appears handsome in his boots. His legs don't
show skinny.

My heart is full of Edward. I'm fearful I love him. I
asked sister Mary-Bernard [her tutor] what would
happen to the soul of one that would marry a Protestand
and she closed her eyes like it hurt her. She said to get on
with me tasks. I expect they would be damned forever in
hell. It may well be I could have some fun before I was
damned.

I think I'll pray for Edward's conversion so I can
marry him. I'll tell him first; tis sneaking to pray behind
one's back. I love Edward with all me heart. I want to be
a noble woman for him and have him for me nine children's father. I think nine a fine number. Had I a sister or
brother I'd be a happy one. Bess thinks tis what makes
me an odd child, being lone as I am.

"As far as the eye can reach . . . nothing but wagons."

Sallie Hester

[*Born 1837*]

In 1849 Craven P. Hester had no need of more money than he was earning as a leading lawyer in Bloomington, Indiana. When he and his family hit the teeming California Trail, it was not for any gold that might lie at the end of it. His wife Martha was a chronic invalid. Perhaps the air and sunshine of the vast open country would do for her what the doctors couldn't. On the chance, the Hesters picked up bag and baggage, left forever the life and friends they had known, and joined the great procession of covered wagons rolling westward. Twelve-year-old Sallie Hester did what hundreds of other Forty-Niners were doing—took along a diary in which to record the great adventure, for her children and grandchildren to read—that is, in case she made it. She closed her diary on October 5, 1871, the day she was married.

Bloomington, Indiana, *March 20, 1849*. Our family, consisting of father, mother, two brothers and one sister, left this morning for that far and much talked of country, California. Our train numbered fifty wagons. The last hours were spent in bidding goodby to old friends. My mother is heartbroken over this separation of relatives and friends. Giving up old associations—for what? Good health, perhaps. The last goodby has been said, the last glimpse of our old home on the hill, and wave of hand at the old Academy with a goodby to kind teachers and schoolmates, and we are off.

New Albany, *March 24*. This is my first experience of a big city. We have been several days reaching it on account of the terrible conditions of the roads. Our carriage upset at one place. All were thrown out but no one was hurt. My mother thought it a bad omen and wanted to give up the trip.

March 26. Took the steamboat *Meteor* this evening for St. Joe [St. Joseph, Missouri, starting point for many wagon trains making the overland trip.] Now sailing on the broad Ohio, toward the far west.

April 14. On the Missouri River, the worst in the world, sticking on sandbars most of the time. Our boat struck another sandbar and was obliged to land passengers ten miles below St. Joe. Having our carriage with us, we were more fortunate than others. We reached the first day an old log hut five miles from town where we camped for the night. Next day an old friend of my father heard of our arrival and insisted that we stay at his home.

SALLIE HESTER

St. Joe. *April 27.* Here we are at last, safe and sound, laying in supplies and waiting our turn to be ferried across the river. As far as the eye can reach, so great is the emigration, you see nothing but wagons. [An estimated 80,000 persons reached California in 1849, probably 55,000 overland.] This town presents a striking appearance—a vast army on wheels—crowds of men, women, and lots of children, and last but not least the cattle and horses upon which our lives will depend.

May 21. Camped on the beautiful Blue River, 215 miles from St. Joe, with plenty of wood and water and good grazing for cattle. Our family all in good health. When we left St. Joe my mother had to be lifted in and out of our wagons. Now she walks a mile or two without stopping and gets in and out of the wagons as spry as a young girl! She is perfectly well. We had two deaths in our train within the past week of cholera—young men going west to seek their fortunes. We buried them on the banks of the Blue River, far from home and friends.

We are now in the Pawnee Nation—a dangerous and hostile tribe. We are obliged to watch them closely and double our guard at night. They never make their appearance during the day, but skulk around at night, steal cattle and do all the mischief they can. When we camp at night we form a corral with our wagons and pitch our tents on the outside, and inside of this corral we drive our cattle, with guards stationed on the outside of the tents.

We have a cooking stove made of sheet iron, a portable table, tin plates and cups, cheap knives and forks (best ones packed away) and camp stools. We sleep in our wagons on feather beds. The men who drive for us

69

sleep in the tent. We live on bacon, ham, rice, dried fruits, molasses, packed butter, bread, coffee, tea and milk as we have our own cows. Occasionally the men kill an antelope and then we have a feast; and sometimes we have fish on Sunday.

June 3. Our tent is now pitched on the beautiful Platte River, 315 miles from St. Joe. The cholera is raging. A great many deaths. Graves everywhere. We are all in good health. Game is scarce; a few antelope in sight. Roads bad.

Fort Laramie, Wyoming. *June 19*. This fort is of adobe, enclosed with a high wall. The entrance is a hole in the wall just large enough for a person to crawl through. The impression you have on entering is that you are in a small town. Men are engaged in all kinds of business from blacksmith up. We camped a mile from the fort, where we remained a few days to wash and lighten up.

June 21. Started over sixty miles of the worst road in the world [from Fort Laramie toward South Pass, where the trail would take them over the Continental Divide] Have again struck the Platte and followed it until we came to the ferry. We had a great deal of trouble swimming our cattle across, taking our wagons to pieces, unloading and replacing our traps. A number of accidents happened here. A lady and four children were drowned through the carelessness of those in charge of the ferry.

Bear River, Wyoming. *July 1*. Lots of Indians in sight, mostly naked, disgusting and dirty looking.

July 2. Passed Independence Rock [a large landmark in central Wyoming.] This rock is covered with names.

With great difficulty I found a place to cut mine. Twelve miles away is Devil's Gate. It's an opening in the mountain through which the Sweetwater River flows. Several of us climbed this mountain [Split Rock]—somewhat perilous for youngsters not over fourteen. We made our way to the very edge of the cliff and looked down. We could hear the water dashing and roaring as if angry at the small space through which it was forced to pass. The scenery was grand, gloomy and wild. We were gone so long that the train was stopped and men were sent out in search of us. We made all sorts of promises to remain in sight in the future. John Owens, a son of the minister, my brother John, sister Lottie, and myself were the quartet.

During the week we went over the South Pass and the summit of the Rocky Mountains.

July 4. Had the pleasure of eating ice. Saw lots of dead cattle left by the emigrants to starve. Took a cutoff. Had neither wood nor water for fifty-two miles. Traveled in the night. At the Green River we lay by two days to rest man and beast after our long and weary journey.

July 29. Passed Soda Springs [Idaho.] Took another cut-off this week called Sublets [Sublette's Cutoff, which shortened the route by bypassing Fort Bridger.] Passed some beautiful scenery, high cliffs resembling old ruins or delapidated buildings.

August 18. This week some of our company left us, all young men. They were jolly, merry fellows and gave life to our lonely evenings. We all miss them very much. Some had violins, others guitars, and some had fine voices. They were anxious to hurry on without the Sunday stops. Roads are rocky and trying to our wagons, and the dust is horrible. The men wear veils tied over their hats as a protection. When we reach camp at night they are covered with dust from head to heels.

Humboldt River [Nevada] *August 20.* We are now 348 miles from the mines. We expect to travel that distance in three weeks and a half. Water and grass scarce. Though the water is not fit to drink—slough water—we are obliged to use it for it's all we have.

September 7. Left St. Mary's, where we camped last Sunday. Traveled six miles. Stopped and cut grass for the cattle and supplied ourselves with water for the desert. Had a trying time crossing it. Several of our cattle gave out and we left one. Our journey through the desert was from Monday, three o'clock in the afternoon, until Thursday morning at sunrise. The weary journey that last night, the mooing of the cattle for water, the cry, "Another ox down," the stopping of the train to unyoke the poor dying brute, to let him follow at will or stop by the wayside and die, and the weary, weary tramp of men and beasts, worn out with heat and famished for water, will never be erased from my memory. Just at dawn in the distance we had a glimpse of the Truckee River, and with it the feeling: Saved at last! Poor cattle; they kept on mooing even when they stood knee deep in water. The long, dreaded desert has been crossed and we are all safe and well. Grass green and beautiful, and the cattle are up to their eyes in it.

September 8. Traveled fourteen miles. Crossed Truckee twelve times.

September 11. Made eighteen miles. Crossed Truckee

River ten times. Came near being drowned at one of the crossings. Got frightened and jumped out of the carriage into the water. The current was very swift and carried me some distance down the stream. In jumping I expected to reach the shore; instead I landed in the water, but was rescued in time all right.

September 14. We passed through the place where the Donner party perished [in the Sierra Nevada Mountains, three years before] having lost their way and being snowed in. Most of them died for want of food. Two long cabins, bones of human beings, tops of trees cut off marking the depth of the snow, was all that was left to tell the tale of that ill-fated party. It was night when we crossed the summit of the Sierra Nevada, and I shall never forget our descent to the place where we are now encamped—our tedious march with pine knots blazing in the darkness and the tall, majestic pines towering above our heads. The scene was grand and gloomy beyond description. We could not ride—roads too narrow and rocky. It was a footsore and weary crowd that reached this camp.

Yuba Valley [California] We are now 108 miles from Sutter's Fort [where gold had been discovered the year before.]

Monday, September 17. Lay by two days. Had preaching under the pines at night.

September 21. Reached Bear Valley by descending a tremendous hill. We let the wagons down with ropes. Left one of our wagons and the springs of our carriage. Cut down trees for our cattle to browse on.

Vernon, California [near San Francisco] *October 6.* Well, after a five-months trip from St. Joe, Missouri, our party of fifty wagons, now only thirteen, has at last reached this haven of rest. Strangers in a strange land, what will our future be?

Fremont, *October 10.* This is a small town on the opposite side of the river from Vernon. My father has decided to remain here for the winter. We have had a small house put up of two rooms made of boards with puncheon [split log] floor.

April 27. Have met a number of nice young men here. I am too young for beaux, but the young men don't seem to think so.

"A prise of 25 cents—that's the part I like."

Margaret O'Brien

[*Born 1937*]

At the time Margaret O'Brien began her diary she was earning a thousand dollars a week as America's leading child actress and trying hard for a three-month award

*from her mother of 25 cents for not forgetting to wash
behind her ears. It was because she could be a great artist
and at the same time a perfectly normal, frecklefaced,
pigtailed little girl, as natural and unspoiled as if she had
never been in Hollywood, that Hollywood and all America "broke up" over her. Lionel Barrymore called her
"the only woman except my sister Ethel who made me
take out my handkerchief in thirty years." She made her
first hit when she was five in "Journey for Margaret." In
the next few years she starred in a dozen big films including "Meet Me in St. Louis," "Music for Millions," "Our
Vines Have Tender Grapes," "Tenth Avenue Angel,"
and "Big City." An Academy Award came in 1944.*

January 15, 1947. This is my birthday and I am ten
years old. Mama, Auntie and Maggie [her cocker span-
iel] and I went to the bakery in Beverly Hills to get my
birthday cake. The baker said it was too big to put in a
box so he put it on a big platter and Mama sat in the
back seat and held it on her lap while Maggie and I sat in
the front with Auntie. Then Mama said, "All I need now
is for Maggie to jump back here." Well, when Maggie
heard her name, that's exactly what she did—she jumped
right in the middle of the cake and splashed whipped
cream all over Mama. Mama looked so funny I wanted
to laugh but I didn't dare so I called Maggie to come
back and that was the worst thing I could have done
because this time she got whipped cream all over Auntie
and me and the front seat. We finally stopped the car and
everybody laughed except Maggie. She was so sad, and I

was too when I saw the big hole in the middle of my cake.

Mama gave me my best present and this is what it is—my new diary.

January 17. Butch Jenkins gave me two white mice for my birthday. Mrs. Hunter came over to take care of me tonight—she is scared to death of mice. She said, "I hear you got some mice for your birthday. Are you sure they are in their cage?" I told a fib because I knew she would have a fit if she found out I let them out to play with. I decided I'd better find them quick, before she saw me, but I couldn't find them. But after dinner, when she was reading her paper, the mice appeared. And she screamed and went and told Mama she was going to leave this instant. But she didn't leave after all—my mice have to instead.

January 22. Mama said if I want to be a lady when I grow up, I better start right now. We have a chart on the bathroom wall [to record washing, brushing teeth, cleaning nails, etc.] I get a blue star each day and a gold star for a perfect week. If I have twelve gold stars at the end, on Sunday I get a prise, which is 25 cents—that's the part I like. But the part I don't like is, if I miss I have to forfeit something.

January 27. We got up early and went to the studio. Mama told Bessie to get some cereal for breakfast for the box tops, so I can get my radar signal ring that glows in the dark.

February 9. Mama finely took me to the amusement pier today. It's the best place—we rode on the boat slide three times but we didn't go on the loop-it-de-loo—we were afraid. I never saw so many games in my whole life. Everything costs ten cents and sometimes you win a prise. I tried to throw some hoops around a square stick but that was hard. I finely won a doll by poppin balloons with some darts. I had two great big spun sugar sticks and a hot dog and Mama says we can come back again.

February 10. A man came out to the set today with four hats. One they are going to use in the picture, but there was another one that was the most beautiful hat I ever saw. I knew it would look just perfect on Mama. It was her favorite color too—American Beauty with American Beauty and chartroose velvit flowers on it and a big bow in the back. I asked the man how much it was and he said sixty dollars. Imagine that!—sixty whole dollars for a hat. He said the reason was—it was a Lili Dashay. I told him I wanted to buy it for Mama but I only had $14 and 65 cents in my bank. And he decided to do it, so he gave me the hat and he's coming back tomorrow for his money. I still think even $14 and 65 cents is a lot of money for a hat. Mama was so happy when she saw it she almost cried. She tried it on and she really looks beautiful in it. She said, "It's the most beautiful hat I ever saw." So now I don't care if I spent my money. I didn't have enough to buy a pony anyway, and where would I keep it if I did have one?

February 14. Today is Valentine's Day. I didn't buy a single one this year, I made them all in school. I gave my prettiest one to Mama, and she loved it. I still can't make up my mind whether it's better to send Valentines or to receive them.

February 15. We went to Graumans Chinese theatre to put my hands and feet and my name in the cement there. Mr. Grauman let me pick out where I would like to sign, so I decided to be between Shirley Temple and Jimmy Durante. I thought I could do it with my shoes on but instead I had to go barefooted. There were lots of people there, and I got embarrassed because they were watching and I got cement all over. Then I put my hand prints in the cement and signed my name underneath. Mr. Grauman said they will stay there forever and ever, and anybody who has his name there can go to the movies free. That's nice. Jimmy Durante had his face in the cement—I wonder if he really had to put it in the wet cement. Then they took some pictures and Mama and I came home.

February 17. The cereal came today so I sent in the box tops for the prise. Mama thought I wanted to eat them, but instead I wanted to cut off the tops because the man on the radio said if you cut off the top of the box and put it in an envelope with ten cents and send it to New York they would send you a weather ring. It is a majic ring that turns white on a clear day and blue on a clowdie day and pink on a medium kind of day. Nancy wanted one too, so I decided to cut off the bottom and send it with another ten cents. I hope the man doesn't mind, but Mama said he would. I don't see why.

March 8. Mama had some ladies over for tea and I got into trouble. Nancy couldn't come over to play because it rained and she has a cold, so I decided to play dress-up. I put on Mama's high heal shoes and put my hair up in a pompadour and then put on one of Mama's long dresses

78

so I would look like a lady of the olden days. All I
needed was a hat and Mama's were too high so I tried on
the visiting ladies hats that were on the bed. I saw one
that was just right—it was the best hat I ever saw and I
wish Mama had one just like it. It was big and floppy
with black velvit top and fussy veils and a stuffed bird
sitting on top. Then the most awful thing happened—I
took it off and the bird fell on the floor. And just
then the ladies were leaving so I hid under the bed. I was
so scared. But they thought my poor dog Maggie did it. I
wonder if I should tell.

March 19. I told and I'm glad I did. Mama said you'd
better call the lady and apologize. So I did and she said,
"Never you mind, I'll glue it right back on." So now my
conscience is clear.

"I put my head on the block."

Theodore Roosevelt
[1858-1919]

Every President of the United States has hoped to be remembered as a great man. Very few are, for true greatness is as rare in the White House as it is anywhere else.

On September 6, 1901, President William McKinley was assassinated. Theodore Roosevelt became President and three years later was elected to a full term.

"Teddy" Roosevelt is remembered, not for what he did but for what he was—a colorful human being who captured the imagination of the America of his time. He had a toothy grin and a zest for living nobody could forget. He said America should "speak softly and carry a big stick." He waved it at a few nations and a few big business men and their corporations, and people liked him for this even though he never hit anybody with it. We could do worse, we think, than to accept his own ap-

praisal of himself: "I am only an average man, but by George I work at it harder than the average!"

When Teddy was ten years old his family spent a summer touring Europe. Here is part of his record of the trip.

JOURNAL OF THEODORE ROOSEVELT OF U.S.A.

When I put "we 3" I mean Ellie [his brother Elliott], Connie [his sister Corinne] and I. When I put "big people" I mean Papa, Mama, and Bamie [his older sister Anna.]

May 12, 1869. We go to Europe today. We sail in the English steamship *Scotia.* It was verry hard parting from our friends. Old Grand Papa came up to us. While going to the docks I cried a great deal.

May 27. Liverpool, England. We went to our cousins' school at Waterloo. We had a nice time but met Jeff Davises son and some sharp words ensued.

June 7. Edinburgh, Scotland. Papa, Mama, Bamie and I drove out to "Auther's [Arthur's] Seat," the highest crag which we made the ascent of. The view was splendid on the top and it was very windey and I bought a sweet cracker.

June 8. An excursion to Abbotsford, Walter Scot's home. There are many curious things in Abbotsford among which were Nupolyan pistols, an Indian neclace of human bones, sir Walter Scot's gun, and others. We then went to Melrose Abby and saw two small dogs fighting.

The smallest (a yellow one) was brave enough while a wagon wheel was between them, and if barking would have done any good, would have won the battle, but finally the wagon moved.

June 9. Edinburgh. Went in a caraige to Roslin. We saw the most interesting castle, and the most dreary kind of Dungens, and then we saw the chapel. One of the pillars had been made by a clerk, and his master had killed him from jealisy and could not make the others so pretty. I went to the village and bought my lunch alone.

June 16. Lemington. We drove to Warick castle of the Saxon Giant. We saw his poridge bowl in which Connie, Ellie and I got into.

June 19. We went in the cars to Oxford. Before we went Bamie, Papa, Mama and I saw an archerry. At Oxford we drove around it and saw some colages.

June 20. Oxford. We went to church in the morning. I had a headache and Connie and Ellie made a tremendous noise playing to my expense and rather laughed when I remonstrated, but I called Bamie and she made them—as they could not play quietly—sit quietly.

June 22. London. I went to the zoological gardens. We saw a great maney animals, zebras, lions, camels, elephants, monkeys and bears, all common to other menageries, but we also saw various kinds of wild asses not common. I was a little disappointed.

June 26. In the morning a doctor came to us and said my lungs were perfect. In the afternoon I went to riding school and I was thrown.

June 28. We three children played in hyde park and then

went to some noted waxworks. I mistook several of them for real persons and was very much amused.

July 1. We three children went to hyde park with Mary Ann [their governess] and got lost from her. We did all we could to find her. We tied my great red cravat to a stick and one remained with it while two hunted in different directions. If one of the hunters saw her he brought her back to the person who was by the red cravat or flag and she waved it and the other hunter came back but if the flag person saw her he or she waved the flag and the hunters came back. Three times we hunted this way and then we took hands and went all round the park and I told the watchman on the beat to tell her if he saw her that we were gone home. Then we did go home.

July 4. Hastings. Hastings town was in the celtesh time before Christ. We had such a nice walk on the cliffs for two miles and coming back we made a feeble attempt at cheering the Fourth of July.

July 10. London. We all went to the tower of London. A kind man dressed like an ancient warden showed us around. I put my head on the block where so maney had been beheaded.

Antwerp, Belgium. *July 14.* I was the first one that got on the continent.

July 16. Hauge [The Hague] We went to the museum. We saw the jacket in which the Prince of Orange was killed and maney other things. We then drove through a park to the summer palace which was very elegant, and we saw the queen. After dinner we saw the winter palace and a barzar. This was the first citty that has horse cars in it.

July 17. Papa told us such a nice story today, about a man who drowned his wife because his wife said his pants was cut with a scisor while he insisted it was cut with a knife.

A venerable tale to prove that woman always gets the last word. The two were in a boat. The man cried "Knife!", his wife, "Scissors!" In a fury, he yelled "Knife!" once more and threw her overboard. In the water, she gasped, "Scissors!" As she rose to the surface, he repeated, "Knife!" She gurgled, "Scissors!" and disappeared. But the third and last time she went down, to his triumphant shout of "Knife!" she held her hand above her head. As it sank beneath the waves, two fingers went through the motions of a scissors.

August 6. Chamonix, France [famed Alpine resort where climbers begin the ascent of Mont Blanc. The Roosevelt family did not attempt that 15,700-foot peak.] We go up the mountain today. It is 8,000 feet high, and some of it was pretty dangerous work. We had mules but I did not go much on them. I found some specimens to keep and we went on a great glacier called "Mother of Ice." We explored the hotel (Connie, Ellie and I) and met with several cross chambermaids.

August 7. we went up to the high and beautiful Glacier which is much higher than yesterday. We had dinner in a hotel on the top. Comeing down I got lost in the woods. Papa and I had strawberries and cream because we walked ahead of the others who were on mules and found them and (without much generosity) then ate them.

August 29. Lucerne, Switzerland. I was very sick on the sofa and lay in bed all day and had to take arrowroot. Mama told me stories and Papa did the same. I think Ellie and Connie the kindest kind of brother and sister.

August 31. I have been homesick all the nights at Luzerne and tonight was no exception to the general rules.

September 9. I sat with one leg in Switzerland and the other in Italy. Soft balmy Italy of the poets!—but we found it cold, dreary, smelly.

September 16. Milan. We got up at six to see the cathedral. We went to the roof and then up to the topmost tower. There are seven thousand statues on the pinicles of the roof and three thousand more to be added. We played in the cells, divesting ourselves of shoes, stockings, garters, cravats, sashes, dresses, pants, jackets. In the romp the strings of my jacket and a butten of my pants were torn and Ellie's butten also, besides getting his sore toe hurt badly, and a little skin was taken off Corinne's hand and her head thomped severly. After this we played at keeping a hotel and travelers coming to him. Connie and I were the travelers and went up staircases for mountains with boxes and bags in hand. I shut the door on Connie's finger and hurt her verry badly.

September 18. To Venice by railway. From the moment we entered Venice till we got to the hotel, Connie abused Venice and called the books story-tellers because there were a good many streets you could walk upon. At last we saw the moonlight on the waters, and I contrasted it with the black gondolas darting about like water bugs.

September 22. We saw a palace of the Doges. It looks like a palace you could be comfortable and snug in, which is not usual.

September 23. To the tower of the Campanile where it is a magnificent view. Mama bought a bracelet which she said would take 15 minutes but took an hour and a half.

September 24. I went to church St. Giorgio Maggiore. The alter is most beautiful, also candleslarbra.

"Some day we shall conquer war and sadness."

Marian Cuca

[1939-1953]

"She was one of us." When Marian died at the age of *14, this is what they said in the neighborhood. In the language of children, it is the highest tribute that can be paid. And in the part of the great city of New York where she lived, all kinds of children—rich, poor, black, white, yellow, Protestant, Catholic, Jewish—all could*

say, "She was one of us." This glimpse into her short, busy life begins when she is in her eleventh year. Three years later, while at a summer camp, Marian was stricken by polio. In two weeks she was dead.

January 1, 1951. Last night I went to the "Dom." That's what I like to call the Yugoslav Home because "Dom" means "home" in Serbo-Croation, the language my Daddy speaks and I'm going to learn. I saw Danny at the Dom and he and Marie were having a good time together. It was sort of a surprise to me, and I was mad at the beginning, but later I got over it. Danny doesn't seem so friendly to me any more. To think when I was ten years old I thought of him as "My Man!" I even wrote a story about him and called it "Love." I still do like him a little bit, though. In fact very much.

January 2. Dear Diary, some day we shall conquer war and sadness, never give up courage. We shall make peace and happiness throughout the world. You are not alone.

January 8. I find that I don't like Danny so much. Allen I like better every day. I <u>really</u> like Johnny, though. Aw, I don't know whom I like!

January 18. Guess what! Today Abby, Louisa, Susie and I organized a crusader's club. I named myself after Allen. My name is Knightress Alleniiss. Sounds funny.

January 20. We all had a wonderful time at Heather's birthday party. It was a Hen party. No roosters.

January 28. In the evening Mother and I went to a concert. Then we had a snack at the cafeteria on Union and Pacific streets. That's where Daddy used to buy

Mommy 5-cent baked apples during the depression.

February 6. Today I was feeling sad. I think of the beauty of the summer which is coming soon, and love, and Peace. Life is so beautiful. After school, walking to Claire's house, I slipped and fell. I felt worse. Later, when Claire and I were walking through the park, all of a sudden I started to cry.

February 9. Right now I'm in Louisa's house. I am sleeping over. Louisa and I decided to call Adam and Allen. First we called Allen. We had practiced what to say. Louisa was to be Willie and I Willie's mother. In practicing we got into hysterics so we decided not to say it was Willie because we would get into more hysterics. We called him and said it was his girl friend, but he was in bed and his father answered the phone. When we called Adam he was at a show, so we said it was Mary Jane.

April 7. After Louisa and I came from a concert we went for a walk in Central Park. It was a most beautiful sight. The cherry blossoms were just starting and everything was turning green. The birds were singing all around. I shall never forget this day. I loved today.

July 1. Saugerties, New York. Well, here I am in camp! I arrived here after a long three-hour ride on a ferry, train and car. I am in a bunk with two girls who are pretty nice.

July 6. I don't think I know of anything as wonderful as sitting around a campfire and telling stories at night after a long hike. And there's nothing more exciting than to lie in a sleeping bag at night and listen to the birds and owls as you try to count the stars.

January 5, 1952. Thinking it over it seems funny. First you go to a party and kiss a boy; and then you go to his house, and he acts like he never saw you before. I went to Rose's again and she said to me, "I was doing a nice slow burn when Michael kissed Janey." I'm beginning to think these kissing games are very silly. I have never kissed Johnny so far—one of the reasons for our strong friendship.

January 25. I'm not Eisenhower. I'm not MacArthur. I'm not Kefauver. I'm just Marian, a girl in 8-1, but I'm still running for president. I feel I'm qualified to run because I am interested in the activities of the students of our school. During my long years as a student I have held various jobs: In the first grade I was monitor of milk and crackers. In the third grade I was paper monitor. In the fifth grade I was president of the phonographic service in my public school. I was president of the first term of the 8th grade and I am now recording secretary of the civics club. Those are just thoughts, dear Diary, if I decide to make a speech and run for president of my class again.

February 4. Today in school a bunch of "toughies" beat up a Negro kid. It seems "They" only get enjoyment out of bloodshed. These things really make me very mad. Why do men have to hate each other so? My God, Hitler Germany started like this. What gets me is, everyone knows kids are getting beaten up, yet they do nothing about it.

March 20. Imagine! It's Spring! Spring at last and the world is as happy and flowery as ever. Janey and I were jumping up and down. I'm really so happy. If anyone likes Spring, it's me! And one of these days I'm going to be real foolish and play hookey!

March 23. I've made a list of my ten favorite friends—boys and girls. Only on the boys' side I have eleven.

January 15, 1953. At our club meeting Albie read a poem he wrote about the Spring. There was one part in it where he states the animals get excited in the spring. We were all in hysterics.

February 3. Reading back in this diary I laugh at my hostile feelings toward the "toughies." I no longer feel justified in calling them that. They are people, very wonderful, warm people, who are only reflecting the society and environment in which they live.

"The most Devilish thing is eight times eight."

Marjorie Fleming
[1803-1811]

Marjorie Fleming was born in the city of Kirkcaldy, Scotland. A few weeks before her ninth birthday she died. Her collected works—some 10,000 words of diary and poems—established her as the youngest world-famous author in history. You will find in the British Dictionary of National Biography *a paragraph in which the compilers of that sedate roll of fame break from their strict objectivity to remark, "Pet Marjorie's life is probably the shortest to be recorded in these volumes, and she is one of the most charming characters."*

When Marjorie was six years old her cousin Isabella Keith came from Braehead to visit the Flemings and remained to take over as governess and teacher. But to make a six-year-old put thoughts into words as Marjorie did—this was not the work of any teacher. "Cousin Isa" realized she had for a pupil a rare human being.

There were others who knew it too, as well if not better than seventeen-year-old Isabella. Sir Walter Scott, who called Marjorie "my bonnie wee croodlin' doo" (cooing dove) said of her, "She's the most extraordinary creature I ever met with, and her repeating of Shakespeare overpowers me as nothing else does."

She died of a brief illness, probably meningitis. Isabella had carefully preserved the child's writings. She gave the manuscript, unedited, to Mrs. Fleming. Then, as happens to many diaries, Marjorie's was laid away, kept in the family, and almost forgotten. Half a century later, quite by chance, a newspaperman saw it and published it, first in a Scottish paper and then as a book.

The world fell in love with the memory of a little girl. Critics used phrases like "the youngest immortal in the realm of letters", and since 1858 millions of readers have

91

agreed and have enjoyed the diary of "Pet Marjorie" in many countries.

Along with the diary the family kept a letter written by Marjorie when she was five and a half years old to her older sister, whose name was also Isabella. It began:

My dear Isabella

I now sit down on my bottom to answer all your kind and beloved letters which you was so good as to write to me. This is the first time I ever wrote a letter in my Life. Miss Potune, a Lady of my acquaintance, praises me dreadfully. I repeated something out of Dean Swift and she said I was fit for the Stage and you may think I was primmed up with majestick Pride but upon my word I felt myself turn a little birsay birsay is a word which is a word that William composed which is as you may suppose a little enraged . . .

William, whoever he was, did not "compose" the word, but the definition is correct; in ancient Scottish "birsay" means "enraged."

And now, from Marjorie's diary:

Today, O today I am going to Braehead but alas my pleasure will be soon damped for I must come home in too days but I wish to stay too months or more for I am very fond of the country and could stay at Braehead all my life.

At Braehead I lay at the foot of the bed because Isabella says that I disturbed her repose at night by con-

tunial figiting and kicking but I was very well and con-
tunaly at work reading Arabin nights entertainments,
which I could not have done had I slept at the top.

> I love in Isa's bed to lie
> O such a joy and luxury
> The bottom of the bed I sleep
> And with great care I myself keep
> Oft I embrace her feet of lillys
> But she has got on all the pillies
> Her neck I never can embrace
> But I do hug her feet in place
> But I am sure I am contented
> And of my follies am repented
> I am sure I'd rather be
> In a smal bed at liberty.

Through Marjorie's diary are scattered many poems.
The next to appear is this "melancholy lay":

> Three Turkeys fair their last have breathed
> And now this worled forever leaved.
> Their Father & their Mother too
> Will sigh and weep as well as you
> Mourning for their Osprings fair
> Whom they did nurse with tender care
> Indeed the rats their bones have cranched
> To eternity are they launched
> There graceful form & pretty eyes
> Their fellow poults did not despise
> A dierful death indeed they had

That would put any parent mad.
But she was more than usual calm
She did not give a singel dam
She is as gentel as a lamb
Here ends this melancholy lay
Farewell poor Turkeys I must say.

At Braehead. Here I pas my life in rurel filicity, festivity & pleasure   I saunter about the woods & forests   Braehead is far far sweeter than Edinburgh or any other place   Every thing is beautiful   some colour is red others green & white but the trees & hedges are the most beautiful, for they are of the most pretty green I ever beheld in all my life.

I confess that I have been more like a little young Devil then a creature for when Isabella went up the stairs to teach me religion and my multiplication and to be good and all my other lessons I stamped with my feet and threw my new hat which she made on the ground and was sulky and was dreadfully passionate   but she never whiped me but gently said Marjorie, go into another room and think what a great crime you are committing letting your temper git the better of you   but I went so sulkely that the Devil got the better of me   but she never never whips me, so that I think I would be the better of it, and the next time that I behave ill I think she should do it   To Day I have been very ungrateful and bad and disobedient   Isabella gave me my writing   I wrote so ill that she took it away and locted it up in her desk where I stood trying to open it till she made me come and read

my bible But I was in a bad humor and read it so care-
lessly and ill that she took it from me and her blood ran
cold but she never punished me She is as gental as a
lamb.

I am now going to tell you about the horrible and
wretched plaege that my multiplication gives me you
can't concieve it—the most Devilish thing is 8 times 8
and 7 times 7 it is what nature itselfe cant endure.

To Day I pronounced a word which should never come
out of a lady's lips it was that I called John a Impudent
Bitch and Isabella afterwards told me that I should
never say it even in joke but she kindly forgave me because I said that I would never do it again.

I must git my spelling first. I acknowledge that this page
is far from being well written. Isabella teaches me my
lessons from ten till two every day, and I wonder she is
not tired to death with me for my part I would be quite
Impatient if I had a child to teach.

In my travels I met with a handsome lad named Charles
Balfour Esq. and from him I got ofers of marage.

The Divel always grins at the sight of the bible; bibles,
did I say? nay, at the word virtue I should like to learn
Astronomy & Geography Miss Potune is very fat she
pretends to be very learned. She says she saw a stone that
dropt from the skies but she is a good christian an anni-
baptist is a thing I am not a member of: I am Pisplikan

[Episcopalian] just now, and a Prisbeteren at Kercaldy, my native town, wich though dirty is clean in the country. Sentiment is what I am not acquanted with.

In the love novels all the heroins are very desperate Isabella will not alow me to speak about lovers & heroins and 'tis too refined for my taste.

Persons of the parlement house are as I think caled Advocakes

A sailor called here to say farewell it must be dreadfull to leave his native country where he might get a wife or perhaps me, for I love him very much & with all my heart, but O I forgot Isabella forbid me to speak about love. Fighting is what ladies is not qualyfied for Alas, we females are of little use to our country & to our friends I remember to have read about a lady who dressed herself in man's cloths to fight for her father women are not half so brave as her, but it is only a story out of Mothers Gooses Fary tales so I do not give it cridit, that is to say I do not belive the truth of it but it matters little or nothing

The Life of Mary Queen of Scots
by M. F.
Poor Mary Queen of Scots was born
With all the graces which adorn
Her birthday is so very late
That I do now forget the date

Her education was in France
There she did learn to sing & dance
There she was married to the dauphin
But soon he was laid in a coffin . . .
She flew to England for protection
For Elisbeth was her connection
Elisbeth was quite cross and sour
She wished poor Mary in her power
Elisbeth said she would her keep
And in her kingdom she might sleep
But to a prison she was sent
Elisbeths hart did not relent
Full ninteen years & mayhap more
Her legs became quite stif & sore
At last she heard she was to die
And that her soul would mount the sky
She was quite overjoyed at this
She thought it was her greatest bliss
The hour of death at last drew nigh
When she did mount the scaffold high
Upon the block she laid her head
She was as calm as if in bed
One of the men her head did hold
And then her head was off I'm told
There ends all Queen Elisbeths foes
And those who at her bend their bows
Elisbeth was a cross old maid
Now when her youth began to fade
Her temper was worce than before
And people did not her adore . . .

There is a thing that I must tell
Elisbeth went to fire & hell
Him who will teach her to be cevel
It must be her great friend the divel.

"Can I please bring you my pomes?"

Howard T. Bissell

[*Born 1955*]

When Howie was in his seventh year he wrote a poem as a valentine for his teacher. In the City of New York there are all kinds of teachers. Second Grader Howie's teacher was only lukewarm to the valentine. But when he showed it to the principal of his school, she fell in love with him. That is how it happened that the valentine and other events recorded in Howie Bissell's diary got into this book. He is nine years old now. He wants to be a psychiatrist when he grows up "so I can help people."

February 14, 1962. Today I rote a valentine for Miss
——. She said she liked it but she didn't take it home. It
goes

Do you know how it works to be happy?
There is one way to do it and that is to give.
There are other ways too.
Another is love.
So here's some—CATCH!

March 21. The first day of spring. Look out the windo. Just look on the trees, the laun, the sun. Now wont you say its a nice day, I would. Today I have roten a pome. It goes

You can try to pin the wind up to the sky—
You can try, yes you can try.
Do you think it will work?
Well you can always try
To pin the wind up to the sky.

April 5. A lot of new things happend. I just got a new claranet. Celia just got a new chalow. And Timmy gets more and more lessens on being pestey. And do you know what happened? I'm 7½. Timmy is 4. and do you know what happend? Alice had a baby and her name is Marjry.

April 16. Today I rote a letter to Miss ——— [his teacher.] It goes

Dear Miss ———

Could I please have pameshen to speak to you privetly? It will only take a minit. It's very inportint becoaes I have a probrom that MUST be solved imdyitly and I need your help. Otherwise I may end up with no glasses. So could I please speak to you today for just a minit.

From Howard

She didn't answer it so I didn't see her.

April 17. Today no answer to my letter.

April 18. Today no answer to my letter to Miss ———.

April 19. Today no answer to my letter so I have roten to Mrs. ———. [the principal] It goes

Dear Mrs. ———

I know your very buizy but could I pleaes speak to you privetly? I have a probrum that must be solved right a way! It is very inportint for Miss ——— not to know about it because: she might feel ambarist and upset if she knew I was going to talk to you inseded of her. This is the probrum

LIST OF PROBRUMS

1. I have tryed very hard to like Miss ——— because she is a kind person but I have been very much upset even thow I tryed.

2. I am VERY BOARD!

3. Miss ——— keeps telling us to read in our readers because she has know time to teatch us new things because she has to keep on writing at her desk, and I have read thows storeys just a MILLYAN TIMES and I can't stand them any more!

4. I keep bringing things for show-and-tell and she won't let me show them. When I brohgt my owl-whtsil from Japan I kept on raising my hand but she won't let me show it and finly it got brocen. The only thing she ever liked was my whalse [whale's] tooth.

5. A boy who sits near me keeps fooling around. He keeps grabing my notebook and glasses. When Miss

—— tells him to stop he *throws* them back! And my glasses coast 25$.

6. I have been looking forward to being in a play because I'd love to be an acter. Then when our class put on a play with the alfabat in it there were some good parts but I was only a capital N.

7. I keep asking for my onaribal menchen siense satifercit but she always says "I'll see." I am very angches to have it.

8. Can I please bring you my pomes?

9. Can you *please* help me solve these probrums?

Love, Howard

May. We selabrate Mother's Day because she does so many things for us and loves us. She cooks and cleans for us, takes care of us, she teaches things to us, she helps us with our probloms. We love her.

June. We selabrate Father's Day because they work to get money to buy things for us, they read to us and teach us how to grow up. Fathers love us and we love our fathers. Fathers take us places too.

Orient Point, Long Island. *July 10, 1962.* I found a shell here. I think it's called a Channeled Whelk [spelled for him] becouce the inside is a pinkish color and the outside is a grayish-white color, also it has little lumps. The animmals that lives inside has no bones, this protaeks it from deathy enemeas. It is a dead shell and proberly has been dead for a few years. The animmal has a tail that comes out through his canal. On it is his eye. When he wants to eat he puts out his mouthe also through the canal. Then the mouth and eye provides food for the animmal. Thank God.

"I will pass with Excellents."

Zoya Kosmodemyanskaya
[1923-1941]

When school was over Zoya left Moscow to spend the summer with her grandparents in the country. Those were happy days. There was peace in the world, and peace and sunshine and fresh air in the village. We have Zoya's diary for only that one season, the jottings of a city child of twelve for whom a dream of living in the country had come true. Six years later Zoya was dead, one of millions killed by the marching men of Germany. When they invaded her country she volunteered for the dangerous assignment of fighting them behind their own lines. She was caught, tortured, and hanged.

May 3, 1936. Moscow. Mama did not go to work today and I was very glad. At school I got a Good for dictation but for literature and arithmetic I got Excellent.

May 12. I was in a strange mood. I wanted to go for a

walk in the street, run and play. But towards evening I dug up the ground for my own private garden. I dream that Mama will buy many different seeds—flowers and vegetables—and then my garden will be lovely.

May 24. Exams start tomorrow. Exams! I do not think of anything else. The main thing is not to be afraid of the teacher and the assistants who will be there. And I know I shall pass with Excellents and certainly nothing less than Goods.

June 11. Today they will tell us who passed and give out report cards and prizes! I got up at half-past eight and went to school. All the children were smartly dressed. Then our study director began his report. It was very quiet in the hall. There were some beautiful books on a table, to be given as prizes. They called out my name. I got Excellent in language and arithmetic and Good in nature and geography. Shura [her little brother] also got good marks. They gave me the very best book—Krylov's fables!

June 26. Mama was still sleeping when I got up. As she had been working until past midnight, I didn't want to disturb her, so Shura and I went for a walk. The water in the pond near our house was warm and clean. We had a bath and dried ourselves on the grass. Then we felt like eating something sour so we went back to the garden. We gathered some sour apples. At about eight o'clock our cousin Slava arrived. He is five years older than I but we get along well. Every day now I think of nothing but the *country. And at last we're going!*

July 2. All yesterday was taken up with preparations for our trip. We didn't even go to bed the whole night. At 4:30 Shura, Slava, Mama and I went to the tram stop. I felt sorry Mama was not coming with us and happy at the same time to be going to the country. I had not been there for five years!

We traveled a whole night and day on the train. At the station we got into a cart and rode to Aspen Woods, where Grandpa and Grandma live. Slava knocked at the door and Grandpa said, "Come in there!" He thought it was the tractor driver dropping in for a visit. Grandma had a pain in the chest but when we arrived she was very glad and the pain stopped. She gave us pancakes, clabber and fresh milk. After that I went for a swim, played with girls in the neighborhood, and in the evening I met my old friend Manya in the village library.

The country air is wonderful! I went to sleep in the kitchen on Grandpa's bed.

July 7. I help Grandma with her work. I like doing what she tells me to. I go and watch the chickens, swim three times a day, and read. I have read a lot of interesting books—*Gulliver in Lilliput*, Gogol's *Inspector General.*

Grandma gives us very tasty things to eat. At the market we buy cucumbers, currants, cherries. But sometimes we have trouble. One day Shura lost his jacket. We went back to look for it but never did find it. And sometimes, when I go to the river and come home late, Grandma is cross with me.

July 15. When there is no work to do I get bored. I have decided to help Grandma all I can. When I got up this morning the idea came into my head to wash the floor. I liked doing it. Then I made some ribbons for myself out of red silk. They came out very well—anyway, no worse than my blue ones.

In the evening we had a thunderstorm. The animals were frightened and our baby goat broke away and Grandma just managed to find him in somebody's garden. Today I wrote to Mama.

July 23. Today I saw my cousin Nina and her brother and their mother coming through the wheat on the common pasture. They live 23 miles from Aspen Woods.

July 26. I was very glad my cousin Nina came. We had lots of fun. Grandma gave us some games—checkers and lotto. But today I didn't get along so well with Nina, Afterwards, though, we made it up and I decided never to quarrel with her again.

July 30. As the sun rose slowly over the awakening earth, a cart drew up, and we said goodby to my cousins Nina, Lelik, and Aunt Anya. In the afternoon I ironed, fetched water, and did other chores.

July 31. By noon it was so hot, there was talk in the village that the water in the brook will start boiling.

Each day, near evening, I go to fetch the goats. There are five of them—Maika, Chernomorka, Baron, Zorka, and one without a name—just Goat. Granny milks them and I carry the milk into the cellar.

August 1. This evening a letter came from Mama. She writes that she is ill and may come here. She has her holiday from the 15th of August and then she will come to us.

August 2. Granny left me to mind the house. She banked up the stove and went out. I made a mess of things. She had cooked macaroni and told me to chop hardboiled eggs into it. I wanted to put the pan of macaroni on the bench. It turned over and the macaroni went flying. I wiped the floor quickly and cooked some more macaroni.

Towards evening Grandma and I went for a swim. The rumors that the brook would boil were not true. It was a hot day, but the water didn't boil.

August 11. In Grandma's kitchen garden there are cucumbers, pumpkins, melons, cabbages, tobacco, tomatoes, and hemp. We have no sunflowers. At planting time Grandma didn't know we were coming so she didn't plant any. The strong hot wind stirs up dust and stings your eyes.

The Russian people are fond of roasted sunflower seeds. They like to munch them as we do popcorn. The hemp in Grandma's garden was an herb. Its tough fibers are used in making cloth and mats. The seed is food for pet birds. A drug can be made from the flowers.

August 15. Early in the morning there was a quiet knock on the door. Shura and Grandma and I jumped out of bed. Mama had come!

August 17. Mama, Shura and I went to the kitchen garden and picked a pumpkin and seven melons no bigger than your hand. Grandma made a porridge out of the pumpkin and dried the seeds. Towards evening Shura, Mama and I went for a swim. How good it is here! But with Mama here it's three times as good!

In the summer of 1941 Adolf Hitler's army struck at Russia and pushed almost to Moscow. Zoya, then 18, joined the partisans, a small secret army of young people who fought back by raiding, burning and blowing up the Germans in the occupied territory. She was sent to the village of Petrishchevo, about a hundred miles northwest of Moscow. There she set fire to houses the German soldiers had taken over. A sentry caught her in the act. He took her to the quarters of the commanding officer, who tried to make her tell who her companions were and where they could be found. She refused, and four men beat her with their belts until the blood came.

Nothing they did could make her talk. A sergeant who saw it all was later taken prisoner by the Russians. He told them, "The little heroine of your people remained staunch. She did not know the meaning of betrayal. She turned blue with the cold, blood flowed from her wounds, but she said nothing."

In the village center the soldiers built a gallows. Next morning they brought Zoya there. They had hung a sign on her with the word "House-Burner." A Russian journalist later described the scene:

"The place of execution was surrounded by ten cavalrymen with drawn sabres, more than a hundred German soldiers and some officers. The village folk had been ordered to assemble but only a few came and some of these, after standing there a little while, quietly slipped away, unable to watch the terrible sight.

"Under the gallows were two boxes, one on top of the other. The executioners lifted the girl onto the boxes and

threw the noose around her neck. Zoya shouted to the little group of remaining villagers, 'I am not afraid of dying! It is a great thing to die for one's people!'

"The executioner kicked out the lower box, which slid along the hard-packed snow. The crowd swayed back. There was a shriek, and the sound of it was flung back by the distant edge of the forest . . ."

"I had a pleasant time with my mind."

Louisa May Alcott

[1832-1888]

Amos Bronson Alcott, father of Louisa, was a philosopher by trade. Louisa loved him dearly but learned early in life that children of philosophers never seemed to have enough to eat. If your father wrote of truth for the love of it, the thing for you to do—if you didn't want the whole family to starve to death—was to write for money.

But even for money, Louisa wrote with an indelible tenderness. And even when she didn't like what she was

*writing about, she couldn't help writing well. When she
was 36 she wrote in her diary, "Mr. Niles [her pub-
lisher] wants a girls' story, and I begin 'Little Women'
. . . though I don't enjoy this sort of thing. Never liked
girls or knew many, except my sisters." So she wrote
about the girls she knew—the four Alcott sisters—and
the result was the most popular girls' book ever written in
America, widely read today as it was nearly a century
ago. After that the Alcotts had all the money they needed.
Louisa, born in 1832, started her diary when she was ten
and the Alcotts were living on a farm near Fitchburg,
Massachusetts.*

September 1, 1843. I rose at five and had my bath. I love
cold water! Then we had our singing lesson with Mr.
Lane. After breakfast I washed dishes and ran on the hill
till nine, and had some thoughts—it was so beautiful up
there. Did my lessons—wrote and spelt and did some
sums; and Mr. Lane read a story, "The Judicious Father", how a rich girl told a poor girl not to look over the
fence at the flowers, and was cross to her because she was
unhappy. The father heard her do it, and made the girls
change clothes. The poor one was glad to do it, and he
told her to keep them. But the rich one was very sad; for
she had to wear the old ones a week, and after that she
was good to shabby girls. I liked it very much, and I shall
be kind to poor people.

As I went to bed the moon came up very brightly and
looked at me. I felt sad because I have been cross today,
and did not mind my mother. I cried, and then I felt

better. I get to sleep saying poetry. I know a great deal.

September 24. I was cross today, and I cried when I went to bed. I made good resolutions, and felt better in my heart. If I only <u>kept</u> all I make, I should be the best girl in the world, but I don't and so am very bad.

October 12. After lessons I ironed. We all went to the barn and husked corn. It was good fun. We worked till eight o'clock and had lamps. I made a verse about sunset:

> *Softly doth the sun descend*
> *To his couch behind the hill.*
> *Then, O then I love to sit*
> *On mossy banks beside the rill.*

My sister Anna thought it was very fine. But I didn't like it very well.

December 19. A long letter from Anna [who was then in Boston] She sends me a picture of Jenny Lind, the great singer. She must be a happy girl. I should like to be famous as she is.

Life is pleasanter than it used to be, and I don't care about dying any more. Had a splendid run and got a box of pine cones to burn. Sat and heard the pines sing a long time. I had a pleasant time with my mind, for it was happy.

November 29. It was Father's and my birthday [his 44th, her 11th] Father asked us in the eve what fault troubled us most. I said my bad temper.

January, 1845. Did my lessons, and in the P.M. mother

read "Kenilworth" to us while we sewed. It is splendid. I got angry and called Anna mean. Father told me to look up the word in the dictionary, and it meant "base", "contemptible." I was so ashamed to have called my sister that, and I cried. We have had a lovely day. All the trees were covered with ice, and it shone like diamonds or fairy palaces.

Wednesday. I am so cross, I wish I had never been born.

Thursday. Read "The Heart of Midlothian" and had a very happy day. Miss Ford gave us a botany lesson in the woods. I am always good there. In the evening Miss Ford told us about the bones in our bodies and how they get out of order. I must be careful of mine, I climb and jump and run so much.

Tuesday. More people coming to live with us. I wish we could be together, and no one else. I don't see who is to clothe and feed us all, when we are so poor now. I was very dismal, and then went to walk and made a poem.

> . . . *O, why these tears*
> *And these idle fears*
> *For what may come tomorrow?*
> *The birds find food*
> *From God so good*
> *And the flowers know no sorrow.*

Concord. Thursday. I had an early run in the woods before the dew was off the grass. The moss was like velvet, and as I ran under the arches of yellow and red leaves I sang for joy, my heart was so bright and the world so beautiful. I stopped at the end of the walk and saw the sunshine out over the wide meadows. It seemed like going through a dark life or grave into heaven beyond. A very strange and solemn feeling came over me as I stood there, with no sound but the rustle of the pines, no one near me, and the sun so glorious, as if for me alone. It seemed as if I <u>felt</u> God as I never did before, and I prayed in my heart that I might keep that happy sense of nearness all my life.

Forty years later Louisa, reading over the diary, wrote in the margin beside this entry: "I have, for I most sincerely think that the little girl 'got religion' that day in the woods when dear Mother Nature led her to God.— L.M.A., 1885."

"All boys are nuts as usuall."
Sylvia McNeely
[Born 1919]

If you are keeping a secret diary, naturally you don't want anybody helping you with spelling or grammar or anything, even if you are only nine. The only way is to go ahead and "right," as Sylvia McNeely does in this "diry," and let the slips fall where they may. So here are some of the notes in which she manages pretty well to record a year of her life. Sylvia's mother was Marian Hurd McNeely, a writer of popular fiction for teen-age girls, who died in 1930—only a few months after the last entry in Sylvia's diary.

January 1, 1929. I'm going to have a Diry.

> *I pity the Bucher,*
> *I pity the cook,*
> *I pity the guy*
> *That tuches this book.*

January 5. Grampa was taken to the hospitle tonight. He is going to be oprated.

January 8. Gramps is 82 today. He got lots of flowers at the hospitle. It seems to lonesome at home here.

January 12. I wrote a poem witch I will put in my diry when I get time.

January 13.

> *A Dream*
> *Tipy toes and midnight were walking*
>   *down the lane,*
> *Filling their fairy buccuts with little*
>   *drops of rain.*
> *I came walking down the lane.*
> *Midnight said to me, would you like to*
>   *see my baby fly from tree to tree?*

113

Surely, I repeated, When does he take
his flight?
Next morning very early before the sun
is bright.
When I woke up next morning
The two had gone away.
So I'll never see that baby
That I planed to see that day.

January 18. Today I tried to right a poem but I didn't seceed. Poems are very easy to right but sometimes I don't seceed.

January 26. This morning mother told me grampa was dead. I cryed.

February 24. I went to Sunday school today. I don't like the Idie of going to the place. My teacher is very thankful of God but she is very homely.

March 13. I took my Lunch to school. The boys wanted to play marbles in the basement. We the girls had to give it up to the <u>little boys</u>, that's always the way with boys.

March 30. I went down town and got 5¢ worth of jelly beans, 5¢ worth of choechlete Easter eggs, 5¢ worth of salted penuts, 5¢ worth of gum drops. I had some candy left over from what I gave mother and daddy so I gave some to Jone my doll for easter.

April 7. The gold-fish is dead. I wrote a poem about him.

Once upon a time there
was a little fish
Right in the middle of

the fish-pond.
This morning he was dead,
He was green instead of red.
O, How it smelled near
the fish-pond.

Monday, April 8. I had a fight with Betty Feller. I had a good one with her too. Later Mrs. Feller phoned mother and told her I hit Betty. I did, too.

Saturday, May 11. It was raining very hard. I took some close over to Betty Kean's house and we dressed up. I took some high heals slippers and some stockings with runers in them. Betty got mad at me but I'm not mad at her.

Wednesday, July 3. Oh Boy tomorrow, fire works day. I got a lot of fireworks today. Grampa always used to buy us fireworks on the fourth but he can't now because he is dead and that makes me feel lonesome still.

July 8. Six of us girls had a show in the side-yard. We got six boys to come and watch so of corse we each got one penney. They didn't like the show and wanted their money back. Boys have never liked any of the shows we had. They din't get it.

July 23. Lee [her twelve-year-old brother] went down to cat fish creek and got the poison ivy. He thought he would try it out and see if he would get it and he rubed it on his hands. He smeard it all over himself. He broke out with it all over. I think he was nuts to do such a thing but all boys are nuts as usuall.

Saturday, September 14. Today I went to a girls house to

make some wine out of elderberries. We got a pan and a spoon. Then we got some elderberries and mashed them up. David Eigalhof had a old rag in his pocket and we draned them threw it and put the wine in a jar. We did not feel like drinking it.

October 21. Mother gave me my alounce today. I got 15¢ for my alounce and five cents for my report. I don't think that was very good. I get 2¢ for every A and 1¢ for every B, but I got mostly C's this time as usuall.

November 6. My birthday. I was ten years old. Jean Gilliam came for dinner. I got a school bag, a doll, a deck of cards, two bars of chocklet, two boxes of candy, and a comb, brush, purse with 42¢ from daddy and a 25¢ piece from Aunt Evlen, a hot water bag for my doll, a little one, and Carol sent me a telgram also. It was the first telgram I ever got. Lee gave me his scees [skis] for my birthday this morning and took them back tonight.

November 9. I have not fought with anybody today, even Lee.

November 28. I got one hundred in Arthmice and in spelling, Geograpy and Fundimentals.

November 27. We are going to have a turkey for Thanksgiving Day. We hope to have it for another meal, at least mother does. I don't. I could eat more than half of it. Last Thanksgiving Grampa was here and I miss him now.

December 10. Betty Russell came to see me tonight after school. We made puzzels. Lee and Bill Pasley are upstairs putting down numbers like this: 47 plus 62 plus 8 minus 3 times 4 divided by 2. Lee said they were making code languege. They think they'll fool me. It's all love stuff. They wright loveness all the time. I hate loveness. The dum boys humed with my comb and put their dirty germs on it.

December 24. Lee and I went to Linwood and took a wreath to Grampa. Both cried while up there.

December 29. Doctor Lily Kinnier came to see daddy and me. I'm going to get up out of bed tomorrow but I don't know about daddy. He has quincy. She said I had a streptacockus sore throat.

December 31, 1929. Goodby good old diry and a happy New year to all.

*"Self-praise smells ugly, let's change
the subject, shall we, all right."*

Benjamin Musser

[1889-1951]

*The writings of Benjamin Musser consist of forty-odd
published volumes of poetry, most of it deeply religious,
and eighty notebooks full of a breezy diary kept over a
twenty-year period, most of it never published. The
poetry he began soon after birth—judging from the product, a little too soon. But he improved, and a book of
poems came out when he was twenty-one. Since then his
work has appeared in more than a hundred anthologies. A
sample, titled "Circles":*

> *A tiny word, and you said nothing more;*
> *You flung it carelessly, and walked away,*
> *Leaving a friend to see, to his dismay,*
> *Circle on circle widening to the shore,—*

Circle on circle that can never turn
Within itself, and draw the ripples in,
And find the sunken word and make it spin
Back to its source of gratefullest rejourn.

The stone is cast, words cannot be unsaid
Whose circles widen even to the dead.

After attending several Episcopal schools, at nineteen
he decided to join the Roman Catholic Church and be-
came a member of the Order of St. Francis. In the period
covered by this part of his diary he was twelve years old
and living in Philadelphia.

THE JOURNAL OR DIARY
OF
BENJAMIN MUSSER, JOURNIOR

I hereby dedicate this journal (however illiterate it may be, for I hope the recipient will forgive all that) to my Conscience and my brother Fred.

October 11, 1901. This morning while cleaning out my closet I came across this book. I have perfect rafts of blank books, scrapbooks and the like, all well filled. My shelves are filled with them, so I wondered what I should do with this. Everybody—at least Julia [his sister] had the same kind of saving habit, and so I could not give this away, nobody would take it. Then I thought of having a journal or diary, and we shall now commence. Doubt if I

shall ever let anyone see this, except chums and perhaps
Fred and Julia, for the writing is fierce.

Monday. I really must write a few lines in here before
school, for I feel gloomy, and whenever I feel melancholy I shall confide in this. Most of all I am sad because
it's Monday, blue Monday, the first schoolday of the
week. Five days before me! Ough! Horrors! I have just
lately begun German, and I like it immensely, although I
can never like any language like I like French. I am
pretty "up" in French. I got first at the end of the year.
Self-praise smells ugly, as Julia says. Let's change the
subject, shall we, all right.

There are the nicest bunch of fellows in the school I go
to now—the Protestant Episcopal Academy—than any
school I have gone too, and I have gone to a lot: two
kindergartens, a primary, the Brooklyn Latin School the
winter before last when I lived in Brooklyn near the
Academy of Music where we use to go to see Weber and
Fields and Lilian Russel. I hope I can stay at this school
now until college. It's the best school of all and in the
best town of all, where nobody ought to live any place
else.

O, on Saturday last I nearly forgot to say we went to
see "The Wizard of Oz", which was fine, especially the
ciclone. Julia has the book about it. It wasn't a real ciclone of course, but they made it look like it on the stage.
Horrors! I must do that algebra.

October 14. Yesterday Billy Bradford and I went to
Wanamakers and had luncheon. Dandy eats. It was
dutch treat. He makes me tired, he is rich and I am not,

and yet he's always borrowing from me at school and never pays back or never treats.

This afternoon I made fudge. It wasn't very good. I make fudge about the way I do algebra.

Mr. Gensamer caught Edward Norris today drawing a sausage machine. Norris knows a lot about machinery and I bet his sausage machine would work all right. You put a live dog in them.

October 17. I am going to read some of Thackeray's books to improve the mind, as Daddy says, at least I will start one this evening. Well, I shall now stop and get settled in a morris chair and read, read, read—until I fall asleep. That's what books that improve the mind do to a fellow. Good night, Ben.

October 19. After school Fred and I went to Reeds, where we met Mother. We went to the boys department and I got the dandiest suit you ever imagined. It is dark brown corduroy norfoke, and the man said a fine quality too. Fred says they always say it's fine. Fred got a long winter coat and a derby hat. O my eye. Then we looked for corduroy caps for His Honorable, and actually went to five different stores, in vain. I came home dead and am to be buried tomorrow.

October 25. The fellows always spit on new clothes to initiate them. I have been making some more things for the church fair—some pictures and calendars, some original and some copied from Gibsons and painted or in ink. Those hand made things are sold very quickly. People seem to think hand made things are nice even if their not just because their hand made. For instance I remember at the fair in Brooklyn for some charity I made some terrible looking pictures and they sold right away and Mrs. Haines sent me home in the middle of the fair to make some more.

October 29. I have a dandy book. It is very exciting. A lady stabs her lover, at least they think she did but she didn't. It is a detective story and is radiantly glorious. Well I must get down to old durn lessons now. Life isn't all Gibson books and detective stories. Away, fond Sherlock Holmes, away! For I to algebra must turn my aching head and throbbing heart. Farewell dear detective stories. I think I'll write one some time. O my eye!

October 30. This afternoon Fred, Julia, Norris and I went to Keith's [theatre] and it was splendid. At the last thing they had sort of lantern slides called sinamatagraph, a most wonderful kind of picture where the people moved. They are just trying the experriment. The pictures were not very clear and not a bit funny, just people walking around, but Norris says he bets it'll be a big thing some day.

October 31. I went out Hallow Eening just to our friends houses. Nothing exciting happened like a couple of years ago when Fred and I were going to the party for the choir boys at St. James Church and we rang a door bell and the lady through a pitcher of water on Fred's best suit and we went home and put on mackintoshes and umbrellas and tied a rope to the lady's bell and went across the street and sat on our porch and pulled the rope and she through about a barrel of water I guess right on a carriage with a baby a man was pushing. That was the most terrible time we ever had on Hallow Een. But we were only children then and didn't know any better.

November 4. I am writing here in my pajamas, ready for bed. It was raining nearly all day, and I certainly feel dreary and old and tired. This was the first day of the church fair. Mother was at one table and she looked so darling selling things.

November 9. I invited Norris to come to luncheon to-morrow but he said he had a prior engagement. He likes to use different words like prior.

November 11. Father thinks my writing is so awful and worse every day, and he showed me some writings of his when he was younger than me, and it was terribly neat but all loops and frills and things and a bird sitting in the middle. A fellow would get arrested if he wrote like that nowadays.

Friday the thirteenth. And it was sort of unlucky too. I had a scrap with one of the fellows at the game, a real fist fight, and he beat me all right. I don't seem to be a born fighter and haven't much strength. I don't even know what the fight was about, except he said I was a sissy and couldn't fight, and I said I could, and then he jumped on me and pounded me just because he was bigger and knew he could lick me. It is all right now, he says it is all right because he licked me. But what did he gain by fighting me when he knew he was bigger and stronger before he started it? I don't believe in wars anyway and I never will as long as I live so help me God.

November 14. Father thinks it's terrible how schools nowadays have so little poetry in them. He's glad to know that at Episcopal Academy we have poems every Friday, only the fellows usually resite the same one every third or fourth week, so we learn three or four and get the same old ones off, it makes it easier only father says it is dishonest. We sometimes take classy things like father would, such as how they brought the good news from Ghent to Aix by Robert Browning. It has so much thrillingness in it.

November 16. We have just gotten back from "Dante" and it was simply great, wonderful. O I'll dream about those graves opening up, they were really only trapdoors on the stage but they looked like graves and the flames bursting out. I love tragedies. My spine felt riggly for hours, and shivery, but I wouldn't have missed it for anything.

November 19. I found in Fred's closet a little theatre which he and I made a year ago and which I loved. He said it could be his and mine together, and we will have plays in it for Julia and her friends. Gee, but we'll have fun! Today I've been writing a play to be acted in it. The play is woven around the French Revolution, dealing with Louis XIV, Marie Antoinette, Cardinal Roan, etc. The theatre is about two feet each way, and has arrangements for the curtains, and is slick.

November 21. Our first play will be next Saturday and will be called "The Guillotine." It is very exciting and terribly tragic. I made it just as tragic as I could so that the audience (Julia) would be fearfully moved and cry maybe. The prison scene is horrible, where they stick

Princess Lamable's head through the bars and tear the dauphin from his mother's arms.

Fred says I am royalist, and I say he bets his life I am, at least regarding France, and Fred said then I ought not to let my own feelings show in things I write. Well, but whose feelings ought to show? That's what writers are for. But he said maybe the audience is not royalist, especially if they're good Americans. Well, anyway, maybe the reader of the Scarlet Letter doesn't believe in Puritans and stern New England laws and punishments, but anyway maybe you can enjoy that book and anyway Thackeray had a right to make it that way if he wanted, whether readers agree with him or whether they don't.

So we argued as the shades of night fell. I have put several notices of the show around the house and am going to make a big poster of it. Fred and I have been busy making the people and scenery. I mean it was Hawthorne not Thackeray.

November 28. It's awful the way I'm so conceeted over nothing much. It's my worst fault. I don't mind telling you, diary, because you can keep secrets. But I'm not snob, for some of my best friends are dirty little poor boys.

November 30. We have just come in from the first skating of the year and my hands are so cold I can hardly write. I am doing a new play for our little theatre. It is about an American girl that is loved by a fine American man and a French count. The count pretends to love her but really wants her millions. She decides to marry the count, goes abroad, but the night before her wedding she dreams that the count only wants her millions. The dream is shown behind a netting. She then runs away and is found by the fine American who came abroad to try to win her back. They then return to America and are married. The count is then accused by some person of murder, and he gets hung on the American girl's wedding day. It is most thrilling, exciting.

Perhaps when I die some body will say I was a very wonderful boy, but they don't say it now. It's funny that way. Such is life.

December 2. The play is called "The One Man" and is very splendid and exciting, but I'm afraid father will say it is a melladrama.

December 13. Well, the play came off all right. We had to have it today for this is the only day Father had time to come. He, Julia and mother all came and enjoyed it immensley. That was a slip of my spelling part of my brain, I mean immensely. Even that doesn't look quite right.

December 14. I came first in class again last week. That puts me head of the class again for the term for commendation day. We have a pretty rummy class for me to come first when I hardly study ever at all!

December 19. Fred and I worked on the next play which is called "Around the World" and is splendid. Fred wrote it. It is about a young man who loves an American girl but he wishes to find if he loves her more than any other girl so he goes abroad in a balloon. The girl loves him, but wants to find if she loves any other man better, so she also goes abroad. In every country they meet, disguised, neither knowing the other one, but both privately declaring that the foreigners are every bit as lovely as Americans. They finely go home. Finely they find it all out and declare that Americans are the best.

January 1, 1902. I have finished reading The Red Triangle and it is simply skablobalous. It is a detective story. A fellow at school named Zara told me once I ought to get some Jessy James books, so I had them on my Christmas list but dad put his foot down. He said "No sir! The line must be drawn somewhere on this detective story insanity and I draw the line at Jessy James. It ruins the taste of the boy for books worth while and puts false ideas in there heads", and it was as good as Jessy just to hear my father rave, only I didn't tell him that.

January 31. It snowed all day yesterday. I have a frightful cold and feel miserable. I wrote a composition today on one of Mark Twain's books, Huckleberry Finn, which I love, but I did not love the composition. It was not interesting like funny Huck and Tom Sawyer, but how can I be expected to pour out splendid language when I use 12 handkerchiefs a day?

"I hope God will forgive me my sins when I die."

Harriet Spencer

[1761-1821]

We Americans honor our dead by talking about their virtues and covering up their frailties. The British tell everything about theirs and honor them anyhow. Until her death in 1821, Harriet, Countess of Bessborough, kept up a long and intimate correspondence with the "singularly handsome and pleasing" Lord Granville. A century later the family published her revealing letters with an explanation that "the marriage vow was taken more lightly in the Regency period than in Victorian times."

Harriet was 19 when she married Lord Bessborough. Bright of mind and good to look at, she numbered among her admirers some of the cleverest men of London, who continued their admiration throughout the appearance of four little Bessboroughs. Her mother, Countess Spencer, worried about "the gayety of her life"

128

and bombarded her with warning notes. "Do you go to the Prince of Wales's ball? For God's sake, take care of your conduct and keep your heart free from too much attachment to the life of dissipation you seem to be plunged into. I think you are in a most dangerous position."

Mama exaggerated. Not because there was no danger of attachments, but because Harriet's husband seemed able to take them quite in the spirit of the Regency period. "There is no evidence," a descendant writes, "that any of Lady Bessborough's friendships seriously interfered with her husband's affection for her." It was true, even of her friendship with Lord Granville, which in due course resulted in a couple of little non-Bessboroughs.

Harriet was 32 when, traveling on the continent, she first met Granville. He was 20. As the publication of her letters revealed long after her death, it was the beginning of something more than romance—an intellectual affinity that made her writing sparkle and that fascinated twentieth century England by the light it shed on her personality and the social and political life of her time. The letters were good all-round reading as the record of a mind rich in many gifts, not least among them affection and a sense of humor.

"I think I ought to be very vain in my old age," she wrote to Granville when she was 36. "I have had three violent declarations of love—one from an old man, another from a very young one, and the third between the other two. You see, there is variety at least. Pray come back. If you stay long in Prussia, heaven knows what

may happen, for I have always heard it remark'd that old women are much more easily flattered and gain'd than young ones, and with reason, for if they don't make haste to express their gratitude, they may chance never to have another opportunity."

When Harriet was 11 years old the Spencer family visited the continent on what was intended to be a brief tour but was drawn out when her father became ill. The little girl's diary is a foretaste of the social whirl that was to carry her along for the rest of her life, and also of her ability to cope with it, both as a participant and an able chronicler.

August 3, 1772. We came to Ghent. Walked on the Grande Place to hear some very pretty Turkish music belonging to the Prince de Ligne, which he sent for on purpose for papa and mama to hear. He is a very pleasant man, and when we were caught in a shower of rain, sent for his coach, which is almost all glass and painted over at bottom with large figures. He would not get in, but ran along in the rain at the side of the coach to take us all out.

August 5. Brussels. We went to a beautiful play in a fine box, all lin'd with looking glass and with a fireplace at the end, like a little room, so that you may sit by the fire and see the play, and there was ice and sweetmeats. Mama shewed us Prince Charles of Loraine, who was in a little box with a grate before it. After the play was over he came into our box. He is a great fat man in a brown coat with a great many ribbands and stars, but seems very good humored. He put his hand upon my head, and said he saw me when I was little, and asked me if I remembered the playthings he shewed me in the Palace, and the fireworks, which I do. He took me back to Princess Charlotte, who admired my dress, not being powdered and curl'd like the little French girls. She gave me a pretty box with some bonbons.

August 12. Mama took us to see the Duchess of Northumberland; she is very fat and has a great beard almost like a man.

August 13. Went to the rooms and danced the Cossack with my sister. We were very much applauded, as they do at the play, particularly by Countess d' Egmont, who said all sorts of fine things to us, and after kissing me very often, put a gold chain about my neck. They say she is very famous for something but I don't know what. She is very tall and straight, and I should think handsome, but she makes one feel afraid of her and she wears a great deal of very red rouge on her cheeks, which I think very ugly. Mons. and Mme. Sarsfield and Mme. Golifet, who is very pretty, walk'd on the Promenade de Sept Heures with us and then to the Princess Esterhazy's. Mme. de Golifet has been married almost two years, and is not yet quite fifteen.

August 18. Mme. de Egmont brought her daughter-in law, Princess Pignatelli, to see us. She is very brown and all covered with jewels.

August 25. A man came today to papa to teach him how he might always win at Pharo, and talked of it as a certainty, telling all his rules, and when papa told him he always lost, the man assur'd him it was for want of money and patience, for that his secret was infallible. Everybody has given him something to play for them, and papa gave him a louis d'or for my sister and me.

September 18. We slept at Liege, then came to Louvain, and from thence to the Duc d' Ahremberg's castle of Hevesley which is called Ease.

September 19. We breakfasted in Mama's room, and then made visits to the different people in their rooms, which is the custom here. After breakfast and visits we went to the Chasse du Sanglier in open carriages. It was a vast wood with roads cut a thousand different ways, which they call une etoile. When we came to the place where the boar was, my sister and I had two little ponies with which we followed a great way, but he ran much farther and faster than was expected, and papa sent us home.

September 21. We went a-hunting again, and came in at the death, after a run of three hours. It is very shocking, for when the boar sees he cannot escape, he turns and defends himself, making a stand in the middle of the dogs, and after tossing them over his head, sometimes wounding the horses, he ran once at the piqueurs. Prince Charles jumped off his horse, and just as the boar was striking at a horse with his tusks, plunged his couteau de chasse in his side.

October 24. Lisle. At half-past five this morning my dear brother left us, and set out for Calais on his way to school with Townshend (the butler) which made us all very melancholy.

October 27. Senlis. We were told the forest was full of

robbers, and we hear terrible whistling all around us, but papa said it was only poachers.

October 28. Paris. Our house is the Hotel de Radziwil.

October 30. Mama took me to St. Germain to see my old abbess Mrs. Trent. I am to stay here all day and go back at night. I am to come every day.

November 6. We went to the partie de chasse. It is St. Hubert's day, who is the saint of hunting. They told us The Royal Family alone had fifteen hundred horses out, and there was a great crowd besides. The Dauphiness (Marie Antoinette, daughter of the Emperor Francis I) is so fair and so handsome, it is impossible not to admire her, but Madame de Provence is quite ugly. The Dauphin is better looking than we expected. Such numbers of people in red, blue, and green gold, glittering in the sun with their piqueurs, servants, horses and carriages, made it a fine sight. At night mama took us to see *d' Oligni* par M. de Voltaire. All the Royal Family were there on one side, and Madame du Barry in a great box on the other. The King (Louis XV) is a handsome old man, but he seemed asleep the greatest part of the play.

November 13. Orleans. The road ugly except one great forest, but there was a shocking sight coming out of it, seven or eight dead bodies broken upon the wheel a few days ago, so that the bodies are quite fresh. It was for a shocking murder of a young woman who was going to have a child, and whom they cut to pieces. Papa thought the horses so good that he rode a great way like our courier.

November 16. Tours. Mama went to look at my grandmama's old house, and I was very glad to see L'Abbe la Bonelle, my old bonne, Mlle. and the Abbess of the pension, who all knew me again and said: Ah! Voila Lady Henriette.

November 20. To Rochfort. The women's dress all along the road is very odd. They wear flannel cloaks and ruffs with a sort of fringe of woolen stuff almost like a mop hanging to their shoulders.

To Saintes. The sitting room of our inn opened into the stables, there was no room in the inn, so my sister and I were wrapp'd up in a blanket, and lay on the floor. Papa says girls of our age should learn not to make a fuss but sleep anywhere.

November 30. Toulouse. On our way to Toulouse we saw a most shocking sight, nineteen or twenty dead bodies hanging on a triangular gallows, and three or four more broke on the wheel, all close to the road.

December 3. We went to the church of the Cordeliers to see a very shocking sight; from something particular in the ground, all the dead bodies that were buried there were preserved as they were, only dried up and black. It is no longer so now, but while it was so, when they began digging to bury new people, there was no room, as all the old dead bodies were still there. So they took them up and put them in some large vaults, where there are several hundreds, some sitting, others lying down, others standing against the walls, in different attitudes and all horrible to look at. Mama and my sister had some of the bodies brought up to look at, as the friars would not let any woman above twelve years old go in. So papa took

me with him alone. I was very much afraid but yet had a
mind to go, and also papa says it is foolish and supersti-
tious to be afraid of seeing dead bodies, so I followed him
down a dark narrow steep staircase that wound round
and round a long way, till they opened a door into a
great cavern. It was lit by a lamp hanging down in the
middle, and the friar carried a torch in his hand. At first I
could not see, and when I could I hardly dared look, for
on every side there were horrid black ghastly figures,
some grinning, some pointing at us, or seeming in pain,
in all sorts of postures, and so horrid I could hardly help
screaming, and I thought they all moved. When papa saw
how uncomfortable I was, he was not angry but very
kind, and said I must conquer it and go and touch one of
them, which was very shocking. Their skin was all dark
brown and quite dried up on the bones, and quite hard
and felt like marble. There was a nun who had great part
of her clothes and veil still on, yet they say she had been
buried five hundred years. Their faces are all very different. The nun was praying, a young man had his hand on
his breast, and the other clenched, and seemed in pain. A
pretty child had such a melancholy look that it took off
from the horror, and I begged papa to let it be the one I
was to touch; an old man grinning shockingly, and terribly distorted, both his face and limbs. Another with a
fine countenance but holding up his finger as if to warn.
He was close to the door. Papa made me observe all
these, as the most remarkable, but there were hundreds
of them. It is very awful and I think I shall never forget
it, and nobody knows how soon they may die. There
were many children of my age, and some younger. I hope

God Almighty will have mercy upon me and forgive me my sins if I die. But I should not like to be in such a place as this.

Montpelier. *December 12.* Mama took us to the Salle des Etats. M. de Perigord represented the King, and sat in a fine chair of State under a canopy, all embroidered with gold fleurs de lis. The Archeveque de Narbonne and all the bishops represent the clergy and sat on his right hand, the noblesse, or barons des Etats on his left; and the Deputies du Tiers Etats sat on benches some steps lower and round the table. We heard a good many speeches, but chiefly on distillation of spirits.

January 18, 1773. Papa thought, as the first English family here, he ought to give a ball on the Queen's birthday. M. de Perigord lent him the Government House, and he let my sister and me both go. The rooms were large but bare walls except the glasses and gilding for the velvet and tapestry. Hangings were taken down when the States closed; but mama hung them over with sheets, with festoons of colored linnen trimmed up with ribbon and flowers, which looked very pretty. We went at seven, the company began coming soon after, but did not begin dancing until eight. At ten supper came. There was one great table where fifty sat and four others of fourteen each. It was served up by the soldiers of the Regiment of Bourbonnais. Their band came first playing a quick march, then a man with his sword drawn, and then fifty soldiers with dishes, which they offered round the table to each person, then plac'd them on the tables. They had their casques on their heads, and great boudins with their swords by their side. All the ladies changed their fine dresses after supper, and came back like paysannes in muslins or linnen with bows of ribbons and flowers. I staid till one hour past twelve, but mama remained till six next morning.

January 29. Poor papa had some terrible operation done by M. le Sevre, the surgeon. Mama says he bore it without once complaining. I hope my dear papa will soon be quite well.

January 31. We saw dear papa today lying on the couch. He look'd very pale, but mama says he is getting well.

February 13. M. Sevre performed another dreadful operation on papa, who never moved or spoke all the while. M. S. assured us all was doing well when he came out, and then he said: Mesdemoiselles, vous devez etre bien fier de votre papa, rendez vous en dignes, et supportez la douleur comme lui, qui ne sait ni flechir ni se plaindre. Les filles d'un heros no doivent pas pleur.*

February 20. There was a horrible thing today. Just before the Salle de Comedie a great gallows was put up, and a poor young man of 18 hung upon it for having robbed his master and squandered away what he had got in very bad company at a house near the theatre. Mama says it is nearly like the story of an English play which she will read to us, called George Barnwell. The shock-

* Girls, you should be proud of your papa, make yourselves worthy of him, and bear up under the pain as he does. He doesn't weaken under this burden, nor does he complain. The daughters of a hero mustn't cry.

ing thing is we see the gallows from all our windows, and papa is not well enough for us to go away.

April 12. We went to la Verone, the Bishop of Montpelier's, to sit under the trees which are already shady. In coming back we saw the road full of people very much dress'd, some on foot, but most on asses or mules, with umbrellas of different colors that made it look very gay and pretty. They told us it was the Protestants coming from their assemblies, which they hold in a garden or field near here. It was what they call their catechumen, to prepare for the first communion, which is always done by questioning them in publick, and their minister takes great pains with them, both with what they ought to do, and the difference between theirs and the Roman Catholic religion, that they may know how to defend themselves, or if necessary, bear persecution, which they are constantly threatened with, for the laws are very severe against them, and when mama asked M. de Perigord leave to go to one of their meetings, he begg'd her not, as he said, his orders were so strict to prosecute and even put to death any minister who held a congregation; if he discovered them, that he was obliged to pretend not to suppose such a thing could be, but that if anybody as much known as mama went, it would be impossible for him to pretend not to know it. The day of communion is kept with great solemnity, that all the relations, .many leagues round, are invited, and even on the common church days they assemble in all weathers, and pray and listen to their preachers in rain and wind and through every danger. Papa bid us observe how much persecution

increas'd zeal for the religion so oppress'd, which he said
was a lesson against oppression and for toleration.

May 7. Paris. Mme. de Damas and Mme. le Roy who
wrote on the Grecian antiquities, came to take us to see
Lucienne, Mme. du Barry's house, which is very fine indeed, particularly the room she lives in. We came back
very late, as the postillions were drunk and fell from their
horses.

May 13. We went to see Marechal Biron's garden.
Marechal B. came out dressed like an old picture but so
good natured he has got us one of the Royal carriages
and six to see the view of the Gardes Royales and
Gardes Suisses on the Plaines de Sablons. He made our
carriage drive along by his as he rode by the soldiers, so
that they seemed to salute us. He told mama he had two
mistresses he loved passionately, his garden and his regiment.

May 26. We went to Versailles and were carried into the
theatre. What is the pit in England is where the royal
family and their household sit, except the King who has a
box in front in the second row, all covered with velvet
and gold, and has a room and every sort of convenience
behind it.

June 5. Amongst the collection of medals in the King's
Library which are very fine they shewed us a bronze one
of the Czar Peter when he went to the mint, and after
looking on for some time at some copper money they
were coining, he desired to be let strike one himself.
They gave him the instrument and on his drawing out the
coin he found he had struck a large gold medal of him-

self, his bust on one side and on the other Fame crowning him.

June 6. We went to Versailles to see the King at High Mass. The musick was very fine. We went afterwards to see the Dauphiness at dinner. She is not regularly handsome, but her complexion and countenance are beautiful, and she has so much grace and dignity. She is very lively and her eyes sparkling. She spoke to mama, kiss'd my sister and me, and gave us flowers. The Dauphin looks stupid but good-natured, and would be handsome if he was not so heavy. We went to the Count and Countess de Provence, which was just the contrary. She is ugly and stupid, he handsome, and they say very sensible.

"I was agreeably surprised in the President."

Samuel Thorne

[1835-1915]

In the America of 1848 not every parent would have let a boy of twelve years go on horseback from Charleston, South Carolina, to New York with a teenager as his only companion. Wealthy leather manufacturer Jonathan Thorne not only consented to it, he planned it. He had taken his son Samuel on a business trip. Also in the party were Lambert Suydam, a few years older than Samuel, and his father. And if Jonathan Thorne knew his own boy, it would be Sam who would take on the responsibility for any fellow-traveler, whatever his age!

Samuel Thorne began his career in his father's business, but later became president of the Pennsylvania Coal Company and director of several railroads and New York banks. On the family acres in Dutchess County, New York, he created a model farm, where he prided himself on his ownership of the finest herd of shorthorn cattle in the country.

In the summer of 1915, while cruising the St. John River in Quebec, he died of a heart attack on board the yacht of James J. Hill, manipulator of railroads and winner with J. P. Morgan of the stock market battle against E. H. Harriman for control of the Northern Pacific which brought on the panic of 1901. Mr. Thorne was 80 years old.

Samuel Thorne's boyhood diary, an account of the trip home from Charleston, was kept in the family until his son and grandson, nearly a century later, decided to print a small edition of it.

Charleston, *April 14, 1848.* Mr. Suydam and father have been talking of sending Lambert and myself home on pony-back. Before breakfast we were hunting around the stables for what we call good ponies which are very scarce. Father found one which he likes very well. He was a red color and 8 years old. 45$ were paid to Master Pepper for him and the bridle. This afternoon I took a ride on my pony which I like very much.

April 15. Mr. Suydam stopped everybody that he met who had a handsome pony asking how much under 40$ they asked for him. After looking around the city Mr. Suydam hit upon a pony which both he and his son were very much pleased with. She is a mare of dark bay color and about 12½ hands high. She is owned by Mr. Paxton, the editor of the Evening News. He asks 60$ for her, the saddle and bridle. She trots and walks very gayley under the saddle. The gentleman says that he would not sell her except that he wishes to travel.

Father bought me a saddle this morning and a pair of saddle bags. I went riding this afternoon out of town a little ways during which my pony was scart. On Tuesday we expect to start for home a-ponyback.

April 18. We started today at 12 o'clock for home with Mr. Hatch, who was to take us to his brother-in-law's to spend the night although it was 6 miles off the road. Today we stopped to let our horses drink at a small creek. Lammy asked Mr. Hatch if there was any danger of his horse getting swamped. He said he did not think there was but still he had better not go in too far. The words were hardly out of his mouth before the pony appeared to be sinking. As soon as Lambert saw her sinking he jumped from her back but he was on his feet sooner than she was for she had attempted to take a roll but as soon as she felt Lammy jump from her back she rose from her knees to her feet.

April 25. Today we went from Winnsboro to Chesterville [South Carolina] which is about 28 miles. The roads were so bad that in some places the mud was up to the horses knees. Today my horse stumbled and I fell over his head.

April 26. Today Lammy's horse stumbled and he fell over his head.

April 27. Today we went from York to Charlotte [North Carolina] which are 30 miles from each other. As Lammy had noticed that my pony had not had any passage in two or three days, I asked several of the Horslers if they knew what ailed him but none of them appeared to know.

April 28. As nobody could give me any information concerning my pony, I asked the farrier's opinion. He said that he had the distemper and that he ought to have some thing to physic him so I bought a pint bottle of castor oil which was administered to him but not without a deal of trouble. We visited this morning the mint where we saw a lump of gold worth $600 or $700. It weighed but 2½ pounds. We also saw a gold mine but it was not in operation. This afternoon the Horse Doctor thought it best to bleed my pony and therefore it was done. The medicine has not yet operated on him.

April 29. As my pony is not well enough to travel, we will have to stay here today and tomorrow. The doctor gave my pony an interjection today which made him have a passage and of course relieved him.

May 3. Day beautiful. Although road good condition, my pony gave out.

May 5. My pony little better. Made arrangements to stay here until Monday, thinking it prudent, hoping to gain time in the end. We are staying with a good but poor farmer. The log house has only one room, in which they eat, cook, sleep, and sit, us among them. The females go out of the room when we go to bed.

May 6. The pony is better.

May 7. Lammy was unwell.

May 18. We saw a large wild turkey running in the road.

May 21. Washington, D.C. First day eve. We arrived in this city yester-afternoon.

May 22. We visited the white house. Going into the East Room, I was introduced to the President's wife [Mrs. James K. Polk] whom I found a very pleasant woman.

May 23. Tonight being reception night, I went to see the President and his Lady again. I was agreeably surprised in the President.

May 25. I have noticed for the past few days that Negroes and log huts began to disappear. The Dutch and Irish are taking the place of the former. [They have been traveling through the northern part of Maryland and southern Pennsylvania.]

May 27. This morning we started from Chambersburg. We have noticed that the farmers have very fancy barns, some of which are better than their houses.

June 8. We left Amboy this morning about 7 o'clock and reached New York about 5 o'clock, where we were met by our parents, brothers and sister, who were overjoyed to see us after having been absent from home about three months.

"Got sent to Princible, had Hell of a time."

Walter Morris

[*Born 1907*]

What does a boy do? For men who have forgotten—
or never known—here, in few words, are many things
a boy does. Walter Morris describes himself as an Adir-
ondack Yankee, raised on skis, venison and oil paints.
Along with several published books, he has done "just
about every job in the realm of the printed word that
gives a man satisfaction while turning his hair gray.
Otherwise I paint pictures or push wood through a bench
saw." Now in his fifties, he has kept a diary of most of his
life. We liked the honesty of this record of a twelve-year-
old as much as we did its brevity.

December 29, 1919. My birthday   I am writing this
diary at the age of 12   I am in 6B
December 30. Whent a skien on Bald Head   fine it was.
January 2, 1920. Found a little kitty in the hall, morn-

145

ing. Afternoon Dad got a pup and I had to put cat out and he ran away. Bought oil paints.

January 3. Painted on bottles all day   flowers.

January 6. Sent in cloak room morning and afternoon.

January 26. Whent over to Main St. school   got a cross teacher.

February 10. Got blotters and white ink. Tomorrow I am going to a archetect for some blue paper.

February 11. I didn't have no money and whene I was going in he looked so cross I changed my mind.

February 19. Max came to my house after school   talked to him about invention.

February 20. Miss Jameson [school teacher] chased me so I stopped   she did it cause I threw snowballs.

March 8. Skipped school in the afternoon and went to Doug Fairbanks.

March 16. No school for me to day cause I got liver trouble.

March 27. Sent letter to Mary Pickford.

April 3. Shot off bomb on Main Street and nearly got pinched.

April 28. It rained and had an awful time with teacher.

May 5. Boxed with Roland   had fun with football played with weejee board.

May 18. had to stay to 4:30. Gee! but I don't care. Learned to walk stilts.

May 22. Got frogs and tadpoles.

May 23. One big frog died and one big one got away.

May 28. had a new teacher   she was awfull but we didn't care   we raised hell.

May 31. Worked all day down to garage.

June 15. had arithmetic exam. Oh! its the hardest I ever had.

June 16. English exam. easy.

June 21. Dad gives me $5 for passing.

June 24. I put my finger in Bucks mouth and he bit it.

June 26. Sent money order for a course in cartooning.

July 9. Sent in lesson II, "The Head." got first lesson back   they said it was good.

July 14. Learned how to dive and open eyes under water.

August 30. SCHOOL! good night.

September 21. Got sent to Princible   had Hell of a time.

October 5. I was driving a car up to house when instead of putting foot on brake I put it on gas and goes in tree bent fender a little.

October 6. Went up in airplane. Done tailspins.

November 22. Sick. got gun and case from Dick   got books.

December 8. A kid keeps picking on me   I can lick him.

December 19. Got Mother's Christmas present all hid.

"I feel like a different girl now."

Mary Garfield
[*Born 1868*]

The record of James A. Garfield was not very promising of greatness as President. But in the eyes of the little daughter he called "Mollie Whack" because she was always falling down (her real name was Mary) this tall, handsome soldier was the greatest man in the world. After his nomination in 1880 a friend gave him a gold pin in the design of a broom—for a clean sweep. He drew twelve-year-old Mollie to him, gave her the pin, and said, "You are worth more to me than a dozen Presidencies." And on July 2, 1881, as Mollie Garfield tried to be cheerful at his bedside in the White House where he lay mortally wounded by a crazed jobseeker's bullet, the President smiled and told her, "You are my brave little darling. I guess your papa will pull through." And Mollie said, "I know you will."

Of what happened after that, she kept her own record.

July 28. Papa has been moved for the first time into another room, sleeping quietly nearly all the time. His temperature rose two degrees but after the doctors dressed the wound it went right down again. How happy I will be when Papa gets well. Oh, I am so sleepy. Good-night.

July 29. It has been a very pleasant day. Papa is slowly improving.

August 1. Papa doing gloriously; improving all the time.

A few weeks later President Garfield was moved to Elberon, a resort on the New Jersey seashore. Once, standing at the bedside and fanning him, Mollie fainted. He cried out to his wife in the next room. "The child fell like a log!"

September 29, 1881. It has been a long time since I wrote in my diary and I feel like a different girl now. We all thought darling Papa was on the sure road to recovery, but we were mistaken. Even the surgeons didn't know anything about the wound. And so after suffering all the tortures that any human being possibly could, he died at 10:35 p.m. on the nineteenth of September.

It seemed so cruel that he should have to die after all the suffering he went through. But if any one deserved reward it is Papa, and I think he has got it. I think if he really is happier than he would be on earth, we ought to try and be comforted. But it is so hard to lose him—there never was a kinder father.

I suppose no one will ever understand. I suspect I am

wicked, but these are my feelings: Guiteau [Charles J. Guiteau, the assassin, who was hanged June 30, 1882] ought to be made to suffer as much and a thousand times more than Papa did—though I suppose he is suffering the kind of torture which is worse than any other kind and that is mental torture. Nothing is too horrible for him and I hope everything that can be done to injure him will be done.

It is beautiful to see how much the people got to love Papa through all his sickness. While we were carrying Papa's remains to Washington we came past Princeton. The whole college was down at the depot and had strewn flowers all along the tracks, and after the train had passed, the boys rushed on the tracks and gathered up the flowers to keep as mementos. At every town and crossing the people were standing, some bareheaded. In Baltimore people had come from miles around with their children, even their babies, hardly expecting to see anything but the train.

We reached Washington Wednesday and staid over until Friday night when we left on a special train for Cleveland. It seemed rather sad to think we were leaving Washington for good, though I don't think I should ever be satisfied to live there again. At Cleveland I went to see Grandma. Poor little Grandma looked very feeble, still much better than I expected to see her. What a wonderful little woman she is—eighty years old and able to stand this terrible affliction. When she saw Hal she said, "Now my dear boy is gone, I have no one to lean on." Dear old Hal said, "Grandma, you have me." I never knew what a noble brother I had until now.

Well, I must tell about Papa now. They took him to the main square where there had been erected a magnificent catafalque in which they let Papa lie in state. The whole city was draped in mourning, even the shanties where the people were so poor they had to tear up their clothes to show the sympathy and respect they had for Papa. I believe if he were able to look down on us he would be deeply touched to see how much everyone loved him.

September 26. We went down to the catafalque to attend the ceremonies, which lasted about an hour and a half. After that Grandma and I went in the carriage following Mama's. The procession was seven miles long, double row. It took us two hours and a half to reach the cemetery, and there we put dear Papa in the receiving vault which was covered with ivy. There was a carpet of flowers clear from the hearse to the vault. There we saw the last of darling Papa, a sweet resting place for such a brave and loving man. Next day at noon we left for the farm at Mentor.

September 29. It seemed very natural to get back to the dear old farm and if it were not for a large vacant something in the family circle which can never be found again we might try and be happy. I like to go around in all the places where Papa loved to go and see all his friends whom he loved so much. But our family can never be the happy one it used to be, without Papa. I am beginning to realize what it is to be without a father.

"I was yelling hard as anything."

"Tishy"
[Born 1937]

"Tishy", nine years old when she began her diary, lived in Toronto, Canada. For her valiant struggle with herself, obviously against heavy odds, we love her. What a wonderful thing it would be if many of her elders who share her weakness—at home, behind the wheel, or before the microphone—were to emulate her in her resolve to quit yelling! For these excerpts from her diary we are indebted to Tuli Kupferberg, of New York City, who edits the publications Birth *and* Swing, *and who has done much excellent and valuable work in the collecting and publishing of writings of children.*

April 22, 1946. I got this book today. I was yelling. I hope I won't any more.

April 23. I got 50 out of 50 in spelling. I am glad God helped me. My socks are nice. God helped.

April 25. I was not good tonight. I hope I will be better tomorrow.

April 27. I was quite good today although I was yelling a bit at night. I think I will be better the next day.

April 29. I was much better today, just as I thought. I was not yelling at all.

April 30. I was crying to myself at night because Gay Box was so meen. She better not be meen.

May 1. I was not yelling today. I hope the robin in the nest will be safe over night. Dear me, I hope I am good.

May 10. I was not yelling today at seven in the morning. I have had a happy day.

May 12. I was yelling hard as anything. I am mad. I made the day unhappy.

May 14. I was not yelling. But I was not very good at the dinner tabble.

May 15. Daddy was so mean tonight. I hope he will be better tomorrow.

June 5. I was not yelling. We found a brown dog which we thought was lost. We fed it and then it went away.

June 12. I was not yelling.

June 13. I was yelling.

June 14. I was yelling in the morning.

June 15. I was not yelling. May God bless me and you.

"I am a boy, and have a right to think differently."

Nathaniel Hawthorne

[1804-1864]

"When I was eight or nine years old," wrote Nathaniel Hawthorne, *"my mother, with her three children, took up her residence on the banks of Sebago Lake in Maine, where the family owned a large tract of land; and here I ran quite wild, and would, I doubt not, have willingly run wild till this time* [forty years afterwards] *fishing all day long, or shooting with an old fowling-piece; but reading a good deal too, on the rainy days especially, in Shakespeare and* The Pilgrim's Progress *and any poetry or light books within my reach. Those were delightful days; for that part of the country was wild then, with only scattered clearings and nine-tenths of it primeval woods . . . I would skate all alone on Sebago Lake with the deep shadows of the icy hills on either hand . . . I would sometimes take refuge in a log cabin where half a tree would be burning on the broad hearth. I would sit in*

the ample chimney and look at the stars through the great aperture through which the flames were roaring up. Ah, how well I recall the summer days also, when with my gun I roamed at will through the woods of Maine!"

Widow Elizabeth Manning Hathorne (spelled thus until Nathaniel slipped a w into it later in life) made the move from Salem, Massachusetts to live in the town of Raymond, deep in the Maine woods, because her brother, Robert Manning, had built a house there for her and the children. Another brother, Richard Manning, lived in Raymond.

When Nathaniel was going into his teens, an occasional fellow-roamer of the woods was William Symmes, mulatto son of a prominent New England lawyer who had never married but had given the child his name. William Symmes, orphaned in infancy, was taken into the home of a Captain Jonathan Britton in the adjoining village of Otisfield.

We give you these facts because they lead into one of the most fascinating enigmas in the history of diaries and diary-keeping—a field replete with literary mystery stories and surprise endings that pop out of attics and old trunks, sometimes centuries after their beginnings.

In 1870 the Portland Transcript *published a story about the town of Raymond. It made note of the fact that although the world-famous author, Nathaniel Hawthorne, dead these six years past, had lived in Raymond in his boyhood, no one remaining in the town had a first-hand recollection of him.*

A few days later a letter came into the office of the paper from William Symmes. It was signed only "W. S.", postmarked Alexandria, Virginia, and bore no return address. W. S. wrote that in an army hospital in 1863 he had "rendered some service during an illness" to a Union soldier quartered in Fairfax County, one Private Small of the 25th Maine Regiment. Small told W. S. his home was in Raymond.

"I then asked him if he knew that Hawthorne, the author, lived there through his boyhood," the letter continued, "but he seemed not to understand my meaning . . . After thinking a few moments, he said, 'You remind me of something. Frank Redo moved a large lot of old furniture from the old Manning house several years ago. I helped him. There was a large mahogany bookcase and a lot of old books, and among them was one entirely in writing, and I feel sure the name of Hawthorne was on the outside. I read portions, and it was a journal of some kind. It was filled with all sorts of witch and ghost stories, and a little of everything. Frank cared nothing for the book and gave it to me. If no one has destroyed it, the thing is safe at home.'

"I said if the book was what he described, it would be a prize to me; and he promised if he got home alive he would send it to me . . . I forgot it, but in the latter part of 1864 it came to me at Camp Distribution by the Sanitary Commission express . . . I have it now and shall keep it while I keep anything . . . On the first page, in a beautiful round hand, is written:

Presented by Richard Manning to his nephew Nathaniel Hathorne with the advice that he write out his thoughts, some every day, in as good words as he can, upon any and all subjects, as it is one of the best means of his securing for future years command of thought and language.

Raymond, June 1, 1816

"*The book has about 250 pages, and was about six by eight inches before it was gnawed [around the edges by mice.] It is written throughout, the first part in a boyish hand, though legibly, and showing in its progress a marked improvement in penmanship.*

"*I am satisfied,*" *the letter from W. S. concludes,* "*that the journal is a genuine one of Hawthorne's. Still it is possible that I have been imposed on, although I cannot conceive why or wherefore . . . If you desire to publish some extracts from this journal, I will furnish them from time to time, my only object being to contribute a little in return for the pleasure I have enjoyed in reading the* Portland Transcript *for three years past.*"

The extracts came in a series of installments and were published in the newspaper. Its editor, Samuel T. Pickard, was excited by the diary but puzzled by the curious way of its coming to light. He leaves us this account:

"*He [W. S.] wrote in pencil on paper evidently torn from some old ledger . . . He never gave me an address by which I could reach him through the mail . . . I communicated with him through [the newspaper's] 'Notices to Correspondents.' Every effort to find him and get sight of the precious journal was futile. I have talked with the elder Radoux [father of the 'Frank Redo' mentioned by the soldier Small. Hawthorne's uncle Richard Manning had died and the elder Radoux had married his widow and come into possession of the house in which Haw-thorne's mother lived.] Radoux said his wife had spoken of a journal kept by her nephew, but that he had never seen it. He believed Small stole it."*

When editor Pickard offered to compensate his myste-rious correspondent for the use of the diary he got no reply. Meanwhile, as the excerpts appeared in print, the newspaper "received scores of letters confirmatory of the names and incidents mentioned." Pickard tracked down some of the boyhood companions Hawthorne had men-tioned, and they recalled events covered in the diary and verified their own participation in them. He also talked to other members of the Hawthorne family and all except Hawthorne's son Julian vouched for the diary's accuracy. Julian simply disclaimed any knowledge of it. "The ex-tracts were so Hawthornesque in style," as Pickard read them, "that I could not doubt their authenticity." Neither could literary critics, who accepted them immediately.

Finally, in the summer of 1871, Symmes wrote to Pickard to say he was soon coming to Maine and would bring the diary with him. This letter he signed "William Sims." But summer passed, and no "Sims." In November a notice appeared in the Georgetown, District of Colum-bia Courier, which began, "Died at Pensacola, Florida, on the 28th [of October] William Symmes, aged 66 years." The obituary revealed that at 21 Symmes had gone to sea and spent the next 25 years of his life as a sailor. In 1852 he drifted into California and stayed eight years. There he met Lafayette C. Baker, who was to become chief of the United States Secret Service during the Civil War. Colonel Baker hired Symmes, not as a *member of his regular force of spies and detectives, but to spy on his own men—a sort of counter-counter-spy —indicating a willingness to place a very considerable trust in him.*

In the last two years of his life, the obituary added, Symmes became a devout churchman and steady reader of the Bible. "Since the war he has lived secluded in Alexandria and Georgetown, not daring to face openly the enemies he made under Baker." Which may explain his use of several aliases and the spelling "Sims."

Since then, so far as is known, the original manuscript of the Hawthorne diary has never been found. Nearly two years after Symmes's death, one more installment came into the office of the Portland Transcript, *sent by someone who signed himself "Dickinson" and who said he had found it among the papers Symmes left in Florida. But Dickinson proved as elusive as Symmes. All efforts of Pickard to locate him failed.*

With a few unimportant omissions, there follows what we believe to be Nathaniel Hawthorne's boyhood diary.

Went yesterday in a sailboat on the Great Pond [another name for Sebago Lake, 31 miles long, 8 miles wide] with Mr. Peter White, of Windham. He sailed up here from White's Bridge to see Captain Dingley and Mr. Ring to take a boat-ride out to the Dingley Islands and to the Images [a rock formation so called because figures painted by the Indians were seen there.] He was also kind enough to say that I might go, with my mother's consent, which she gave after much coaxing. Since the loss of my father, she dreads to have anyone belonging to her go upon the water. [Captain Nathaniel Hathorne of Salem died of yellow fever in Surinam when Nathaniel junior was four years old.]

It is strange that this beautiful body of water is called a "Pond." The geography tells of many in Scotland and Ireland, not nearly so large, that are called "Lakes." It is not respectful to speak of so noble, deep, and broad a collection of clear water as a "Pond." It makes a stranger think of geese, and then of goosepond. Mr. White, who knows all this region, told us that the streams from thirty-five ponds, large and small, flow into this, as he calls it, Great Basin.

We landed on one of the small islands that Captain Dingley cleared for a sheep pasture when he first came to Raymond. Mr. Ring said he had to do it to keep his sheep from the bears and wolves. A growth of trees has started on the island, and makes a grove so fine and pleasant that I wish almost that our house was there.

On our way from the island to the Images, Mr. Ring caught a black spotted trout that was almost a whale and weighed, before it was cut open, after we got back to uncle Richard's store, eighteen and a half pounds. The men said that if it had been weighed as soon as it came out of the water it would have been nineteen pounds. This trout had a droll-looking hooked nose, and they tried to make me believe that if the line had been in my hands I should have been obliged to let go or have been pulled out of the boat. They were men, and had a right to say so. I am a boy, and have a right to think differently. We landed at the Images, when I crept into the cave and got a drink of cool water.

In coming home we sailed over a place, not far from the Images, where Mr. White has at some time let down a line 400 feet without finding bottom. This seems strange, for he told us that his boat, as it floated, was only 250 feet higher than the boats in Portland Harbor, and that if the Great Pond was pumped dry, a man standing on its bottom, just under where we were, would be more than 150 feet lower than the surface of the water at the Portland wharves. [From the boy's puzzlement over this, we may conclude as Mr. White doubtless did, that young Hawthorne was more at home with words than with figures.]

Coming up the Dingley Bay, had a good view of Rattlesnake Mountain, and it seemed to me wonderfully beautiful as the almost setting sun threw over its western crags streams of fiery light. If the Indians were very fond of this part of the country, it is easy to see why. Beavers, otters, and the finest fish were abundant, and the hills and streams furnished constant variety. I should have made a good Indian if I had been born in a wigwam. To talk like sailors, we "made" the old hemlock stub at the mouth of the Dingley Brook just before sunset, and sent a <u>boy</u> ashore with a hawser, and were soon safely moored to a bunch of alders.

After we got ashore Mr. White allowed me to fire his long gun at a mark. I did not hit the mark, and am not sure that I saw it at the time the gun went off, but believe rather than I was watching for the noise that I was about to make. Mr. Ring said that with practice I could be a gunner, and that now, with a heavy charge, he thought I could kill a horse at eight paces!

Mr. White went to Uncle Richard's for the night, and I

went home and amused my mother with telling her how pleasantly the day had passed. When I told her what Mr. Ring said about my killing a horse, she said he was making fun of me. I had found that out before.

Swapped pocket-knives with Robinson Cook yesterday. Jacob Dingley says that he cheated me; but I think not, for I cut a fishing-pole this morning and it did well. Besides, he is a Quaker and they never cheat.

After this item appeared in the Portland Transcript, *editor Pickard managed to track down both Robinson Cook and Jacob Dingley. Mr. Cook wrote: "There can be no doubt of the truth of Nat's records, nor has he used any fictitious names. I did not at first distinctly recollect of swapping knives with him, but after considering, the whole affair is fresh in my mind.*

Two kingbirds have built their nest between our house and the millpond. The male is more courageous than any creature that I know about. He seems to have taken possession of the territory from the great pond to the small one, and goes out to war with every fish-hawk that flies from one to the other over his dominion. The fish-hawks must be miserable cowards to be driven by such a speck of a bird. I have not yet seen one turn to defend himself.

Captain Britton, from Otisfield [Jonathan Britton, who took two-year-old William Symmes into his home after the death of the mulatto infant's white father] was at Uncle Richard's today. Not long ago uncle brought

162

here from Salem a new kind of potatoes called "Long Reds." Captain Britton had some for seed, and uncle asked him how he liked them. He answered, "They yield well, grow very long, one end is very poor and the other good for nothing."

I laughed about it after he was gone; but uncle looked sour and said there was no wit in his answer, and that the saying was stale. It was new to me, and his way of saying it very funny. Perhaps uncle did not like to hear his favorite potato spoken of in that way, and if the captain had praised it he would have been called witty.

Captain Britton promised to bring "Gulliver's Travels" for me to read the next time he goes to Portland. Uncle Richard has not the book in his library.

This morning the bucket got off the chain and dropped back into the well. I wanted to go down on the stones and get it. Mother would not consent, for fear the wall might cave in, but hired Samuel Shane to go down. In the goodness of her heart she thought the son of old Mrs. Shane not quite so valuable as the son of the widow Hathorne. God bless her for all her love for me, though it may be some selfish. We are to have a pump in the well after this mishap.

Washington Longley has been taking lessons of a drumming master. He was in the grist-mill today and practiced with two sticks on the half bushel. I was astonished at the great number of strokes in a second; and if I had not seen that he had but two sticks, should have supposed he was drumming with twenty.

Major Berry went past our house with a large drove of sheep yesterday. One, a last spring's lamb, gave out—could go no further. I saw him down near the bridge. The poor dumb creature looked into my eyes, and I thought I knew what he would say if he could speak, and so asked Mr. Berry what he would sell him for. "Just the price of his pelt, and that will bring 65 cents," was the answer. I ran and petitioned mother for the money, which she soon gave me, saying with a smile that she tried to make severe but could not, that I was "a great spendthrift." The lamb is in our orchard now, and he made a bow (without taking off his hat) and thanked me this morning for saving him from the butcher.

Mr. March Gay killed a rattlesnake yesterday, not far from his house, that was more than six feet long and had twelve rattles. This morning Mr. Jacob Mitchell killed another near the same place, almost as long. It is supposed they were a pair and that the second one was on the track of its mate. If every rattle counts a year, the first one was twelve years old. Eliakim Maxfield came down to mill today and told me about the snakes.

Mr. Henry Turner of Otisfield took his axe and went out between Saturday and Moose ponds to look at some pine-trees. A rain had just taken off enough of the snow to lay bare the roots of a part of the trees. Under a large root there seemed to be a cavity, and on examining closely, something was exposed very much like long black hair. He cut off the root, saw the nose of a bear, and killed him, pulled out the body, saw another, killed that, and dragged out its carcass, when he found there was a third one in the den, and that he was thoroughly awake too; but as soon as the head came in sight it was split open with the axe, so that Mr. Turner alone, with only an axe, killed three bears in less than half an hour, the youngest being a good-sized one, and what the hunters call a yearling. This is a pretty great bear story, but probably true, and happened only a few weeks ago; for John Patch, who was here with his father, Captain Levi Patch, who lives within two miles of Saturday Pond, told me so yesterday.

A young man named Henry Jackson, Jr. was drowned two days ago up in Crooked River. He and one of his friends were trying which could swim the faster. Jackson was behind but gaining; his friend kicked at him in fun, thinking to hit his shoulder and push him back, but missed and hit his chin, which caused him to take in water and strangle, and before his friend could help or get help, poor Jackson was (Elder Leach says) "beyond the reach of mercy." I never saw Henry Jackson—he was a young man just married. Mother is sad; says she shall not consent to my swimming any more in the mill-pond with the boys, fearing that in sport my mouth might get kicked open, and then sorrow for a dead son be added to that for my dead father, which she says would break her heart. I love to swim, but shall not disobey my mother.

I can, from my chamber window, look across into aunt Manning's garden this morning and see little Betty Tarbox flitting among the rosebushes and in and out of the arbor like a tiny witch. She will never realize the calamity that came upon her brothers and sisters that terrible night when her father and mother lay within a few rods of each other in the snow, freezing to death. I love the elf because of her loss and still, my aunt is much more to her than her own mother, in her poverty, could have been.

The storm lasted nine days. No food was left in the house for the Tarboxes and their five children. Mr. Tarbox went five miles to get supplies. Struggling through deep drifts, he fell exhausted before he could make it quite back to the house. He hung the bag of provisions on a tree limb and called for help. His wife rushed out, found him, covered him with her shawl, and tried to bring the food in for the children. But the snow was too deep, the cold too intense. She was overcome. Two days later the bodies of the parents were found in the snow. Mrs. Manning adopted four-year-old Betty, youngest of the children.

Fishing from the bridge today, I caught an eel two-thirds as long as myself. Mr. Watkins tried to make me believe that he thought it a water moccasin snake. Old Mr. Shane said that it was a "young sea sarpint, sure." Mr. Fickett, the blacksmith, begged it to take home for its skin, as he said for buskin strings and flail strings. So ends my day's fishing.

Went over today to see Watkins make bricks. I have always thought there was some mystery about it, but I can make them myself. Why did the Israelites complain so much at having to make bricks without straw? I should not use straw if I was a brick-maker; besides, when they are burned in the kiln, the straw will burn out and leave the bricks full of holes.

Polly Maxfield came riding to mill today on horse-back. I wish with all my heart that I was as daring a rider, or half so graceful.

This morning I saw at the grist-mill a solemn-faced old horse, hitched to the trough. He had brought for his owner some bags of corn to be ground, who, after carry-ing them into the mill, walked up to uncle Richard's store, leaving his half-starved animal in the cold wind with nothing to eat while the corn was being turned to meal.

I felt sorry, and nobody being near, thought it best to have a talk with the old nag and said, "Good morning, Mr. Horse, how are you today?" "Good morning, young-ster," said he, just as plain as a horse can speak, and then said, "I am almost dead, and I wish I was quite. I am hungry, have had no breakfast, and must stand here tied by the head while they are grinding the corn, and until my master drinks two or three glasses of rum at the store, and then drag him and the meal up the Ben Ham hill and home, and am now so weak that I can hardly stand. Oh, dear, I am in a bad way," and the old creature cried—I almost cried myself.

Just then the miller went downstairs to the meal trough. I heard his feet on the steps, and though not thinking much what I was doing, ran into the mill, and taking the four-quart toll-dish nearly full of corn out of the hopper, carried it out and poured it into the trough before the horse, and placed the dish back before the miller came up from below.

When I got out the horse was laughing, but he had to eat slowly because the bits were in his mouth. I told him that I was sorry, but did not know how to take them out, and should not dare to if I did, for his master might come out of the store suddenly and see what I was about. "Thank you," said he, "a luncheon of corn with the bits in is much better than none. The worst of it is, I have to munch so slowly that my master may come before I finish it and thrash me for eating his corn, and you for your kindness."

I sat down on a stone out of the wind, and waited in trouble for fear that the miller or the owner of the corn would come and find out what I had done. At last the horse winked and stuck out his upper lip ever so far, and then said, "The last kernel is gone;" then he laughed a little, then shook one ear, then the other, then shut his eyes as if to take a nap.

I jumped up and said, "How do you feel, old fellow; any better?" He opened his eyes, and looking at me kindly, answered, "Very much," and then blew his nose exceedingly loud, but he did not wipe it; perhaps he had no wiper. I then asked if his master whipped him. "Not much lately; he used to, till my hide got hardened, but now he has a white oak goad-stick with an iron brad in its end, with which he jabs my hindquarters and hurts me awfully." I asked him why he did not kick up and knock his tormenter out of the wagon. "I did try to once," said he, "but am old and was weak and could only get my heels high enough to break the whiffletree, and besides lost my balance and fell down flat. Master then jumped down and, getting a cudgel, struck me over the head, and I thought my troubles were over. This happened just before Mr. Ben Ham's house, and I should have been finished and ready for the crows if he had not stepped out and told master not to strike again, if he did he would shake his liver out. That saved my life; but I was sorry, though Mr. Ham meant good."

The goad with the iron brad was in the wagon, and snatching it out, I struck the end against a stone and the stabber flew into the mill-pond. "There," says I, "old colt," as I threw the goad back into the wagon, "he won't harpoon you again with <u>that</u> iron."

The poor old brute knew what I said well enough, for I looked him in the eye and spoke horse language. So he turned his long upper lip away back and laughed again, I thought a little exultingly.

Very soon, however, a tear came into his eye and he said, "My young friend, do you know how long horses live?" I answered that I had heard that some lived thirty years. "Oh, dear!" said he, "I am sorry. I am twenty-four and have been hoping that I should die before snow fell; it does not seem that I can possibly go through another winter," and the tears began to run again.

At that moment the brute that owned the horse came out of the store and down the hill towards us. I slipped behind a pile of slabs. The meal was put in the wagon, the horse unhitched, the wagon mounted, the goad

picked up, and a thrust made; but Dobbin was in no
hurry. Looking at the end of his stick, the man bawled,
"What little devil has had my goad?" and then began
striking with all his strength; but his steed only walked,
shaking his head as he went across the bridge, and I
thought I heard the ancient Equus say as he went,
"Thrash as much as you please; for once you cannot
stab."

I went home a little uneasy, not feeling sure that feed-
ing the man's corn to his own horse was not stealing, and
thinking that if the miller found it out he would have me
taken down before Squire Longley.

*Robinson Cook, the one-time playmate who had
swapped knives with Hawthorne, told Editor Pickard
that he remembered and recognized the hard master. "He
was a worthless, tyrannical, cruel man, past middle
age, with a large family of boys and girls who had to look
out for themselves. He and his son would come together
to the mill. I have seen them occasionally at the store. In
bitter cold days the horse would have to stand without
covering while the northern blast was whistling through
his hair and over the chafed places worn tender by the
harness. Without food or shelter he would have to remain while father and son played cards in the store to
decide which should pay for the drinks."*

This morning walked down to the Pulpit Rock hill and
climbed up into the pulpit. It looks like a rough place to
preach from and does not seem so much like a pulpit
when one is in it as when viewing it from the road below.

It is a wild place and really a curiosity. I brought a book and sat in the rocky recess and read nearly an hour. This is a point on the road known to all teamsters. They have a string of names for reference by which they tell each other where they met fellow-teamsters or where their loads got stuck, and I have learned them from those who stop for drinks at the store. One meets another near our house and says, "Where did you meet Bill ———?" "Just this side of Small's Brook," or "At the top of Gay's Pinch," "At the Dry Millpond," "Just the other side of Lemmy Jones's . . ." I have heard these answers till I have them by heart, without having any idea where the places are, excepting the one I have seen today.

While on the bridge, near the pulpit, Mr. West, who lives not far away, came along and asked where I had been. On my telling him, he said no money would hire him to go up to that pulpit; that the devil used to preach from it to the Indians long, long ago; that on a time when hundreds of them were listening to one of his sermons a great chief laughed in the devil's face, upon which he stamped his foot and the ground to the southwest, where they were standing, sank fifty feet, and every Indian went down out of sight, leaving a swamp to this day.

He declared that he once stuck a pole in there, which went down easily several feet but then struck the skull bone of an Indian, when instantly all the hassocks and flags began to shake and he heard a yell as if from fifty overgrown Pequots; that he left the hole and ran for life, and would not go back to the bog again for the best farm in Raymond. Mr. West also said that no Indian had ever been known to go near that swamp since, but that when-

ever one came that way, he turned out of the road near
the house of Mr. West and went straight to Thomas
Pond, keeping to the eastward of the Pulpit Rock, giving
it a "wide berth." Mr. West talked as though he believed
what he said.

A peddler named Dominicus Jordan was today in
uncle Richard's store, telling a ghost story. I listened in-
tently but tried not to seem interested. The story was of a
house, the owner of which was suddenly killed. Since his
death the west garret window cannot be kept closed,
though the shutters be hasped and nailed at night; they
are invariably found open the next morning and no one
can tell how or when the nails are drawn.

There is also on the farm an apple-tree, of the fruit of
which the owner was particularly fond, but since his
death no person has been able to get one of the apples.
The tree hangs full nearly every year; but whenever any
individual tries to get one, stones come in all directions,
as if thrown from some secret infernal battery or hidden
catapult, and more than once those making the attempt
have been struck. What is more strange, the tree stands
in an open field, there being no shelter near from which
tricks can be played without exposure.

Jordan says that it seems odd to strangers to see that
tree loaded with apples when the snow is four feet deep;
and what is a mystery, there are no apples in the spring;
no one ever sees the wind blow one off, none are ever
seen on the snow, nor even the vestige of one on the
grass under the tree; and that children may play under
and around it while it is in blossom, and until the fruit is

large enough to tempt them, with perfect safety. But the moment one of the apples is sought for, the air is full of flying stones.

He further says that late one starlight night he was passing the house and, looking up, saw the phantom walk out of the garret window with cane in hand, making all the motions as if walking on terra firma, although what appeared to be his feet were at least six yards from the ground; and so he went walking away on nothing, and when nearly out of sight, there was a great flash and an explosion as of twenty field-pieces—then—nothing!

This story was told with seeming earnestness, and listened to as though it was believed. How strange it is that almost all persons, old or young, are fond of hearing about the supernatural, though it produces nervousness and often fear. I should not be willing to sleep in that garret, though I do not believe a word of the story.

The lumbermen from Saccarappa are getting their logs across the Great Pond. Yesterday a strong northwest wind blew a great raft of many thousands over almost to the mouth of the Dingley Brook. Their anchor dragged for more than a mile, but when the boom was within 20 or 30 rods of the shore it brought up and held, as I heard some men say who are familiar with such business.

All the men and boys went from the mill down to the pond to see the great raft, and I among them. They have a string of logs fastened end to end and surrounding the great body, and the string is called the boom. A small strong raft, it may be 40 or 50 feet square, with an upright windlass in its center, called a capstan, is fastened to some part of the boom. The small raft is called "head works," and from it, in a yawl boat, is carried the anchor, to which is attached a strong rope half a mile long. The boat is rowed out the whole length of the rope, the anchor then thrown over, and the men on the "head works" wind up the capstan, and so draw along the acres of logs.

After we got down to the shore several of the men came out on the boom nearest to us, and striking a single log, pushed it under and outside. Then one man with a gallon jug slung to his back, taking a pickpole, pushed himself ashore on the single log—a feat that seemed almost miraculous to me. This man's name was Reuben March, and he seemed to be in no fear of getting soused, though the top of the log was just out of water. This masterly kind of navigation he calls "cuffing the rigging." Nobody could tell me why they gave it that name.

March went up to the store and had the jug filled with rum (the supply having run out on the head works) and made the voyage back in the way he came. His comrades received him with cheers and after sinking the log and drawing it back under the boom, proceeded to try the contents of the jug, seeming to be well satisfied with the result of his expedition.

It turned out that March only rode the single log ashore to show his adroitness, for the yawl boat soon came round from the head works and brought near a dozen men, in red shirts, to where we were.

I was interested listening to their conversation, mixed with sharp jokes. Nearly everyone had a nickname. March was "Captain Snarl"; a tall, fierce-looking man who had just filled my idea of a Spanish freebooter, was "Doctor Coodle." The rum seemed to make them crazy, for one who was called "Rub-a-Dub" pitched Doctor Coodle head and heels into the water. A gentlemanly man named Thompson, who acted as master of ceremonies, or Grand Turk, interfered and put a stop to what was becoming something like a fight. Mr. Thompson said that the wind would go down with the sun, and that they must get ready to start. This morning I went down to look for them, and the raft was almost to Frye's Island.

I have read "Gulliver's Travels" and do not agree with Captain Britton that it is a witty and uncommonly interesting book. The wit is obscene and the lies too false.

Day before yesterday Mr. Thomas Little, from Windham Hill, Mr. M.P. Sawyer, of Portland, Mr. Thomas A. Deblois, a lawyer, Mr. Hanson of Windham, and Enoch White, a boy of my own age, from White's Bridge, came up to the Dingley Brook in a sailboat. They were on the way to Muddy River bog for a day's sport, fishing and shooting ducks. Enoch proposed that I should go with them. I needed no urging, but knew how unwillingly my mother would consent. They could wait but a few minutes, and uncle Richard kindly wrote a note asking her to be willing to gratify me this time.

She said "Yes," but I was almost sorry, knowing that my day's pleasure would cost her one of anxiety. However, I gathered up hooks and lines, with some white salted pork for bait, and with a fabulous number of biscuit split in the middle, the insides well buttered, then skillfully put together again, and all stowed in sister's large work-bag and slung over my shoulder, I started, making a wager with Enoch White as we walked down to the boat, as to which would catch the largest number of fish.

The air was clear, with just breeze enough to shoot us along pleasantly without making rough waves. The wind was not exactly after us, though we made but two tacks to reach the mouth of Muddy River. The men praised the grand view after we got into the Great Bay. We could see the White Hills to the northwest, though Mr. Little said they were eighty miles from us, and grand old Rattlesnake Mountain to the northeast, in its immense jacket of green oak, looking more inviting than I had ever seen it, while Frye's Island with its close growth of great trees, growing to the very edge of the water, looked like a monstrous green raft floating down to the southeastward. Whichever way the eye turned, something charming appeared.

Mr. Little seemed to be familiar with every book that has ever been written, and must have a great memory. Among other things, he said, "Gentlemen, do you know that this should be called the sea instead of Great Pond; that ships should be built here, and navigate this water? The surface of the Sea of Galilee, of which we read so much in the New Testament, was just about equal to the surface of our sea today." And then he went on to give a geographical description of the country about the Sea of Galilee and draw parallels between places named in the New Testament and points in sight. His talk stole my attention until we were fairly at Muddy River mouth.

Muddy River bog is quite a curiosity. The river empties into the pond between two small sandy capes or points, only a short distance apart; but after running up a little between them, we found the bog to widen to fifty or sixty rods in some places and to be between two and three miles long. People say that it has no bottom and that the longest pole that ever grew may be run down into the mud, and then pushed down with another, and this may be repeated till the long poles are all gone.

Coarse tall water-grass grows up from the mud over every part with the exception of a space five or six rods wide running its whole length and nearly in the middle, which is called the channel. One can tell at first sight that it is the place for pickerel and water-snakes.

Mr. Deblois stated something that I never heard before as a fact in natural history: that the pickerel wage war on all fishes except the trout, who is too active for him; that he is a piscatorial cannibal; but that under all circumstances and in all places he lives on good terms with the water-snakes.

We saw a great many ducks but they seemed to know that Mr. Sawyer had a gun, and flew on slight notice. At last, as four were flying and seemed to be entirely out of gunshot, he fired, saying he would frighten them if no more, when to our surprise he brought one down. The gun was loaded with ball, and Mr. Deblois told him that he could not do it again in a million times. Mr. Sawyer laughed, saying that he had always been a votary of chance and that as a general thing she had treated him handsomely.

We sailed more than a mile up the bog, fishing and

trolling for pickerel, and though we saw a great many, not one offered to be caught; but hornpouts were willing, and we caught them till it was no sport. We found a man there who had taken nearly two bushels of pouts. He was on a raft and had walked from near the foot of Long Pond, in Otisfield. Mr. Little knew him, and intending to have some fun, said, "The next time you come to Portland I want half a dozen of your best jews'-harps. Leave them at my store at Windham Hill. I need them very badly."

The man deliberately took from the hook a large pout that he had just pulled up, and laying his fishing-pole down, began to explore solemnly in his pockets and brought out six giant jews'-harps carefully tied to pieces of corncob. Then he tossed them into our boat to Mr. Little, saying, "There they are, Tom, and they are as good ones as I ever made. I shall charge you fifty cents for them."

Mr. Little had the worst of the joke, but as the other men began to rally him, he took out the silver and paid the half-dollar; but they laughed at him till he told them if they would say no more about it he would give them all the brandy they could drink when they got home.

Mr. Deblois said he would not be bribed, and that he would tell Peter White when he got to Windham Hill. Mr. Little said he would not have Peter White know it for a yoke of steers.

After fishing till all were tired, we landed on a small dry knoll that made out into the bog, to take our luncheon. The men had a variety of eatables. The question was started whether Enoch and I should be invited to drink and they concluded not to urge us as we were boys and under their care; so Mr. Deblois said, "Boys, anything to eat that is in our baskets is as much yours as ours. Help yourselves. But we shall not invite you to drink spirits."

We thanked them and said we had plenty of our own to eat and had no relish for spirits, but were very thirsty for water. Mr. Little had been there before and directed us to a spring of the best of water that boiled up like a pot from the ground just at the margin of the bog.

Before starting to return, the bet between Enoch and myself had to be settled. By the conditions, the one who caught the largest number of fish was to have all the hooks and lines of the other. I counted my string and found twenty-five; Enoch made twenty-six on his. So I was about turning over the spoils when Mr. Sawyer said my string was largest—that there was a mistake. So he counted and made twenty-six on mine and twenty-five on Enoch's. We counted again, and found it was as he said, and Enoch prepared to pay the bet, when Mr. Sawyer again interfered, saying that Enoch's string was certainly larger than mine and proposed to count again. This time I had twenty-four and Enoch twenty-seven. All the men counted them several times over, and until we could not tell which was which and they never came out twice alike.

At length Mr. Deblois said with solemnity, "Stop this, Sawyer. You have turned these fish into a pack of cards and are fooling all of us." The men laughed heartily and so should I if I had known what the point of the joke was. Mr. Deblois said that the decision as to our bet would have to go over to the next term.

After starting for home, while running down the bog, Mr. Sawyer killed three noble black ducks at one shot, but the gun was not loaded this time with ball. Mr. Hanson struck with his fishing-pole and killed a monstrous water-snake. Mr. Little measured a stick with his hands, and using it as a rule, declared him to be five feet long. If I thought such snakes ever went over to Dingley Bay I never would go into the water there again.

When we got out of the bog into the open water we found a lively breeze from the northwest, and they landed me at the Dingley Brook in less than an hour and then kept on like a great white bird down toward the Cape and for the outlet. I stood and watched the boat till it was nearly halfway to Frye's Island, loathe to lose sight of what had helped me to enjoy the day so much.

Taking my fish, I walked home and greeted mother just as the sun went out of sight behind the hills of Baldwin. The fish were worthless, and it made me sweat to carry them, but I thought I must have something to show for the day spent. After exhibiting them to mother and sister, and hearing the comments as to their ugliness, and much speculation as to what their horns were for, I gave them to Mr. Lombard, who said pouts were the best of all fish after they were skinned.

I have made this account of the expedition to please uncle Richard, who is an invalid and cannot get out to enjoy such sport, and wished me to write and describe everything just as it happened, whether witty or silly, and give my own impressions. He has read my diary, and says it interested him, which is all the reward I desire. And now I add these lines to keep in remembrance the peculiar satisfaction I received in hearing the conversation, particularly of Mr. Deblois and Mr. Little.

Raymond, August, 1818.

In searching and selecting for this and other anthologies from among hundreds of diaries, we have run across some that were obvious fakes, some that seemed to have been written up afterwards from notes that may have been genuine, and some that have left us uncertain for a variety of reasons. All these we have excluded if the evidence of tampering was convincing.

We believe it would be very difficult to forge a diary like the one you have just read—the product of a personality that reveals itself so abundantly in other writings by the same individual. To turn out a microscopically perfect forgery of a ten-dollar bill would be easy by comparison; and that, we are told, has never been done.

Not because we have any doubt of the authenticity of this diary, then—on the contrary, we don't see how it could have been written at all if not by the boy Hawthorne—but because of a curious decision by editor Pickard and an interesting bit of publishing history, we add this postscript.

Pickard, like all good newspapermen, was a stickler for "getting it right"—names, identities, places, dates. He checked this diary in depth, went to Hawthorne's family, his boyhood friends, to everyone he could find who might have had some connection with it, and almost all of them had given him reason to feel satisfied it was genuine.

For a quarter of a century after it appeared in his news-paper, he remained so.

But newsprint crumbles and goes to dust. A Haw-thorne diary, even a boyhood one, deserved better than that. Pickard wrote what he knew about the diary and his strange experience in coming by it, arranged and anno-tated the extracts, and in 1897 brought out Hawthorne's First Diary *between hard covers under the imprint of the respectable Boston publishing firm of Houghton Mifflin.*

The first edition was only 1,000 copies. But there never was a second printing. For suddenly, just at that time, Pickard decided the diary was a hoax!

Why? Because of one entry beginning, "A young man named Henry Jackson, Jr., was drowned two days ago up in Crooked River . . ." Henry Jackson, Jr., did drown in Crooked River, but not when the diary said he did—in fact, Pickard learned, the tragedy had taken place several years later, at a time when Hawthorne was no longer living in Raymond! Pickard went further into the local records. He found that another Henry Jackson had also drowned in Crooked River. Curiouser and curiouser!— as the bewildered editor remarked, Henry Jacksons seemed to have a talent for drowning in Crooked River. But this one had done so when Nathaniel Hawthorne was only four years old.

Pickard gave up. He destroyed the plates and recalled from the bookshops all unsold copies of Hawthorne's First Diary. *Of those that were sold, probably very few are extant today. We found one in the Rare Book Divi-sion of the New York Public Library. File copies of the* Portland Transcript, *which ceased publication in 1910,*

*are in the New York Public Library and the Library of
Bowdoin College. Up to now, only in such carefully
guarded sanctuaries as these could Hawthorne's readers
—and they are still legion—have found this diary.*

*Obviously, Pickard did what he thought was right and
what he had to do. There it was, in the diary—that mis-
timed drowning—and no third Henry Jackson could be
found obliging enough to have repeated the performance
at just the time when Pickard needed it in the records.
There were no three ways about it—the Hawthorne
diary was a fake and nobody could argue the point with
him.*

*We think we can argue it. In the first place, William
Symmes, if he had had the tremendous skill required for
such a forgery, and the time, and some way of getting the
necessary data—a feat we can't imagine—would still be
without any motive apparent to us. Money is out, and so
is any notion of personal credit for bringing the manuscript to light, since Symmes had not given Pickard his
real name at any time.*

*As for explanations of the discrepancy, admittedly
none could be proved. But explanations we can imagine
—implausible ones, to be sure, of a kind Pickard did not
consider, yet should have. If we set ourselves up as
judges to rule out the implausible, then by all means let
us begin by denying the existence of the human species!
Granted the single misstatement in the diary. But
mightn't it have begun, for example, with young Hawthorne himself, in deliberately telling a lie for the sake
of—what? A dramatic addition to his diary? A story of
scaring his mother, just for the fun of showing himself*

how much she loved him? A mention of a tragedy that had taken place when he was only four, updated to suit his storyteller's taste, and then perhaps given a few final corrective touches by Symmes, who knew about the second Henry Jackson's drowning in Crooked River?

Who knows? Implausible, certainly. But we think Pickard had to swallow a greater implausibility when he chose to deprive the public of his book. For isn't it easier to assume that there must be some explanation of that single flaw, even though we don't know what it is, than to believe that William Symmes or anyone else, other than the boy Hawthorne, could possibly have fabricated this diary?

We leave it at that.

"I was made for triumphs."

Marie Bashkirtseff
[1860-1884]

"Suppose I were to die now, suddenly. My family would discover this diary and destroy it. Nothing would remain of me—nothing! It is this that terrifies me!"

Six months after Marie Bashkirtseff wrote this, she was dead. But her diary was not destroyed. Since 1890, when it was published, it has been read by millions of people in many countries as one of the world's great personal records.

In the society of her time, Marie was the girl who "had everything"—high spirit, charm, brains, talent, beauty, rank in the nobility, wealth, all in full measure—everything, that is, except health and happiness. She was born in Russia. When she was ten her family left that country, and "home" for her was almost any place where high society gathered, mainly Paris. She wanted to be a painter and worked so hard at it she became ill. But she wanted everything else too—romance, adventure, hero-worship. Several times in her diary is the line, "Oh, to think we live but once and life is so short!" For her, it was so short—finished by tuberculosis at the age of 24.

Today her painting is all but forgotten. But her diary has been reprinted again and again. The original is written in French. It begins when Marie is twelve years old.

Nice, France. *January, 1873.* O my God! Grant me happiness in this life and I will be grateful! But what am I saying? It appears to me that I have been placed in this world to be happy. Then make me happy, O my God! Please, God, grant that the Duke of H. may be mine! I will love him and make him happy. I will be happy too. I will do good to the poor (I know it is a sin to think we can buy God's favor by doing good works, but I don't know how else to express myself.)

I love the Duke of H. but I can't tell him so. And even

if I did he would pay no attention to me. In fact, he doesn't even know I exist! When he was here in Nice I had some purpose in going out, in dressing myself. I used to go out on the terrace in the hope of seeing him go by on the promenade, even for an instant and at a distance. His face always stood out from among the vulgar faces of Nice. But now!—now he is gone! And I am grief-stricken not to see him any more on the promenade. My God, assuage my grief!

Yesterday after dinner all went into the great drawing-room and the girls begged me to sing. They practically went on their knees to me, children as well. We laughed a great deal. I sang "Santa Lucia" and "The Sun Is Risen" and some others. They were so delighted they all embraced me frantically. If I could have such an effect on the public I would go on the stage this very day. I get such a thrill out of being admired for something more than my clothes! Truly, I am transported by these words of praise from children. What would it be like, then, if I were admired by others?

I was made for triumphs and emotions. The best thing I can do is to become a singer. If the good God would only preserve and strengthen my voice, perhaps I should enjoy the fame I long for. I should have the happiness of being celebrated and admired, and in that way, the man I love might be mine. If I remain as I am, there is little hope that he will notice me, let alone love me. But when he sees me surrounded by my glory, in the midst of triumphs! Men are so ambitious! And of course I shall be received in society, since I am of noble birth. Then my life would be perfect, and that is why I dream of glory, fame, of becoming known throughout the world.

I can see Monsieur le Duc de H. coming to me with the others to throw himself at my feet! But he shall not meet with the same reception as those others. Ah, my dear, you will be dazzled by my splendor and you will love me! You will behold me in all my glory. Yes, you deserve for a wife only such a woman as I hope to become. I am not ugly, you know. I am even pretty—yes, rather pretty than ugly. I am extremely well-formed, with all the grace of a statue. I have tolerably fine hair. And I have a coquettish manner that is quite fetching and I know how to conduct myself toward men. Yet I am a modest girl, too, and I would never give a kiss to any other man than my husband.

Friday, March 14. This morning I heard the sound of a carriage in the Rue de France. I looked out and saw the Duke of H. driving by with four horses on the promenade. No one bears himself as he does. He has the air of a king when he is driving in his carriage.

I shall be happy with my husband, for I will not neglect myself the way some wives do. I will dress to please him then just as I am dressing now in the hope of pleasing him the first time I meet him.

Friday, December 30. Today I had on a quaint oldfashioned dress, my little petticoat and black velvet coat, and over it the tunic and sleeveless jacket, and it all looked very well, probably because I knew how to wear the dress and carry myself well. I looked like a little old lady of twelve years. I know I was very much noticed.

(But what I don't know is *why* they all look at me—whether it is because I appear ridiculous or because I am pretty. I would reward well anyone who would tell me the truth. I have a mind to ask someone, some young man, if I am pretty. Perhaps, I deceive myself! Well anyhow, if it's a delusion I would rather hang on to it because it's a flattering one. What would you have? In this world it is necessary to look at things in their best possible light. Life is so beautiful—and so short)

Oh, I had almost forgotten (what a shame) the absence of the Duke! It seems as if the gulf that separates us is so impossibly wide! How can I imagine he would ever be mine? He no more thinks of me than he does of last year's snow. I do not exist for him.

If we remain in Nice for the winter, there may still be hope for me. But if we leave for Russia all my hopes will vanish. I am going through a time of supreme anguish. A change in my whole nature is taking place. How strange it is!

This morning I pointed out a passing coal peddler to Mlle. Colgnon, my governess, and said, "Look how much that man resembles the Duke of H!" She smiled and said, "Oh, nonsense!" All the same, it gave me an indescribable thrill to pronounce his name.

I am in despair about my gowns. They have caused me many tears. I went with my aunt to two dressmakers, but neither was any good. I shall write to Paris for gowns. I can't bear the ones they make here.

I shall be so happy if the Duke would only take notice of me.

May 6, 1874. Praying to God last night, when I came to

the part where I asked that I might know the Duke, I shed tears. Twice already God has listened to me, once when I asked Him for a croquet set, and the second time when I asked Him to help me learn English. What a consolation it is to write this! Already I am calmed down. But I am very much afraid that if the Duke should ever read this diary he would think it silly, especially my confessions of love.

June 9. I have begun to study drawing. But I feel tired, weak, and unable to work. The summers in Nice are killing me. Nobody is here. I am ready to cry. Now I am crying. A tear has fallen on the page. Nothing diverts my thoughts from <u>him.</u> It has been so long since I have even heard his name mentioned! It seems to me as if he were dead.

I want very much to own a horse and Mama has promised me one. How happy I am! Did anyone ever see a little girl like me with a racehorse? What a furor I shall stir up! What colors should my jockey wear? Gray? No, green and pale rose. Ah, what a creature I am, what a selfish, miserable creature! Why not give something from my overflowing cup to the poor? Mama gives me money. From now on I shall give half of it to the poor.

Monday, October 13. I was studying my lesson today when little Heder, my other governess who teaches me English said to me, "Do you know that the Duke of H is going to marry Duchess M?" I put the book closer to my face and hid behind it, for suddenly I was as red as fire. I felt as if a sharp knife had been plunged into my heart. My God, save me from despair! My God, pardon my sins! Do not punish me for them! All is ended—ended!

Friday, October 17. Today as I was playing the piano the newspapers were brought in. The first words on which my eyes fell told of the marriage of the Duke of H. O, divine charity! What have I read? My God, what have I read?

We now skip many pages of Marie's diary. But to round out the story of her Great Love for the Duke, here is an entry written three years later, when she is nearly seventeen.

Paris, *October 5, 1877* . . . By the way, whom do you think I saw in the Champs Elysees today? None other than the Duke of H driving by in a carriage! The handsome, vigorous young man of other days, with the yellow locks and the delicate mustache, now looks like a big bloated Britisher. His face is very red and he has little red whiskers growing from his ears to the middle of his cheeks. Ho hum! Three years change a man greatly. At the end of half an hour I stopped thinking of him.

"Too men squis out the blubber."

Laura Jernegan
[*Born 1862*]

A whaling voyage might keep a man away from home two or three years. For that reason, many a Yankee skipper of a century ago took his wife to sea with him. If she liked it, well and good. If she didn't he took her anyhow.

Captain Jared Jernegan, of Martha's Vineyard, was 37 when he married pretty, 22-year-old Helen Clark. Chasing whales was the only kind of work Captain Jared knew how to do. But that he did well—could earn up to $16,000 on a single voyage. Off he sailed, without Helen. But the years were long and lonely on the Pacific or in the Arctic, and after a few more, he sent for his wife and little daughter Laura.

From her neighbors on the Vineyard, Helen Jernegan heard what life was like on a New England whaleship with a length of 100 feet and beam of 30 and a captain's cabin of two tiny staterooms—day after day, month after month on the vast, empty waste of the "South Sea." But

191

she liked the sea—or said she did when Jared sent back his message—and she joined him. Jared, unlike the skipper in O'Neill's play Ile, *wasn't so cruel or selfish as to force her to go to the Arctic with him. During the season when the chase took him there, he left his family in Honolulu.*

In 1868 they sailed again on the bark Roman, *out of New Bedford. During the five months around Cape Horn, Helen made a "log cabin" quilt of 2,310 pieces. Two hours each morning she spent teaching Laura the three R's. By this time there was another member of the family, two-year-old Prescott. When they reached Honolulu, Prescott had been at sea so long the land terrified him, and when he was told to step out of the boat to the dock, he held back and cried!*

After 33 years of whaling, Captain Jernegan died in 1899. Helen lived in the home on Martha's Vineyard until she was 94. Laura grew up to be a beautiful woman and married an officer of a revenue cutter.

When Laura was six, her mother thought keeping a diary would be good practice in writing. Sometimes it was hard going—"I cant think of much to write"—but she kept at it faithfully until she was nine. Here is part of it.

December 1, 1868. It is Sunday and a very pleasant day. I have read two story books. This is my journal. Good Bye for To Day.

The story books were about Prudy, heroine of a series that was very popular at the time, by the American author Rebecca S. Clarke.

Tuesday, 14. To day Papa is making a mark to show the men where the whles arer. Good Bye For To Day.

A "mark" was a flag used by the skipper to signal from the crow's nest to the men in the boats.

Saturday, 5. Papa spoke the ship Annawan. Capt. Russel came on board of the Roman. Good Bye For To Day.

Monday, 7. They have taken four sperm whales. It is nice fun to see them. Good Bye For To Day.

Wednesday, 9. The men are boiling the blubber that makes the oil. Good Bye For To Day.

Saturday, 12. We had a tempest last night and a squall this morning. Papa spoke the ship Chnticleer and reported our oil. We have 60 barrels of sperm oil. Good Bye For To Day.

Sunday, 13. It is quite rough to day. There is a ship in sight. We have put on our flannels. Good Bye For To Day.

Monday, 14. Mama is making patch work. Good Bye For To Day.

Tuesday, 15. The men are stowing the oil down. We have 4 ducks on board of our ship. Good Bye For To Day.

Friday, 18. The wind blows very hard. We had ducks for dinner. I study my lessons every day. Mama has given me some wosted and I am making a toilet cushion. Good Bye For To Day.

Monday, January 4, 1869. We past by Cape Horn to

day. It is a large black rock. Some of the rocks look like the steeple of a church. Good Bye For To Day.

Wednesday, 6. The men caught a goney and we had it on deck.

A sea bird that followed the ship for scraps. The men, bored nearly to death, would fish for it by tying a piece of pork on a line.

Monday, 11. We have had a gale two days. I am getting along with my lessons nicely.

Friday, 15. We have been in sight of Tres Montes [Chile]. The gonneys have been flying around the ship. Good Bye For To Day.

Saturday, 16. Prescott is on the floor looking at the pictures. Good Bye For To Day.

Sunday, 17. Papa spoke the ship Mornin Star. Capt. Allen came on bord of the ship Roman. Uncle Nathen came on bord of us at one oclock. Good Bye For To Day.

The meeting with "Uncle Nathen" was by appointment, made by letter six months before, to take place at an agreed longitude and latitude, and was carried out exactly at the time set. The Jernegan brothers had not seen each other for four years.

Monday, 18. Uncle Nathen came in bord and spent the forenoon. He gave us some sweet potatoes and some limejuice and some coconuts and a few pumpkins. Good Bye For To Day.

Tuesday, 19. Papa opened one of the coconuts. It is soft inside. Prescott loves them. Thare is a fly on my finger. He has flew of now. Good Bye For To Day.

Monday, 25. This afternoon Papa and Mama went ashore of Juan Fernandes [where lived Alexander Selkirk, prototype of Robinson Crusoe, 1704-09.] She brought me a basket of flowers. Good Bye For To Day.

Monday, February 1, 1869. It is a calm day and very pleasant. Papa has made two boat sails. P.S. I have made eight babies.

Wednesday, 3. Papa is nailing boards on the deck. Prescott has got some nails and pounding them in a board.

Thursday, 4. Mama is making a toilet cushion. It is made of red and green wosted. Papa has made Prescott a hat out of my shaker. We had green peas for dinner.

Friday, 5. Papa saw diamond fish from the mast head.

Saturday, 6. I shall finish my third reader this afternoon. Papa is making a jib. Prescott gos to bed evry moning at ten oclock.

Sunday, 7. Papa saw a maring spike bird. It has one feather for a tail.

Monday, 8. Mr. Wilbur struct a fish this forenoon. The fish is albacore.

Tuesday, 9. Papa saw some whales from the mast head.

Wednesday, 10. Papa has got two whales.

Thursday, 11. The men have just finished boiling the oil. I have just commenced my geography. I like it very much. We had green peas for dinner.

Friday, 12. They have taken 40 teeth out of the largest sperm whale. The deck is very clean and white.

Sunday, 14. We have four chickens on board of the ship. We have six pigs on board. Papa is up the mast. Mr. Dougherty is hanging out his clothes.

Monday, 15. Papa is making a sail. Stuard has given me six wine glasses.

Tuesday, 16. The men have killed one of the pigs. We have five now.

Wednesday, 17. I have had my lessons perfect.

Thursday, 18. I have just finished a story book called Little Prudy. Papa saw some grampuses.

Friday, 19. I have had my lesons perfect. I am doing sums in division. Mama is making some new waists. Papa is getting latitude. The men have been getting water.

Saturday, 20. I have had my lessons perfect two day.

Tuesday, 9. We have 195 barrels of sperm oil. There is a ship in sight. We are most to Honolulu.

Honolulu, *Monday, September 28, 1870.* It has blown real hard for two days. Honolulu is a real pretty place. Mama is making a dress for me. Papa is up north where it is cold. He will come back pretty soon. I have two kittens here and one aboard the ship.

Bark Roman, *February 10, 1871.* We have 135 barrels of oil, 60 of humpback and 75 of sperm. We had too birds, there is one now. One died. There names were Dick and Lulu. Dick died. Lulu is going to. Prescott has got a little dog, its name is Tony. We have not seen a ship since we have left Honolulu. I am in the forth reder, and the fith righting book.

Saturday, 11. Lulu died last night. I am eight years old and Prescott is four. We are to have fresh mutton for dinner. Papa put up a hammock for Prescott and me. Mama is going to make a sack for herself. Papa is fixing the sink.

Sunday, 12. Papa made a trap and caught 5 mice, and mama has some hens that have laid 37 eggs. The man at the mast head first, siad he saw a whale. I hope we shall get him. We have had dinner. We had mutton for it.

Monday, 13. It has rained all the morning and is very unpleasant. Papa has been fixing the sink and it runs real nice. We had corn for dinner and we had baked potatoes for supper.

Tuesday, 14. Mama has 44 eggs. we saw a ship her name was the lizzyrosy. Papa spoke her. we saw a black fish this morning and Papa lowered the boats, they did not catch any. we lowered the boats this afternoon but have not caught any yet but I hope we shal.

Wednesday, February 15. we had sammon for breakfast. we saw a ship today it was the Emmile Morgan. Mrs. Dexter came on board and we had a gam. papa has just goon on board to get some papers. he is comeing back pretty soon.

Thursday, 16. It is quite pleasant today, the hens have laid 50 eggs. Papa came home last night and broght lots of papers and books. Mrs. Dexter sent Prescott and I some candy. I am going up now to swing. Papa is fixing the water closet. Prescott is eating eggs. he loves them. so do I. We are going aboard of the ship Emily Morgan to see some dogs. I think I shal have a good time. I went on board the Emile Morgan and Mrs. Dexter gave me some cards to play with, and a bottle of hair oil. and she gave me a little dog but we forgot him.

Friday, 17. Papa is makeing a book-case. we had biskit for supper. I cant think of much to write. Papa is fixing the water closet.

Saturday, 18. It has been quite rough this afternoon. I want to go to Honolulu very much. We saw a jumpper [a fish that broke water] Papa thougt it was a sperm whale but it was not. Mama has 60 eggs.

Sunday, 19. I cant think of much to write. we had pancakes for supper. they were real good. the Longitude was 117-23. I dont know what the Latitude was.

Monday, 20. We saw whales this morning, we lowered the boats and we got six, the men are cuting them in now. Papa said the men would get 2 cut in to night but I think we shal only get one cut in. Prescott is up on deck seeing the men cut the whale in. the first Mate got 2 and the Second Mate got 2 and the third Mate got too. I cant think of much to write. I am going up on deck to see the men cut in the whale. Mama has 70 eggs. the men have got 2 whales cut in. I dont no whate we had for supper. it is most bed time. I cant think of much to write.

Tuesday, 21. the men are cutting in the whales. they smel dredfully. we got a whale that made 75 barrels. the whales head made 20 barrels of oil. the whales head is as big as four whole rooms. and his body as long as one ship. the men have got 5 whales cut in, they have throne some of the whale over board. it is fun to see them cut the whales in. I just went up on deck and the men were just geting the last pease. when they get done they all hury, hury, and five and forty More [refrain of a chantey.] Papa said he would put some whales down in my journal, but I dont think so. I am going up on deck. the men have just began to boil out the blubber.

Wednesday, 22. the men are boiling out the blubber in the try pots. the pots are real large. when the men are going to boil out the blubber, too men get in the pots and squis out the the blubber and are way up to there knees of oil. when the men at the mast head say there she blows, Papa gives them 50 pounds of tobacco. Prescott is up on deck, and Mama too. I cant think of much to write. I went to bed last night and got up this morning. we had baked potatoes for supper. and biscute. would you like to hear some news   well I dont know of any.

"We made blood sisters."

Susan Robben
[Born 1955]

What do little girls do? Is life just sugar and spice and everything nice? For pretty little blue-eyed Susan Rob-

ben it's all of that plus getting your teeth knocked out and making pledges in real blood and flirting with restaurant men for strategic reasons and picketing homes of crabby neighbors. Susan gives us a moppet's-eye view of life as it is lived in Levittown, New York and pretty much the way it is in suburbia all over America. Susan, eldest child of five, started her diary when she was eight years old. She did it because John Robben, her daddy, had been keeping one ever since she was born, and even before that. And for Susan, this was reason enough to try it herself.

February 24, 1963. Today my daddy, two sisters and I went to Bethpage Park. It was snowing. It was a beauiful day. We walked four miles. The snow sounded like rain.

February 27. I marked the papers for the teacher at school. It is realy very fun.

February 28. Today I went to a restaurant. I had a boy friend there. His name was Jim. He gave me ice cream. He gave me flowers. He was a very nice man. He was the sheff. I think he cooks.

March 6. Last night my daddy brought me home a prisom. I brought my prisom to school.

March 9. Today I was very sick. I think I have the mumps.

March 10. Today I was sick too. But I felt fine. I felt like I was not sick. But I think I was sick. But I realy felt good. I felt like running and jumping all over.

May 1. I picked flowers for a May basket for my mother.

200

And do you know what waked her up? The fresh flowers I picked!

May 11. Today my father moded the lawn. I raked it. I like to moe the lawn. I have lots of fun every day.

May 13. Today is catacisom. We had a examination test. I am positif I got 100.

May 14. Today we brought Figaro our cat to the animal hospital.

May 15. Today we got Figaro our cat back. And I think he does not want to be home. He cannot go outside or eless he might get into another fight.

June 3. Today Pope John XXIII died. I like him very much. I wish he did not die.

June 8. Today Robert Corbet knocked my tooth out by bumping into my mouth. My father said I might get about 50 cents for that, or 25 cents. I will tell you on the next page how much I get.

June 9. I got 35 cents.

June 10. At music we had to sing by ourselves. I sang a song that its name was Where Does It Come From? I will sing it to you.

Where does it come from?
Where does it come from?
I tell it to you now.
Sponges come from the botom of the sea.
Bananas they grow on the tall banana tree.
Gather cocoa beans and what you've got?
Pleanty choco-lot
For putting in the pot.

I like that song. I think I am going to get A in music.

June 19. Today for the first time Gail Greenfield and I had a cut and we made blood sisters. This is how we did it. Paula Greenfield got some of my blood and put it on Gail's cut and got some of that blood and put it on my cut. And that's how we got to be blood sisters.

June 29. Today we went to Westbury to see a muscicle show called Carnervle. It was about a girl who ran away from home because she did not get a noff food. She met a man called Marco. He was a madgishon. He was very good with the magic.

September 2. We went to our cousins house for a barbara-q.

October 27. I played football. I did not catch one ball.

November 1. Today I am starting to go all over the world in my inmagination.

November 23. I wrote poems today. I wrote a lot of poems.

BALLOONS
You cannot eat a balloon
With a spoon
Anyhow you cannot eat a balloon
With a spoon
Because you would chouk

January 2, 1964. Today is my mother's and father's anerversiry. They put on a record and danced awhile.

March 11. Just because I could not help laughing and I looked around the room the teacher put me in the corner. She says if we get good report cards we do not deserve them. I think she is very wrong.

March 17. At school today instead of staying in for lunch we went out. Always when we go out the boys chase the girls or the girls chase the boys. I was not on the girls side.

March 25. Today Peter Schacter came over my house.

March 26. Today Peter Schacter my boy friend came over my house.

May 28. Mr. Greenfield took Warren Schimpf's ball. It was a tennis ball. We were piceding [picketing] and yelled WE—WANT—THE—BALL. The newspapermen came and took a picture.

May 29. Mr. Greenfield gave Warren his ball—SLICED. Now we are piceding and saying we want a new ball. Today a story is in the newspaper. A policeman came twice and said we cannot play in the street.

June 6. Today our whole family except my father went fishing. I caught a blowfish. Janet caught a bagel. I got a fish hook caught in my hand. I went to the hospital by ambolance.

July 18. This boy who works at a refresment stand gave me a free soda.

July 25. I made a chocolate cake for Papa's birthday. He said it was the best chocolate cake he has ever tasted.

September 21. Today at school we had phisical phitnis.

October 4. Daddy and I went to the Schacters. When Peter saw me he ran.

October 8. Gail Greenfield and I went to the Village Green. We met Peter Schacter on the way. He is getting to be more friendly.

"Not for my own fame . . ."

Bruce Frederick Cummings
[1889-1919]

He hoped to become a naturalist—not a great one, just a "learned" one. Shy, small for his age, and sick most of his life, Bruce Frederick Cummings had to be taken out of school. His beloved British countryside was his classroom, the wild things in it his subjects. And something there was, in thought and word, that drew him, delighted him, a moth circling the brightness with only half a wing. It all went into his diary, which he wrote under the pen name of W.N.P. Barbellion. At age 30 he died of multiple sclerosis. But a few months earlier "Barbellion's" diary was published. He called it Journal of a Disappointed Man. *And the fame he had never wanted came to him—not as a naturalist, but as a writer.*

January 17, 1903 [at age 13] Went with L. out catapult [slingshot] shooting. L. spotted what he thought to be some wild duck and brought one down, hitting it right in the head. He is a splendid shot. We discovered on examining it that it was <u>not</u> a wild duck at all, but an ordinary tame duck—a hen. We ran away, and tonight L. tells me he saw the farmer enter the poultry shop with the bird in his hand.

April 2. Many people go for a walk and yet are unable to admire Nature simply because their power of observation is untrained. I have used the term "study of nature", but it cannot be called a <u>study.</u> It is a pastime of sheer delight, with naught but beautiful dreams and lovely thoughts, where we are urged forward by the fact that we are in God's world which He made for us to be our comfort in time of trouble. Language cannot express the joy and happy forgetfulness during a ramble in the country. I do not mean that all the ins and outs and exact knowledge of a naturalist are necessary to produce such delight, but merely the common objects—Sun, Thrush, Grasshopper, Primrose, Dew.

April 21. S. and I have made a little hut in the woods out of a large natural hole in the ground by a big tree. We have pulled down branches all around it and stuck in upright sticks as a paling. We are training ivy to grow over the sticks. We smoke cigarettes here and hide the packets in a hole under the roots of a tree. It's like a sort of cupboard.

December 24. Went out with L. to see the squirrels again. We could not find one and were just wondering if we should draw a blank when L. noticed one clinging to the bark of a tree with a nut in its mouth. We gave it a good chase but it escaped into the thickest part of the fir tree, still carrying the nut, and we gave up. Later on L. got foolishly mischievous—owing, I suppose, to our lack of sport—and unhinged a gate which he carried into a copse and threw it on the ground. Just then he saw the squirrel again and jumped over the hedge into the copse, chasing it from tree to tree. Having lost it, he climbed a fir tree up to a squirrel's nest at the top and sat there, and I, below, was just going to lift the gate back when I looked up and saw a farmer watching me, menacing and silent.

I promptly dropped the gate and fled. L., from his squirrel's nest, not knowing what had happened, called out to me that there was nothing in it. The man looked up and asked who he was and who I was. L. would not say and would not come down. The farmer said he would come up. L. answered that if he did, he would spit on him. Eventually L. climbed down and asked the farmer for a glass of cider. The latter gave him his boot, and L. ran away.

January 13, 1906. I have always had one ambition—to be a great naturalist. That is, I suppose, a child's fancy, and I can see my folly in hoping for such great things. Still, there is no reason why I should not become a learned naturalist if I study hard. I hope that whatever I do, I shall do in the hope of increasing knowledge of truth, and not for my own fame. This entry may suggest that I am horribly conceited. But really I am as humble as possible. I know I have advanced beyond many others, and I know I shall advance further, but why be conceited? What a short life we have, and what heaps of glorious work to be done!

February 26. Although it is a grand achievement to have added but one jot or tittle to the sum of human knowledge, it is grander still to have added a thought. It is best for a man to try to be both poet and naturalist—not to be too much of a naturalist and so overlook the beauty of things, or too much of a poet and so fail to understand them or even perceive those hidden beauties only revealed by close observation.

"When I am old and in a remembering mood . . ."

Catherine Elizabeth Havens
[1840-1939]

Stamford, Conn. Feb. 19 [1939]—Lacking six months of being 100 years old, Miss Catherine Elizabeth Havens, retired school teacher who taught music here, died today of pneumonia after a brief illness . . . When 80 years old Miss Havens published a book, "The Diary of a Little Girl in Old New York."

—The New York Times

It began, "I am ten years old today, and I am going to begin a diary. My sister says it is a good plan, and when I am old and in a remembering mood I can take out my diary and read about what I did when I was a little girl."

Three score and ten years later she was in a remembering mood. Sister Charlotte was long dead, but Kitty Havens hadn't forgotten her suggestion. She took out her diary, was amused, showed it to a publisher, and so was he. And so, too, were we, when half a century more had passed and we read one of the few remaining copies of the little book.

Kitty was the fourteenth and last child of Rensselaer Havens, wealthy New York merchant and ship owner. The Havenses had come to America early on, and from the outset had proved a thrifty and burgeoning lot, with five main branches of the family spreading over New England, New York, and down the seaboard. In 1733 Jonathan Havens bought a large tract of land on Shelter Island, an enchanted, otherworldly isle a hundred miles from New York City, near the eastern end of Long Island. There he built an imposing "manor house." When Kitty started her diary in 1849, two of her aunts were living on the Shelter Island estate.

"The first thing I can remember," she wrote, "is going with my sister in a sloop to visit my aunts on Shelter Island. We had to sleep two nights in the sloop." Her father she described as "a very old gentleman." At the time she wrote, he was 77, and Kitty's mother—his second wife—was 48. Three of her half-sisters were nearly *as old as her mother. One of them, Charlotte, conducted a private music school and Kitty was among her pupils.*

When she grew up, Kitty taught music too. She joined the faculty of the Catherine Aiken School for Girls in Stamford. One of her colleagues there was a visiting Frenchman named Georges Clemenceau who many years later at the age of 76 was to become premier of his country and to be called, in World War I, "the Tiger of France." Clemenceau spent three years in America, studying our democracy—years which he later described as the happiest of his life.

We suppose we have no business wondering why the owner of such a sprightly personality as the one revealed in Kitty Havens's diary never married—many such persons don't—but we wondered anyhow. One present-generation Havens—a married woman—told us, "It's been traditional in all five branches of us that there's one in every family who lives a very long life and never marries—usually the most interesting one of the brood."

August 6, 1849. I am still living in our Ninth Street house [near University Place, New York City.] It is a beautiful house and has glass sliding doors with birds of Paradise sitting on palm trees painted on them. And back of our dining room is a piazza, and a grape vine, and we have lots of Isabella grapes every fall.

It has a parlor in front and the library in the middle and the dining room at the back. On the mantel piece in the library is a very old clock that my father brought from France in one of his ships. It has a gilt head of Virgil on top, and it is all gilt, and stands under a big glass case, and sometimes I watch my father when he takes off the case to wind up the clock, and he has to lift it up so high and his hands tremble so, I am afraid he will break it.

Sometimes I think we shall never move again. I think it is delightful to move. I think it is so nice to shut my eyes at night and not know where anything will be in the morning, and to have to hunt for my brush and comb and my books and my et ceteras, but my mother and my nurse do not feel that way at all.

I forgot to say I have a little niece, nearly as old as I am, and she lives in the country. Her mother is my sister, and her father a clergyman, and I go there in the summer, and she comes here in the winter, and we have things together like whooping cough and scarlatina. Her name is Ellen, and she is very bright. She writes compositions, but I beat her in arithmetic. I hate compositions unless they are on subjects I can look up in books.

Besides my niece I have a dear cousin near my age. Her father died in New Orleans and her mother then came to New York to live. She brought all her six children with her and also the bones of seven other little children of hers who had died in their infancy. She brought them in a basket to put in the family vault on Long Island.

I think spelling is very funny. I spelt infancy infantsy and they said it was wrong but I don't see why because if my seven little cousins died when they were infants they must have died in their infantsy, but infancy makes it seem as if they hadn't really died but we just made believe.

Anna is my dearest friend. She and I are together in school, but now they have moved way up to Fifteenth Street, but I walk up every morning to meet her and we walk down to school together.

Sometimes we get some of the big girls' books and carry them in our arms with the titles on the outside so the people we pass will see them. I like to take Miss D's geometry. There is a Miss Lydia G. who goes to our school and she is very sweet and beautiful and one day our minister's son was walking to school with her and carrying her books and I was just behind them and I saw him give her a beautiful red rose and I guess he was making love to her and perhaps asking her to marry him, for she blushed when she said goodby. He is going to be a clergyman like his father. I hope they will be happy.

Saturdays I go up to Anna's, and on Irving Place between Fourteenth and Fifteenth Streets there is a rope walk and we like to watch the men walk back and forth making the rope. It is very interesting.

New York is getting very big and building up. I walk some mornings with my nurse before breakfast from our house in Ninth Street up Fifth Avenue to Twenty-third Street and down Broadway home. An officer stands in front of the House of Refuge on Madison Square, ready to arrest bad people, and he looks as if he would like to find some.

Fifth Avenue is very muddy above Eighteenth Street and there are no blocks of houses as there are downtown but only two or three on a block. Last Saturday we had a picnic on the grounds of Mr. Waddell's country seat way up Fifth Avenue [at Thirty-seventh Street] and it was so muddy I spoiled my new light cloth gaiter boots.

I have a beautiful green and black changeable silk visite [a loose-fitting unlined coat] but my mother said it looked like rain and I could not wear it and it never rained a drop. It has a pinked ruffle all around it and a sash behind.

Miss Carew makes my things. She is an old maid and very fussy, and Ellen and I don't like her. She wears little bunches of curls behind her ears, and when she is cutting out she screws up her mouth and we try not to laugh, and my mother says Miss Carew is well born and much thought of and only works for the best families.

There is another person called Miss Platt who comes to sew carpets and although we don't despise her, which would be very wicked for my mother says she comes of an excellent old Long Island family, yet Ellen and I don't like to have her use our forks and drink out of our cups. She is very tall and thin and has a long neck which reminds Ellen and me of a turkey gobbler and her thumbnails are all flattened from hammering down carpets and she puts up her front hair in little rings and sticks big pins through them. Ellen and I try to pick out a nicked cup for her to use so that we can recognize it and avoid it.

The wife of one of my brothers thinks I am too fond of pretty clothes and she sent me a Valentine about a kitten wanting to have pretty stripes like the tiger and how the tiger told the kitten she had a nicer life than he did, out in the cold, and that she ought to be contented.

August 15. My father is a very old gentleman. He was born before the Revolutionary War. I have three sisters who are nearly as old as mother. We have the same father but different mothers, so they are not quite my own sisters; but they say they love me just the same as if we were own. Two of them got married and went away to live with their husbands, but one whose name begins with C is not married. I will call her sister C in my diary. She has a school. She is educating me.

I love my music lessons. I began them when I was seven years old. Our piano is in the middle room between the parlor and the dining room, and my teacher shuts the sliding doors, and Ellen peeked through the crack to see what I was doing but she was only six years old.

My teacher is very fond of me. Last year my sister let me play at a big musical party she had and I played a tune from "La Fille du Regiment" with variations. It took me a good while to learn it and the people all liked it and said it must be very hard. My mother has had all my pieces bound in a book and my name put on the cover.

I love my music first, and then my arithmetic. Sometimes our class has to stand up and do sums in our heads. Our teacher rattles off like this as fast as ever she can, "Twice six less one, multiply by two, add eight, divide by three, how much?" I love to do that.

I have a friend who comes to school with me named Mary L. She lives on Ninth Street between Broadway and the Bowery. She and I began our lessons together and sat on a bench that had a little cupboard underneath for our books. She has a nurse named Sarah. Sometimes Ellen and I go there and have tea in her nursery. She has a lot of brothers and they tease us. One time we went and my mother told us to be polite and not to take preserves and cake but once. But we did, for we had raspberry jam and we took it six times but the plates were dolls' plates and of course my mother meant tea plates. My brother laughed and said we were tempted beyond what we were able to bear, whatever that means. He says it is in the Bible.

I hate my history lessons. Once a girl in our class asked our teacher if what we learned in history was true or only just made up. I suppose she thought it was good for the mind, like learning poetry.

I know a little girl who has a stepmother, and she has her own child and she dresses her own child prettily but she makes the stepchild wear nankeen pantalettes and when she plays in the Parade Ground the boys tease her and call her Ginger Legs and she is very unhappy. It is a very sad case.

I meant to write about the time three years ago when I went with my father to Brady's Daguerrean Gallery, corner of Tenth Street and Broadway, to have our picture taken. My father was seventy-four and I was seven. It is a very pretty picture but people won't believe he isn't my grandfather. He is sitting down and I am standing beside him and his arm is around me and my hand hangs down and shows the gold ring on my forefinger. He gave it to me at New Years to remember him by. I wore it to church and took off my glove so that Jane S. who sits in the pew next to me would see it but she never looked at it. We introduced ourselves to each other by holding up our hymnbooks with our names on the corner so now we speak.

Ellen and I are afraid of the sexton in our church. He

looks so fierce and red. Once in a while my sister takes me down to the Brick Church on Beekman Street where our family went before I was born. We generally go on Thanksgiving Day. Dr. Springer is the minister. He married my parents and baptized all their children. Mr. Hull is the sexton and he puts the coals in the foot-stoves in the pews. Sometimes the heat gives out and the lady gets up in the pew and waves her handkerchief and Mr. Hull comes and gets her stove and fills it again. When church begins he fastens a chain across the street to keep carriages away.

September 21. My parents went up to Saratoga in August for two weeks to drink the water. They always stay at the Grand Union Hotel. Some time they will take me. It takes my mother a long time to pack, particularly her caps. She has a cold that comes on the nineteenth day every August. She calls it her peach cold and says it comes from the fuzz on the peaches she preserves and pickles. It lasts six weeks and is very hard to bear. It makes her sneeze and her eyes run and it is too bad for she has sweet brown eyes and is very beautiful and when she was a girl she was called "the pink of Maiden Lane" where she lived.

This summer I went up to my sister's, my own sister, at Old Church. Maggy, my nurse, took me in a carriage from Hathorn's Livery Stable on University Place to Catherine Slip on the East River, where we get into a steamboat—sometimes it is the Cricket and sometimes the Cataline—and we sail up to the Sound to the landing where we get off to go to Old Church, and then we get into the stagecoach to ride to my sister's parsonage. I was so wild to get there and to see Ellen and the rest of them that I could hardly wait to have the driver let down the steps for me to get in.

I just love it at Old Church. We play outdoors all day; sometimes in the barn and the hayloft and sometimes by a brook across the road behind a house where three ladies live who never have married, although they have a vine called Matrimony on their porch. They have a brother Augustus and his wife Laura who visit them sometimes. They live in New York and the sisters make a great time over their visit. Then they open their best parlor. The three sisters of Mr. Augustus are Charlotte and Angeline and Eliza. Miss Charlotte is going to be married. Miss Angeline has lost some of her teeth and she keeps little pieces of wax on the mantel piece and sticks them in when company comes.

It is lovely on Sunday at Old Church. My brother-in-law is in the pulpit, and his pew is in the corner of the church and there are two pews in front of us. On pleasant days when the window is open behind us we can hear the bees buzzing and smell the lilac bush, and out on the salt meadows in front of the church we sometimes—alas! —hear old Dan F. swearing awfully at his oxen as he is cutting his salt grass, which it is very wicked of him to cut on the sabbath. He has only one eye and wears a black patch over the other one and Ellen and I are afraid of him and run fast when we pass his house.

A nice gentleman sits in front of us in church and brings little sugar plums and puts them on the seat beside him for Katy (Ellen's sister) to pick up, as she is very little and it keeps her quiet. One time this gentleman went to sleep in church and his mouth was open and Katy had a rose in her little hand and she dropped it into his mouth but he did not mind because she was so cunning.

I could write lots about Old Church and the good times I have there. My sister's father-in-law is Governor of the State [Hamilton Fish] and sometimes he and his wife drive over and spend the day with my sister and her husband who is their son. Once when my sister called us to come and get dressed as they were going to arrive soon, Ellen said to me, "You needn't hurry, he isn't your grandfather." She felt so proud to think he was the Governor. But my father is her grandfather too, and he is much finer looking than the Governor; and my mother says she is very proud of my father for he stands very high in the community—whatever that means. One time I was very angry with my father. It was about the Ravels.

October 1. I stopped to get rested a fortnight ago and then I forgot about my diary. I will now tell about the Ravels. They act in a theater called Niblo's Theater and it is corner of Broadway and Prince Street. My biggest own brother goes there with some of his friends to see the plays and he said he would take me to see the Ravels. But when my father heard about it he would not let me go. He said he did not think it was right for Christians to go to the theater. I went out on our front balcony and walked back and forth and cried so much I hurt my eyes.

October 15. My eyes are so bad that I could not write in my diary, and Maggie takes me to Dr. Elliot and he puts something in that smarts awfully. He has two rooms and all the people sit in the front room, waiting, and his office is in the back room, and they have patches over their eyes—some of them—and sit very quiet and solemn. On each side of the folding doors are glass cases filled with stuffed birds and I know them all by heart now and wish he would get some new ones.

Ellen is here and we have fun. We have been down to Staten Island to one of my sisters. She has ice cream on Thursdays so we try to go then. One day I ate it so fast it gave me a pain in the forehead and my brother-in-law said I must warm it over the register and I did and it all melted and then they all laughed and said he was joking but he gave me some more.

My brother-in-law is a dear old gentleman but he is very deaf. He has a lovely place and every kind of fruit on it and there is a fountain in front with pretty fish in it. The farmer's name is Andrew and when he goes to market Ellen and I go with him in the buggy and we always ask him to please take us past Polly Bodine's house. She set fire to a house and burned up ever so many people, because there is a wax figure of her in Barnum's Museum. Maggie takes us there sometimes and it is very instructive.

My mother remembers when the City Hall was being built, and she and Fanny S. used to get pieces of the marble and heated them in their ovens and carried them to school in their muffs to keep their hands warm. She loves to tell about her school days and I love to hear her.

December 10. My eyes are better and I will write a little when I can. Ellen and I went shopping alone. We went to

Bond's Dry Goods Store on Sixth Avenue just below
Ninth Street to buy a yard of calico to make an apron for
Maggie's birthday. We hope she will like it. It is good
quality, for we pulled the corner and twitched it as we
have seen our mothers do and it did not tear. Ellen and
I call each other Sister Cynthia and Sister Juliana, and
when we bought the calico Ellen said, "Sister Cynthia,
have you any change? I have only a fifty-dollar bill papa
left me this morning," and the clerk laughed. I guess he
knew Ellen was making it up.

Sometimes we play I am blind and Ellen leads me
along on the street and once a lady went by and said to
her little girl, "See that poor child, she is blind," and
perhaps when I get old I may be really blind as a punishment for pretending. But once Maggie was walking behind us and she called out, "Hurry, children, don't walk
so slow," only she always calls us by our names out loud,
Katy and Ellen. I don't think grownup people understand
what children like—we love to dress up in long frocks
and I guess all little girls like to, for my mother did.
When she was about twelve years old she put on her
mother's black lace shawl and walked out on Broadway
in it, and her cousin, Katy Lawrence, met her in front of
St. Paul's Church and saw the shawl dragging on the sidewalk and my mother looking behind to see if it dragged
and she told my grandmother about it and my mother
was punished. I know it was wrong but it must have been
lovely to think that it really dragged and that people were
looking at it.

There is a bakery kept by a Mr. Walduck on the corner of Sixth Avenue and Eighth Street and they make

delicious cream puffs and when I have three cents to spare I run down there right after breakfast, before school begins, and buy one and eat it there.

I hope Ellen will stay all winter. She is full of pranks and smarter than I am if she is younger and I hope we will have lots of snow. When there is real good sleighing my sister hires a stage sleigh and takes me and a lot of my schoolmates a sleigh ride down Broadway to the Battery and back. The sleigh is open and very long and has long seats on each side and straw on the floor to keep our feet warm and the sleigh bells sound so cheerful. We see some of our friends taking their afternoon walk on the sidewalk and I guess they wished they were in our sleigh!

Stages run through Bleecker Street and Eighth Street and Ninth Street right past our house, and it puts me to sleep when I come home from the country to hear them rumble along over the cobblestones again. There is a line on Fourteenth Street too and that is the highest uptown.

I roll my hoop and jump rope in the afternoon sometimes in the Parade Ground on Washington Square and sometimes in Union Square. Union Square has a high iron railing around it and a fountain in the middle. My brother says he remembers when it was a pond and the farmers used to water their horses in it. Our Ninth Street stages run down Broadway to the Battery and when I go to the ferry to go to Staten Island they go through Whitehall Street and just opposite the Bowling Green there is a sign over a store, "Lay & Hatch" but they don't sell eggs.

January 2, 1850. Yesterday was New Year's Day, and I had lovely presents. We had 39 callers and I have an ivory tablet and I write all their names down in it. We have to be dressed and ready by ten o'clock to receive. Some of the gentlemen come together and don't stay more than a minute; but some go into the back room and take some oysters and coffee and cake and stay and talk. My cousin is always the first to come, and sometimes he comes before we are ready and we find him sitting behind the door on the end of the sofa because he is bashful. The gentlemen keep dropping in all day and until long after I have gone to bed; and the horses look tired, and the livery men make a lot of money.

Next January we shall be half through the nineteenth century. I hope I shall live to see the next century [which she did with 39 years to spare] but I don't want to be alive when the year 2000 comes, for my Bible teacher says the world is coming to an end then, and perhaps sooner.

January 14. My Staten Island sister gave me a nice silk dress, only it's a soft kind that does not rustle. I have a green silk which I hate and the other day I walked too near the edge of the sidewalk and one of the stages splashed mud on it and I am glad, for it can't be cleaned.

Maggie, my nurse, is a very good woman and reads ever so many chapters in her Bible every Sunday and she said one day, "Well, Moses had his own troubles with all the children of Israel." I suppose she was thinking about the troubles she has with us children. I have a little bit of a hymn book that was given to one of my sisters (not own) "by her affectionate mother." It was printed in 1811 and is called "The Children's Hymn Book" and some of the hymns are about children sleeping in church and they are very severe and I don't have to learn them.

221

We used the book "Watts & Select" in our church and I know lots of them. There is a hymn I have learnt, and in it, it says:

Like young Abijah may I see
That good things may be found in me,

and my sister says when she was a little girl and learned it, she always thought that when Abijah died they cut him open and found sugar plums in him. Sometimes when the sermon is very long Ellen and I count the bonnets to keep ourselves awake. She chooses the pink ones and I take the blue and she generally gets the most.

This is my mother's birthday and my grandmother came to dinner. My mother is forty-nine today, and I hope she will live to be a hundred.

April 12. Minnie B. and Lottie G. and Mary P. and I have a sewing society and we sew for a fair but we don't make much money.

May 15. My grandfather had a ship called the Snow and he used to tell people he had seen Snow in June more than three feet deep and they wouldn't believe him.

July 15. I have not written in my diary for ever so long, but now school has just closed for the summer and I have more time. We had a new study last winter, something to strengthen our memories. The teacher was a Miss Peabody from Boston and she has a sister married to a Mr. Nathaniel Hawthorne, who writes beautiful stories.

We had charts to paint on, and stayed after school to paint them, and one-half of the page was a country and the other half was for the people who lived in that country, and the country was painted one color and the people another color, and this is the way it will help us to remember, for Mesopotamia was yellow and Abraham who lived there was royal purple, and so I shall never forget that he lived in Mesopotamia but I may not remember after all which was yellow, the man or the country, but I don't suppose that is really any matter so long as I don't forget where he lived.

August 6. This is my birthday again and I am now eleven years old.

"Laughterre is apt to seize me."

Anna Green Winslow
[1759-1779]

Long before the Revolution, many American colonists believed war with England was coming. Joshua Winslow, a fifth-generation descendant of the Winslows of Boston, was an army officer who had served as Commissary-General of the British forces in Nova Scotia. His daugh-

ter Anna was born there. The Winslows went back to New England and Joshua bought the house in Marshfield that was later to be the home of Daniel Webster. In 1770 Joshua was so sure of the coming conflict with the mother country that rather than remain to turn against his King, he took his wife with him back to Nova Scotia. They left eleven-year-old Anna in Boston to live with an aunt while she finished her education.

Just before he left, Anna's "Honoured Papa" told her to keep a diary so that he would know of everything that happened to her while he was away. Neither he nor Anna had the faintest expectation that the diary would ever be printed, and many times reprinted, and that people would still be enjoying it two hundred years later!

Boston. *November 29, 1771.* My aunt Deming gives her love to you and says it is this morning 12 years since she had the pleasure of congratulating papa and you on the birth of your scribling daughter. She hopes if I live 12 years longer that I shall write and do everything better than can be expected in the past twelve.

November 30. My company yesterday made four couple at country dansing; danceing I mean. In the evening young Mr. Waters hearing of my assembly, put his flute in his pocket and played several minuets and other tunes, to which we danced mighty cleverly. But Lucinda [a slave girl] was our principal piper.

I am to leave off my black ribbins tomorrow, & am to put on my red cloak & black hatt—I hope aunt wont let me wear the black hatt [which her mother had sent her] with the red Dominie, for the people will ask me what I have got to sell as I go along the street if I do. Dear mamma, you dont know the fation here—I beg to look like other folk. You dont know what a stir would be made in sudbury street, were I to make my appearance there in my red Dominie & black Hatt.

My aunt Deming dont approve of my English.

December 6. Yesterday I was prevented dining at unkle Joshua's by a snow storm which lasted till 12 o'clock today, I spent some part of yesterday afternoon and evening at Mr. Glover's [Nathaniel Glover, father of her friend Polly and a business partner of John Hancock.] When I came home, the snow being so deep I was bro't home in arms. The snow is up to the peoples wast in some places in the street.

December 14. The weather and walking have been very winter like since the above hotch-potch, pothooks & trammels. I went to Mrs. Whitwell's last wednessday— you taught me to spell the 4 day of the week, Mamma, but my aunt says that it should be spelt wednesday.

My aunt also says that till I come out of an egregious fit of laughterre that is apt to sieze me & the violence of which I am at this present under, neither English sense nor anything rational may be expected of me.

December 24. Elder Whitwell told my aunt that this winter began as did the Winter of 1740. How that was I dont remember but this I know, that today is by far the coldest we have had since I have been in New England. The walking is so slippery & the air so cold that aunt chuses to have me for her scoller these two days. And as tomorrow will be a holiday, so the Pope and his associates have ordained, my aunt thinks not to trouble Mrs. Smith [her sewing teacher] with me this week.

Anna, like other Bay Colony children, was taught by her Puritan parents to frown on Christmas celebrations. It wasn't until the Nineteenth Century that Christmas was accepted in New England as a time of rejoicing and exchanging of gifts. Bostonians gave each other New Year's day presents.

December 27. I keept Christmas at home this year & did a very good day's work, aunt says so. How notable I have been this week I shall tell you by & by. How strangely industrious I have been this week, I will inform you with my own hand—at present, I am so diligent that I am oblig'd to use the hand & pen of my old friend, who being near by is better than a brother far off. I dont forgit dear little John Henry so pray mamma, dont mistake me.

December 28. Last evening I finished my shift. I began my shift at 12 o'clock last monday, have read my bible every day this week & wrote every day save one.

December 30. Unkle has just come in with a letter from Papa in his hand (& none for me) by way of Newbury. I am told my Papa has not mention'd me in this Letter. Out of sight, out of mind.

January 1, 1772. I wish my Papa, Mama, brother John Henry & all the rest of my acquaintance a Happy New Year, I have bestow'd no new year's gift as yet. But have received one very handsome one, viz. the History of Joseph Andrews [novel by Henry Fielding] abreviated. In nice Guilt and flowers covers. This afternoon being a holiday I am going to pay my compliments in Sudbury Street [where lived her aunt Elizabeth Storer, with whom Anna spent much of her time.]

January 4. I was dress'd in my yellow coat, my black bib & apron, my pompedore shoes, the cap my aunt Storer sometime since presented me with (blue ribbons on it) & a very handsome loket in the shape of a hart she gave me—the past [paste] pin my hon'd Papa presented me with in my cap, My new cloak & bonnet on, my pompedore gloves, &c. And I would tell you that for the first time they all lik'd my dress very much. My cloak & bonnett are really very handsome, & so they need be. For they cost an amasing sight of money, not quite £45 tho' Aunt Suky said that she suppos'd Aunt Deming would be frighted out of her Wits at the money it cost. I have got one covering, by the cost, that is genteel, & I like it much myself.

January 11. I have attended my schools every day this week except wednesday afternoon when I made a setting up visit to Aunt Sukey & was dress'd just as I was to go to the ball.

I heard Mr Thacher preach our Lecture last evening Heb. 11.3. I remember a great deal of the sermon, but a'nt time to put it down. It is one year last Septr. since he was ordain'd & he will be 20 years of age next May if he lives so long.

January 17. I told you the 27th Ult that I was going to a constitation with Miss Soley. I have now the pleasure to give you the result, viz. a very genteel well regulated assembly which we had at Mr. Soley's last evening, miss

Soley being mistres of the ceremony. Mrs. Soley desired
me to assist Miss Hannah in making out a list of guests
which I did some time since, I wrote all the invitation
cards. There was a large company assembled in a handsome, large, upper room in the new end of the house. We
had two fiddles, & I had the honor to open the diversion
of the evening in a minuet with Miss Soley.

Our treat was nuts, raisins, Cakes, Wine, punch, hot &
cold, all in great plenty. We had a very agreeable evening
from 5 to 10 o'clock. For variety we woo'd a widow,
hunted the whistle, threaded the needle, & while the company was collecting, we diverted ourselves with playing
of pawns, no rudeness Mamma I assure you. Aunt Deming desires you would <u>perticulary observe</u> that the elderly
part of the company were <u>spectators only</u>, they mix'd not
in either of the above describ'd scenes.

*"Pawns" was a popular kissing game of the day. Since
all the guests at this party were girls around Anna's age,
except for a few chaperons, her description of the "scenes"
could hardly have come as much of a shock to mama.*

I was dress'd in my yellow coat, black bib & apron,
black feathers on my head, my past comb, & all my past
garnet marquesett & jet pins, together with my silver
plume—my loket, rings, black collar round my neck,
black mitts & 2 or 3 yards of blue ribbin (black & blue is
high tast) striped tucker and ruffels (not my best) & my
silk shoes compleated my dress.

January 18. Yesterday I had an invitation to celebrate
Miss Caty's birth-day with her. She gave it me the night

before. Miss is 10 years old. The best dancer in Mr
Turner's school, she has been his scoller these 3 years.
My aunt thought it proper (as our family had an invita-
tion) that I should attend a neighbor's funeral yesterday
P.M. I went directly from it to Miss Caty's rout.

January 25. Honoured Mamma, My Honoured Papa has
never signified to me his approbation of my journals,
from whence I infer that he either never reads them or
does not give himself the trouble to remember any of
their contents, tho' some part has been address'd to him,
so, for the future, I shall trouble only you with this part
of my scribble.

February 9. My honoured Mamma will be so good as to
excuse my useing the pen of my old friend just here,
because I am disabled by a whitloe [inflammation] on
my fourth finger & something like one on my middle
finger, from using my own pen; but altho' my right hand
is in bondage, my left is free; & my aunt says it will be a
nice oppertunity if I do but improve it to perfect myself
in learning to spin flax. I am pleased with the proposal &
am at this present exerting myself for this purpose. I
hope, when two, or at most three months are past, to give
you occular demonstration of my proficiency in this art,
as well as several others.

My fingers are not the only part of me that has suffer'd
with sores within this fortnight, for I have had an ugly
great boil upon my right hip & about a dozen small
ones—I am at present swath'd hip & thigh, as Samson
smote the Philistines, but my soreness is near over. My
aunt thought it highly proper to give me some cooling
physick, so last tuesday I took ½ oz Globe Salt (a dis-

agreeable potion) & kept chamber. Since which, there has been no new eruption & a great alteration for the better in those I had before.

I have read my bible to my aunt this morning (as is the daily custom) & sometimes I read other books to her. So you may perceive, I have the use of my tongue & I tell her it is a good thing.

I tell my Aunt I feel a disposition to be a good girl, & she pleases herself that she shall have much comfort of me today.

February 10. This day I paid my respects to Master Holbrook [her writing master] after a week's absence. My finger is still in limbo as you may see by this writeing. I have not paid my compliments to Madam Smith, for altho I can drive the goos quill a bit, I cannot so well manage the needle. So I will lay my hand to the distaff, as the virtuous woman did of old.

February 12. Aunt Green gave me a plaister for my fingure that has near cur'd it, but I have a new boil, which is under poultice, & tomorrow I am to undergo another seasoning with globe Salt.

February 13. Everybody says that this is a bitter cold day, but I know nothing about it but hearsay for I am in aunt's chamber (which is very warm always) with a nice fire, a stove, sitting in Aunt's easy chair, with a tall three leav'd screen at my back, & I am very comfortable. I took my second (& I hope last) potion of Globe salts this morning.

Valentine day. My cousin Sally reeled off a 10 knot skane of yarn [which Anna had spun from flax] today.

My valentine [first man she saw that day] was an old country plow-jogger. Aunt says niece is a whimsical child. *February 18.* Another ten knot skane of my yarn was reel'd off today. Aunt says it is very good. My boils and whitloes are growing well apace, so that I can knit a little in the evening. You see how I improve in my writing, but I drive on as fast as I can.

February 21. My Grandmamma sent Miss Deming, Miss Winslow & I one eighth of a Dollar a piece for a New Years gift. I have made the purchase I told you of a few pages agone, that is, last Thursday I purchas'd with my aunt Deming's leave, a very beautiful white feather hat, that is, the out side, which is a bit of white hollond with the feathers sew'd on in a most curious manner, white & unsullyed as the falling snow, this hat I have long been saving my money to procure for which I have let your kind allowance, Papa, lay in my aunt's hands till this hat which I spoke for was brought home. As I am (as we say) a daughter of liberty I chuse to wear as much of our own manufactory as pocible. But my aunt says I have wrote this account very badly.

Papa I rec'd your letter dated Jan. 11, for which I thank you, Sir, & thank you greatly for the money I received therewith.

February 22. I have spun 30 knots of linning yarn and (partly) newfooted a pair of stockings for Lucinda, read a part of the pilgrim's progress, coppied part of my text journal (that if I live a few years longer I may be able to understand it, for aunt sais that to her the contents as I first mark'd them were an impenetrable secret) play'd some, tuck'd [ate] a great deal, laugh'd enough, & I tell aunt it is all human nature, if not human reason.

March 4. I have just now been writing four lines in my Book almost as well as the copy. But all the intreaties in the world will not prevail upon me to do always as well as I can, which is not the least trouble to me tho' it's a great grief to aunt Deming.

March 9. Now, Hon'd Mamma, I must tell you of something that happened to me today, that has not happen'd before this great while, viz My Unkle & Aunt both told me I was a very good girl.

I have been writing all the above gibberish while aunt has been looking after her family—now she is out of the room—now she is in—& takes up my pen in my absence to observe, I am a little simpleton for informing my mamma that it is a great while since I was prais'd because she will conclude that it is a great while since I deserv'd to be prais'd. I will hence forth try to observe their praise & yours too. I mean deserve. It is near candle lighting.

March 11. Boast not thyself of tomorrow; for thou knowest not what a day may bring forth. Thus king Solomon, inspired by the Holy Ghost, cautions, Pro. XXVII. i. My aunt says this is a most necessary lesson to be learn'd & laid up in the heart. I am quite of her mind.

I have met with a disappointment today & aunt says I may look for them every day—we live in a changing world—in scripture call'd a vale of tears. There has been a steady rain—so no visiting as I hoped this day, & this is the disappointment I mentioned on t'other page.

March 19. I must inform you (pray dont let papa see this) that yesterday I put on No 1 of my new shifts [made of the linen she spun] & indeed it is very comfortable. It is long since I had a shift to my back. I dont know if I ever had till now—It seem'd so strange, too, to have any linen below my waist.

My aunt Deming says it is a grief to her that I don't always write as well as I can, I can write <u>pretily.</u>

March 28. This minute I have receiv'd my queen's night cap from Miss Caty Vans—we like it. Aunt says that if the materials it is made of were more substantial than gauze, it might serve occationally to hold anything measur'd by an ½ peck, but it is just as it should be, & very decent, & she wishes my writing was <u>as</u> decent. But I got into one of my frolicks upon sight of the Cap.

April 13. I have now before me, hon'd Mamma, your favor dated January 3. I am glad you alter'd your mind when you at first thought not to write to me. I hope you will answer this "viva vosa" as you say you intend to. Pray mamma who larnt you lattan?

May 25. Yesterday towards evening I took a walk with cousin Sally to see the good folks in Sudbury Street & found them all well. I had my HEDDUS roll on [a fashionable and elaborate hair-do which consisted of a roll sometimes weighing as much as fourteen ounces] aunt Storer said it ought to be made less, Aunt Deming said it ought not to be made at all. It makes my head itch & ach & burn like anything, Mamma. This famous roll is not made <u>wholly</u> of a red Cow Tail, but is a mixture of that & horsehair (very course) & a little human hair of yellow hue that I suppose was taken out of the back part of an old wig, all carded together and twisted up. When it first came home, aunt put it on [me] & my new cap on it, she then took up her apron & mesur'd me, & from the roots of my hair on my forehead to the top of my notions I mesur'd above an inch longer than I did downwards from the roots of my hair to the end of my chin. Nothing renders a young person more amiable than virtue & modesty without the help of fals hair.

Now all this mamma, I have just been reading over to my aunt. She is pleas'd with my whimsical description & grave (half grave) improvement, & hopes a little fals English will not spoil the whole with Mamma. Rome was not built in a day.

There is no official record of Anna's death. No grave-stone has been found. The Winslow family believes she died of tuberculosis at Marshfield in 1779, the twentieth year of her life.

"Have I been busy this year! Whew!"

Marilyn Bell
[born 1942]

Marilyn Bell was twelve when she began her diary. She was born in Holdensville, Oklahoma. Her family moved to the little town of Crescent, about 25 miles north of Oklahoma City, and there she went to school, then to Northwestern University, and finally to the University of Oklahoma. Wherever she went she was popular. Today, in her early twenties, she still is. She lives in New York City, works, and writes plays.

THIS BOOK IS THE PERSONAL PROPERTY
OF MARILYN BELL, CRESCENT, OKLAHOMA.
PLEASE REFRAIN FROM GLANCING ON ITS
PAGES. IN OTHER WORDS, KEEP OUT.
(Maybe some day, you know—"Marilyn
Bell, The Story of Her Life.")

September 7, 1954. About a month ago I wrote a fan letter to Laraine Day, my favorite movie actress. Yesterday I nearly fainted when I received a personal note from her! I'll always keep it. New York Giants doing swell! Hope I don't have to miss too much of World Series for school. I'm reading David Copperfield and it gets longer every day.

October 24. Yesterday the band went to Norman. I play flute and sometimes help carry the bass drum. If I ever get to become an actress, which I'm determined to be, I want to meet all the great people and have them want to meet me. Made the Honor Roll at school! Got a handkerchief from Tetsuo, my Japanese pen pal.

November 29. Kueta, Jenny and I have been looking forward to our forthcoming trip to Hollywood. We're going to run off Christmas! We decided today to get one of Kueta's dad's coffin crates from his undertaker business and wrap ourselves up in it and send it special delivery to Liberace—or something. Can't wait. Am now 13—respectably.

December 10. We played a darn good basketball game against the Mulhall girls even if the score doesn't show it. We really had them scared! Final 39 them, 26 us. I sank 18 points.

December 22. Mother, Dad and Janie [her older sister] went to Guthrie, but I have been playing tennis and lousing around town. Got a beautiful doll from Tetsuo for Christmas. Will probably send him a book. Finished David Copperfield!

January 22, 1955. Have I been busy this year! Whew!

Basketball mainly, is jamming up all other duties. We played Jones—ugh!—43-27. I hit 19 points. Played Deer Creek in a good close game. We led at half. Then—ugh! I've been working on snazzy hook shot.

February 1. Might as well tell that we beat Deer Creek—yes, <u>us!</u> 48-47! Still can't believe it.

February 5. I've been reading my first Shakespeare lately. I really like it, don't think it's hard to understand if you read carefully. The television is broken so I've accomplished something today. Cleaned room and downstairs, practiced music, read, helped Daddy on March of Dimes money.

February 20. A terrible catastrophe has just confronted my life. It will ruin everything. While the older kids spend Sunday afternoons limousining around in their Fords and Chevies, I sit home, not allowed <u>even a meager 15 minutes a week</u> to drive the car. If I can earn $300 a summer for the next few summers some way, then when I'm old enough I'll simply purchase my own jalopy. That's it! P.S. How am I gonna earn $300? <u>That is the question.</u>

March 1. I have spring fever and really feel great. Virginia and I are going to California. Got a letter on Japanese wrestling from Tetsuo. He's a kill. Think I had about 15 points per game average in basketball. I'll double that next year. I'm gonna <u>work.</u> I guess Virginia and I probably won't get to do what we've dreamed about—seeing Beverly Hills together. I'm going out there with the family on vacation and she probably won't go at all.

April 12. I'm reading Uncle Tom's Cabin. Sure is slow reading. Forgive these gripes, but lately things have been Miserable. Great were Academy awards! Kelly and Brando (drool).

April 19. I dreamed last night I visited Richard Widmark and he lived at Roman Nose Park. I guess the reason is that there's a lifeguard at the swimming pool at Roman Nose that looks a lot like Widmark. What next?

May 7. I've hit upon a new person that is really an asset to anyone's life. It's Mrs. Fanny Cress, whom I'll never forget in all my life. She lives half a mile west of Hopkins in a cute little house all by herself. Is she a scream! She mows the lawn; washes everything on a scrub-board; eats five biscuits, egg, orange juice and coffee for breakfast; keeps a garden; loves poetry; canasta queen—and is 86 years old! She possesses one of the most alert minds in town. It's really fun to be around her as she's comical with some sense of humor. You'd never dream—86 years old! She wants me to come and see her more often and you can bet I am! In band we are scheduled to March at Enid Wednesday night. I've gotten my arms real tan and I sure look funny with white legs and brown arms. By the way, I'm not carrying the bass drum at Enid. Johnny is. Whew.

May 20. Last night Marilyn Tackitt had a slumber party. We slumbered from 5:30 A.M. to 8:00 A.M. The rest of the time was engaged in a show, cards, wrestling, eating (made a cake at 4 A.M.) and watching TV. Today I had to reveal my ambition to Mr. Dyar. I will not be a dramatics teacher, but a drama coach. Much better, don't you think? Actually I'd like to go higher than that. Ligitimate stage. I know it will have to be strictly talent that gets me anywhere, because I'm not stupid enough to think I've got the looks. Anyway, I wanta act.

Editors' note: She was mistaken about her looks—either that or she certainly changed. Ten years later, when the editors met Marilyn, she was quite beautiful.

June 14. This year has been full of unforgetable experiences. Like Jenny's and my notes and giggles in science class, our first smoke (and last) on band trip, our split malts, troubles with teachers, skipping last hour, and oodles of other times. They were fun, but I do hope I mature next year! Most of this summer has been spent keeping up with the Giants and going to town with Nancy and planning trip to West Coast. Mother gave me a permanent yesterday and it was awful. So was the result, but I'm getting it all cut off so who cares?

July 25. I've been clear to California since seeing this little book! Gee, it was a wonderful trip and I saw Television City in Hollywood where many network shows are telecast. I saw Beverly Hills and Farmers Market and movie studios and Liberace (and his car) and watched De Mille direct. I had the most wonderful trip of my life and I can't put all the things we did into words. It was just G-R-E-A-T! You know what I'm gonna be when I get through school? A Californian! I know (when I'm nearly 20) I'll want to work in the summer and maybe study in summer stock or travel around (on a shoestring) but at any rate make something out of my opportunities as a college co-ed. Think of it—me in college! It won't be so terribly long now. My fielding is improving.

August. This is Sunday morning and we are all staying home from church. There are a lot of relatives here for the funeral. I am just very glad God had me at a church convention when grandmother died. They called me and told me about 10 P.M. Her death seemed a beautiful beginning to the real life—in heaven. Of course it would have been much sadder if grandmother wasn't a good, very good Christian. But I do know she was, so she is happy and I am happy for her. Life is looking brighter. We started family devotions with the Bible. I'm hoping and praying this will bring us all much closer.

September 18. Last night we went watermelon-swiping but didn't find any. New band teacher is a real cat. We all love the little guy.

September 27. Mother said tonight she thought in ten years I would be married. Imagine that! Of course I won't be. I'll probably be directing high school plays in Australia or something.

November 3. Well, I guess I now begin my life of crime. I'm a delinquent, no doubt. From this point on, this here lil book is definately private! I'm in trouble with daddio. I skipped school (study hall) and the dance tonight. Nobody interesting was there so I went to a show with Judy. So natcherly daddy comes up to watch us dance! Oh well, I'm done anyway. Honestly, I might as well have some fun out of my newly acquired reputation and rob a bank! The next page of this diary may be written from my cell. (It ain't funny!)

November 6 [the next page] Tonight I had a lot of fun at Church.

"Children in old times were not as bad as they are now."

Caroline Cowles Richards
[1842-1913]

When Caroline Cowles Richards was seven years old and her sister Anna four, their mother died. Caroline and Anna went to live with their grandparents—their mother's parents—who had already brought up eleven children of their own and were living alone in their big house in the village of Canandaigua, New York. How much Grandma and Grandpa Beals knew about taking care of children, and loving them, and making them happy, comes through in this account of more than a century ago. Caroline began her diary after she had been living with them a couple of years.

November 21, 1852. I am ten years old today, and I think I will write a journal and tell who I am and what I am doing.

I have lived with my Grandfather and Grandmother ever since I was seven years old, and Anna too, since she was four.

Anna and I go to school. Mr. James C. Cross is our teacher, and some of the scholars say he is cross by name and by nature, but I like him. He gave me a book by the name of "Noble Deeds of American Women" for reward of merit in my reading class.

Today a nice old gentleman by the name of Mr. William Wood visited our school. Wood Street is named after him. He had a beautiful pear in his hand and said he would give it to the boy or girl who could spell "Virgaloo", for that was the name of the pear. I spelt it but it was not right. A little boy named William Schley spelt it right and he got the pear. I wish I had, but I can't even remember now how he spelt it. If the pear was as hard as its name, I don't believe anyone would want it.

People must think this is a nice place for children, for Grandpa and Grandma had eleven of their own before we came. Mrs. McCoe was here to call this afternoon, and she looked at us and said, "It must be a great responsibility, Mrs. Beals." Grandmother said she thought "her strength would be equal to her day." This is one of her favorite verses.

Friday. We asked Grandmother if we could have some hoopskirts like the Seminary girls and she said no, we were not old enough. When we were downtown Anna bought a reed for 10 cents and ran it into the hem of her

underskirt and says she is going to wear it to school tomorrow. I think Grandmother will laugh out loud for
once when she sees it, but I don't think Anna will wear it
to school or anywhere else. She wouldn't want to if she
knew how terrible it looked. Mrs. McCarty told us Monday that Mrs. Brockle's niece was dead, who lives next
door to her. Grandmother sent us over with some things
for their comfort and told us to say we were sorry they
were in trouble. We went, and when we came back Anna
told Grandmother I said, "Never mind, Mrs. Brockle,
some day we will all be dead." I am sure I said something
better than that.

Wednesday. Mr. Cross had us speak pieces today in
school. Two boys spoke "The boy stood on the burning
deck whence all but him had fled." William Sly was one,
and he spoke his the best. When he said, "The flames that
lit the battle wreck shone round him o'er the dead," we
could almost see the fire, and when he said, "My father,
must I stay?" we felt like telling him no, he needn't. We
played snap-the-whip at recess today and I was on the
end and was snapped off against the fence. It hurt me so
that Anna cried.

Tuesday. I could not keep a journal for two weeks because Grandfather and Grandmother have been very sick
and we were afraid something dreadful was going to happen. We are so glad they are well again. Grandmother
was sick upstairs and Grandfather in the bedroom
downstairs, and we carried messages back and forth for
them. When Grandmother came downstairs the first
time, she was too weak to walk, so she sat on each step
till she got down. When Grandfather saw her, he smiled

and said to us, "When she will, she will, you may depend
on't; and when she won't she won't, and that's the end
on't." But we knew all the time he was very glad to see
her.

Sunday, March 20, 1853. Grandmother gave us "The
Dairyman's Daughter" and "Jane the Young Cottager"
by leigh Richmond to read. I don't see how they happened to be so awfully good. Anna says they died of
"early piety" but she did not say it very loud. Anna
learned:

>A   *In A-dam's fall*
>*We sinned all.*

>B   *My B-ook and heart*
>*Shall never part.*

>C   *The C-at doth slay*
>*And after play.*

When she came to the end of it and said,

>Z   *Z-accheus he did climb a tree*
>*His Lord to see*

she said she heard someone say,

>*The tree broke down and let him fall*
>*And he did not see his Lord at all.*

Grandmother said it was very wicked indeed to speak

light of the story of the Lord and she hoped Anna would try and forget it.

Sunday. Today the Sacrament of the Lord's Supper was held in our church and Mr. Daggett baptized several little babies. They looked so cunning when he took them in his arms and not one of them cried. I told Grandmother when we got home that I remembered when Grandfather Richards baptized me in Auburn, and when he gave me back to Mother, he said, "Blessed little lambkin, you'll never know your grandpa." She said I was mistaken about remembering it, for he died before I was a year old, but I had heard the story so many times I thought I remembered it.

November 22. I wrote a composition today and the subject was "Which of the Seasons Is the Pleasantest?" Anna asked Grandmother what she should write about and Grandmother said she thought "A Contented Mind" would be a very good subject, but Anna said she never had one and didn't know what it meant, so she didn't try to write any at all.

November 23. We read our compositions today. One of the girls had a prophecy for a composition and told what we were all going to be when we grew up. She said Anna was going to be a missionary and Anna cried right out loud. I tried to comfort her and told her it might never happen, so she stopped crying.

Saturday. We took our music lessons today. Miss Hattie Heard is our teacher and she says we are getting along well. Anna practiced her lesson over sixty-five times this morning before breakfast and can play "Mary to the Savior's Tomb" as fast as a waltz.

January 1, 1854. About fifty little boys and girls at intervals knocked at the front door to wish us a Happy New Year. We had pennies and cakes and apples ready for them. The pennies especially seemed to attract them, and we noticed the same ones several times.

Tuesday. A gentleman visited our school today whom we had never seen. Miss Clark, the teacher, introduced him to us. When he came in Miss Clarke said, "Young ladies," and we all stood up and bowed and said his name in concert. We girls think he is a very particular friend of Miss Clark. He is very nice looking but we don't know where he lives. Laura Chapin says he is an architect. I looked it up in the dictionary and it says one who plans or designs. I hope he does not plan to get married to Miss Clark and take her away and break up the school, but I presume he does for that is usually the way.

Monday. There was a minister preached in our church last night and some people say he is the greatest minister in the world. I think children in old times were not as bad as they are now.

Wednesday. Grandmother sent Anna and me up to Butcher Street after school today to invite Chloe to come to dinner. We told her we should think she would rather invite white ladies, but she said Chloe was a poor old slave, and as Grandfather had gone to Saratoga, she thought it was a good time to have her. She said God made of one blood all the people on the face of the earth, so we knew she would do it and we didn't say any more.

When we talk too much Grandfather always says N.C. (nuff ced).

May 26. There was an eclipse of the sun today, and we were very much excited looking at it. General Granger came over and gave us some pieces of smoked glass. Miss Clark wanted us to write compositions about it, so Anna wrote, "About eleven o'clock we went out to see if it had come yet but it hadn't come so we waited a while and then looked again and it had come and there was a piece of it come out of it."

Monday. When we were on our way to school this morning we saw General Granger coming, and Anna had on such a homely sunbonnet she took it off and hid it behind her till he had gone by. When we told Grandmother she said, "Pride goeth before a fall." I never heard of anyone who knew so many Bible verses as Grandmother. Anna thought she would be sorry for her and get her a new sunbonnet, but she didn't.

Sunday. Grandmother always comes upstairs to get the candle and tuck us in before she goes to bed herself, and some nights we are sound asleep and do not hear her but last night we only pretended to be asleep. She kneeled down by the bed and prayed aloud for us, that we might be good children and that she might have strength given to her from on high to guide us in the strait and narrow path which leads to life eternal. Those were her very words. After she had gone downstairs we sat up in bed and talked about it and promised each other to be good and crossed our hearts and hoped to die if we broke our promise. Then Anna was afraid she <u>would</u> die but I told her I didn't believe we would be as good as that, so we kissed each other and went to sleep.

Friday. Miss Clark told us we could have a picnic down to Sucker Brook this afternoon and she told us to bring our rubbers and lunches by two o'clock. But Grandmother was not willing to let us go. Grandfather took us to ride, to see old Mrs. Sanborn and old Mr. and Mrs. Atwater. He is ninety years old and blind and deaf, so we had quite a good time after all.

Sunday. Reverend Mr. Dickey of Rochester, the agent for the Seaman's Friend Society, preached this morning about the poor little canal boy. His text was from the 107th Psalm, 23rd verse: "They that go down to the sea in ships." He has the queerest voice and stops off between his words. When we got home Anna said she would show us how he preached, and she described what he said about a sailor in time of war. She said, "A ball came— and struck him there—another ball came—and struck him there—he raised his faithful sword—and went on— to victory—or death!" I expected Grandfather would reprove her but he just smiled a queer sort of smile and Grandmother put her handkerchief up to her face. I never knew anyone who liked to go to church as much as Grandmother does. She says she would rather be a doorkeeper in the house of God than to dwell in the tents of wickedness. They don't have women doorkeepers and I know she would not dwell a minute in a tent.

"I don't fit with the little ones nor the big ones!"

Tatyana Tolstoy
[1865-1950]

*If preaching were doing, no long-faced Puritan could
have matched the capacity for self-denial of affluent, high-
born Leo Tolstoy, who liked to ask the peasants, "Why
do you call me 'Count'? I am one of you—just plain
Leo." For the last thirty years of his life the good gray
"peasant" of Yasnaya Polyana maintained a pose of ex-
treme austerity and relied on his family not to let him slip
from posture into practice. The responsibility for saving
him from himself he placed mainly on his wife Sonya,
who proved quite up to it. Thus it was that the great
Russian novelist could renounce money in his writings and
at the same time channel a heady flood of royalties into
Sonya's lap; could go about wearing the garb of serfdom
and at the same time rule over the broad ancestral acres
and the huge mansion in Tula province; could crusade
fiercely against the evils of drink and at the same time*

249

contemplate the profitable manufacture of vodka on the estate.

There was room in the house of Tolstoy for both love and hate, and neither was very long absent. And there were singing and dancing and a noisily desperate pursuit of many arts. "Sometimes people who are together," wrote Tolstoy, "if not hostile to one another are at least estranged in mood and feeling, till perhaps a story, a performance, a picture, or even a building, but oftenest of all music, unites them as by an electric flash, and in place of their former isolation or enmity they are conscious of union and love."

But Tatyana, his eldest daughter and prettiest of the thirteen children Sonya bore him—Tatyana who as a little girl would be in love now with Nicky Kislinsky, now with God knows whom, Tatyana who loved to play-act—went too far. She was a butterfly, that one. What good was it to a writer, to be adored and worshiped by a child who paid no attention to the things he wrote? Then suddenly, when she was 22, Tatyana rose to the level of his ideas and ideals and swallowed them hook, line and sinker. Such was her zeal that Tolstoy was not only delighted; he was a little uncomfortable. Working like a housemaid, going into the fields with a scythe like any common hand—was she, once again, going too far?

It looked that way to both parents, but especially to Sonya as the years rolled by and "Tanya" rejected one eligible suitor after another until she was turned 34. Then she fell in love. This time there was no play-acting. She would marry Sukhotkin, the old friend of the family,

*even if he was a simple country squire, an aging wid-
ower, even if he did have a potbelly and six children!*

*Tolstoy never displayed the unlovely side of his nature
more vividly than he did in a letter he wrote to Tatyana
on receiving the news of her engagement:*

*". . . I certainly cannot answer your letter as you would
like me to. I understand that a debauched man saves himself by getting married. But it is difficult to understand
why a pure girl should let herself be chained in that gal-
ley. If I were a girl I would not get married for anything
in the world. As for falling in love, knowing it is not a
beautiful, poetic and lofty feeling but an evil, morbid one,
I would not open the door to it but protect myself from it
as carefully as we guard ourselves against far less dangerous diseases such as diphtheria, scarlet fever or typhus."*

*Tatyana married the man she loved. As it turned out
for her, this particular form of ill health proved a happy
one, resulting in a little "Tanichka." In time her parents
became reconciled to her marriage, especially her father,
who found nothing morbid in the chess games he played
nightly with Sukhotkin. Tatyana lived to the age of 85,
spending her last 20 years as a widow in Rome.*

*The following part of her diary begins when she is 13,
that time in her life when her father saw in her only
frivolity, but in which she obviously understood more
about herself than he did.*

November 11, 1878. We have two donkeys. Going out, they walk. But coming home, if you let them, they gallop. One is called Bismarck, the other MacMahon. I have a governess, Mlle. Gachet. Masha [her sister Maria, age 7] has Annie, who is English. The boys [Sergey, 15; Ilia, 12; and Lev, 9] have M. Nief, and little Andrew [then one year old] has a Nanny. We also have a Russian teacher who lives in our house with his wife and two-year-old son and eight-year-old stepdaughter, and other teachers who live out for drawing, Greek, music and German.

November 12. We went to call at the Baron's today [Baron Delvig, whose daughters Rossa and Nadia were close friends of Tatyana.] It was very jolly. When we arrived only Baron Bode was there with some very little girls I didn't know. We began playing blind man's buff, but then the Kislinskys came. Nicky played, but the Delvigs' piano is horrid and the little ones made a terrible row, so you could hear nothing. He played pieces from Lucia di Lammermoor and very many Beethoven sonatas. Then we danced a waltz.

I danced with Nicky. While we were dancing he asked me if I was dancing the quadrille. I said yes, then saw I had misunderstood him and said no. Then he invited me to do the quadrille. I danced the first one with him, and waltzes with everybody. Barbara Kislinsky sent for costumes to do some tableaux vivants, but as there was not much time, we gave it up. I awfully didn't want to leave but it couldn't be helped. As it was, little Andrew had not been suckled for four hours. Outside it was very dark and muddy. We had brought a lantern to light the way but it wasn't needed. Papa had walked out to meet us.

November 13. Pretty boring today. I did all my homework very badly, but what I did for the priest was fierce. The music teacher came and brought his fiddle with him, and he played with Sergey accompanying, but Sergey got lost because he didn't count and it was not a great success. I think it was a Haydn sonata. In the evening Papa played duets with him.

The reason I did my lessons so poorly was that all the time I should have spent on them I was reading Count Sollohub's comedies to pick out something for us to do. Mama has chosen one—The Studio of a Russian Artist —very amusing and charming. If we and the Delvigs are not enough of a cast, Mama, if Papa agrees, is thinking of inviting Nicky Kislinsky. I was delighted, but then the whole thing was dropped. Pity!

Papa and our music teacher are playing at this moment. I should like to know whether music affects everybody as it does me. Mama once said she thought I didn't understand music. Is it possible that other people like it more than I do? When music is played, such an overpowering mood takes possession of me! I think I like Nicky because he plays so well. While he was playing I could not understand how other people could take no notice and go on chatting about other things.

Like father, like daughter. As a young amateur Tolstoy often sat at the piano three or four hours, and at the time was widely accredited with a command comparing well with that of many professionals. Sonya often com-

*mented on the violent effect music had on him. Paul
Boyer, a friend, wrote of one occasion when Tolstoy
played Chopin for him. "At the fourth Ballade his eyes
filled with tears. 'Ah, the animal!' he cried, and suddenly
rising, left the room."*

November 14. I knew, when Mama went to Tula and
saw all our friends, she would want to invite nearly
everybody [to the performance of the play] but Papa
doesn't like that and never agrees willingly. Mama thinks
Nicky's mother won't let him come alone but would let
him come with the Delvigs.

At the moment we all are sitting writing our diaries—
Ilia and I, and Mama sent Lev to bring his. Lev tried
writing in it but it won't go and he's given it up.

We have been looking at the illustrations intended for
War and Peace, Papa's book, which were not printed
because it would cost too much.

November 15. Again nothing done, only Sergey and I
planning what we shall do when we live in Moscow. Ilia
was scolded today at dinner for doing his lessons badly.
Papa went hunting and got three hares and one fox. We
counted up today how many he has got this autumn and
it came to fifty-five hares and ten foxes.

November 17. Ilia has been very naughty. Just before
dinner M. Nief had to scold him and Ilia took a wet
sponge and would have thrown it if he had dared. Then
Lev said, "Throw! He won't kill you for it, will he?" So
Ilia actually did fling the sponge and hit M. Nief right in
the face. He had to go without dinner for that.

November 18. After dinner our drawing master came. He brought me a little head he has done of himself. Very nice. I should like to learn some day to draw like that. Had a letter from Rossa Delvig to say they are all ill and cannot come [for the play] How tiresome they are!

November 19. We all spent the morning drawing. Then the boys went to Yassenki [railway station about three miles from the house] to see the Emperor passing through. They didn't see the Emperor at all, only his cooks.

November 26. Spent the morning with my teacher drawing a foot. It is very hard to make the shadows well. We haven't been going out because we have coughs. Ilia has been unbearable lately and we don't go near him. Little Andrew is out of sorts—teething, no doubt. Sergey makes me want to throw up with a Strauss waltz—*Du und du* . . .

December 1. The ground is covered with snow this morning. Please God it stays. This long autumn has been so dreary.

December 5. A letter from Nadia Delvig. She says she is going to three dances. I'm frightfully envious. I hope when I am sixteen I will go out a lot too. Rossa Delvig has sent another play, Granny Mischief, and that is what we shall act. The one we chose first I don't like now because there are too many male parts in it and I should have had to play one of them. Also, Nadia would have had very little to do. After all, I can't snatch the best part and she have almost nothing.

Deep snow, nine degrees of frost last night.

January 5, 1879. A whole month since I last wrote in my
diary. Since then we have had the Christmas tree and our
play. On the tree I had opera glasses, notepaper with my
own initials, and a ring from Granny in Petersburg. Then
Mama gave me Papa's works and an English novel Jane
Eyre, also a cut-glass bottle for my dressing-table and
two vases.

On January 3 we did Granny Mischief and the Vice-
Uniform, which was pretty poor because Sergey, who
played the lead, and Ilia forgot their lines. I saw Nicky
Kislinsky, the first time in nearly a month, but he only
stayed about half an hour.

I have bought a toboggan for 20 kopeks and have
been out on our run several times. But we haven't been
able to skate once. As soon as they get the pond clear of
snow there's another fall. One night we all went out in
four one-horse sleighs, but there were terrible drifts and
it was almost impossible to drive. I was awfully afraid.

I have made myself a German costume and we have
all dressed up a number of times.

Nicky went to Moscow for the whole of the Christmas
holiday, and I am going there, and after that we probably
won't see each other for a long, long time.

At our plays we had terrifying people in the audience
—Prince Obolenski [Nicholas, a distant cousin of Tolstoy who lodged with the family in Moscow while he
attended the university and many years later, after the
death of his first wife, was to marry Tatyana's sister
Masha] and Prince Urusov [vice-governor of Tula province and long an admirer of Tolstoy]; also, there were so

many of our own household peasants and people from the village that the hall was crammed full.

Yesterday there were spots on Lev's cheeks. Mama thinks it may be measles, because he's hoarse too and coughs. She has written to the doctor to ask his advice. Papa has been in bed all day with a high fever. Mama wanted him to take some medicine but he refused. He doesn't like medicines and never takes them.

January 6. The doctor writes to say that it looks as if the boys have measles. So the trip to Moscow is off. How tiresome! After breakfast read Jane Eyre. Papa's no better, still in bed. Ilia coughing, Lev's spots worse. Read Prudy in English, and how I did laugh!

January 14. Lessons have begun. We are supposed to be going to Moscow, but now there's Sergey with a sore throat! And Mama's frock still not sent from Petersburg. She has ordered one of black silk, but it still is not ready. Today, if Sergey's throat trouble hadn't started, I should be in Tula, and I should see Nicky; he has gone back there from Moscow, and when Rossa came to my name-day party on the 12th she promised that if I came today she'd have Nicky there for me. O dear, how tiresome, that horrible Sergey getting a sore throat! We had thought that Lev was getting measles and sent for the doctor, but the doctor says it's because he poured some perfume over himself. On the tenth Mr. Fet [a poet, friend of Tolstoy] came and brought us a huge box of candy.

January 29. Friday evening arrived back from Moscow. Went to the opera twice. Saw The Masked Ball and then

Linda di Chamonix. The first I did not like because they sang badly, but the other one was wonderful. And yet, I had expected that opera would make a much more powerful impression on me and that I should go absolutely crazy over it—and I didn't. Yesterday Prince Urusov came and promised to get us tickets for the theatricals in Tula.

February 8. I have been to the theatricals. I saw Nicky and we had a talk, but in the second and third intermissions he strolled about with one of the B. girls. A frightful frump!

March 31. Tomorrow is Easter Sunday. All the eggs are colored. I have seventeen, twelve done with prints and silk transfers. The day before yesterday Mama called on the Delvigs in Tula. She was told that when the Kislinskys left for Moscow, Nicky ran into the Delvigs and asked them to give me his regards. Then he blushed and added that he meant them for Sergey too, and for all the folk at Yasnaya.

The roads are frightful. Yesterday we drove to church, to the Good Friday service, and nearly drowned the horse.

Andrew has become such a comical little thing! He is eighteen months old now. He is beginning to speak, but cannot walk.

May 29. Yesterday we made a trip to Kozlovka [another nearby railway station] to see the Emperor, but saw nothing of him as he was not in the train we met but another that we couldn't wait for. A school boy said I was a jolie fille.

June 1. Slept in Mama's room last night as Papa has gone
to Pirogovo [home of his brother.] All day today I have
been terribly bored and have not known what to do with
myself. I can't play dolls with the little ones and I have
absolutely nothing to do. Yesterday I made a frock and
played with Big Masha [a cousin] but today I told her
I'm not going to play with her any more and now she's
hurt and says I've been horrid to her. So that now it
seems I've quarreled with everybody all round. Now I
can't think what I shall do to get through the summer.
Well, first I'll get up early and write up my diary, then do
a little work—all the time alone, of course—then there'll
be nothing to do all the rest of the day. Now, with
Sergey, it's different. He will go fishing, or for a walk, or
after mushrooms or berries. But I shall have to depend
first on Annie, then on the little ones; and if they don't
want to go for a walk I'll have to stay at home and be
bored. It's all right for them—four little girls—but I am
all by myself; I don't fit with the little ones nor with the
big ones.

February 4, 1882. What a long time since I've put anything in my diary! But life has now become so miserable
for me that I've made up my mind to do something which
I find entertaining, something I like. Since I last wrote in
my diary I have changed a lot. I have become quite big.
In some things I've changed for the better, in some for
the worse. First, I have begun to like dressing up; but I
don't think that's bad—only silly. I have begun thinking
a lot and arguing things out with myself. But the worst
thing of all, I have become terribly vain, and whatever I
do, I hate it if others don't notice it and praise me, so that

I am very nasty to anybody who doesn't appreciate me.

Unfortunately, I am not now in love with anybody, and I miss that terribly. Nicky Kislinsky clung to me the whole evening and put on such airs—but all in vain. I held myself in. Rossa Delvig says he's a fop, and I believe her. I should awfully like to see him again. Then it would be decided. As it is now, I am in love one moment and out the next.

"i dont know what i cried for."

Henry Augustus Shute

[1856-1943]

Twelve-year-old Henry Augustus ("Plupy") Shute twirled his pencil on a period, closed his diary for the last time, stuck it away, and—knowing nothing about what diaries can do to change people's lives—forgot it. Thirty-two years later, now a police court judge in his home town of Exeter, New Hampshire, he was rummaging through a closet. The diary turned up. The local paper ran it serially. There was so much talk around town about it that he sent it to a Boston publisher. In 1902 it came out as a book under the title, The Real Diary of a Real Boy. *It was an immediate national best-seller—the biggest thing that ever happened to Judge Shute. When he died in 1943 the* Boston Globe *said he "had opened the doors to understanding of small boys everywhere."*

January 1, 1868. Had an awful time in school today. me and Cawcaw Harding set together. when we came in from resess Cawcaw reached over and hit me a bat and I lent him one in the snoot and he hit me back. we was jest fooling but old Francis [the teacher] called Cawcaw up front to lick him.

i thought if i went up and told him he wood say noble boy go to your seat, i wont lick neether of you. anyway i knew that Cawcaw wood tell on me and so i told old Francis i hit Cawcaw first and old Francis said Harry i have had my eye on you for a long time, and he jest took us up and slammed us together and then he wood put me down and shake Cawcaw and then he wood put Cawcaw down and shake me till my head wabbled and he turned me upside down and all the fellers looked upside down and went round and round, and somehow i felt silly like and kind of like laffin.

i dident want to laff but coodent help it. and then he talked to us and sent us to our seats and told us to study, and i tried to but all the words in the book went round and round and i felt awful funny and kind of wabbly, and when i went home mother said something was the matter and i told her and then i cried. i dont know what i cried for becaus i dident ake any.

father said he wood lick me at home when i got licked at school and perhaps that was why i cried. ennyway when father came home i asked him if he was agoing to lick me and he said not by a dam site and he gave me ten cents and when i went to bed i got laffin and cryin all to once and coodent stop and mother set in my room and kept her hand on my forred till i went to sleep.

February 5. Got to the head in spelling today. old Francis makes us all stand up in the ile and gives us a lot of words to spell and then we wright them down on our slates and then the head feller or girl changes slates with the foot feller or girl and so on and then old Francis wrights the words on the blacboard and then we mark each others slates.

John Flanygin was the foot feller and had my slate. well, most of Johns words was wrong. but John marked mine all write. i gess John dident know it, but there was four or five of my words spelled wrong. i set out to tell old Francis but dident dass to becaus he licked me for teling that i paisted Cawcaw Harding that time. so i kept still and kept at the head and John kept at the foot. i hope John will do it again tomorrow.

February 16. beat in spelling today.

February 17. beat in spelling today.

February 19. beat in spelling today. old Francis is agoing to give a prise tomorrow. i told father i was pretty sure to get it and he said it will be the first one. Aunt Sarah asked him if i took many prises. and he said he dident get much of a prise when he got me. i gess he wont say that tomorrow when i bring my prise home.

February 20. i didn't get the prise. you see, yesterday John Flanygin spelt more words write than Gimmy Fitsgerald and Gimmy went to the foot. when we marked slates Gimmy marked 9 of my words wrong out of twenty and i had to go down most to where John Flannygin was. old Francis said he dident beleave i had ought to have staid at the head so long as i did and i was afraid he wood lick me and John, but he dident. he said he was ashamed and disapointed. but i gess he was not the only one who was disappointed. i had told Pewt and Beany i wood treat on what father wood give me for getting the prise. Pewt and Beany was both mad, and are going to lay for Gimmy.

April 2. been trying to get rid of some warts. Pewt says if you hook a piece of pork after dark, rub it on the warts and say arum erum irum orum urum and nurum three times, turn around twice, and throw the pork thru a window, then the warts will be all gone the next day. me and Beany is going to try it tomorrow.

April 3. brite and fair. dident get a chance to hook the pork.

April 4. The band played in the band room tonite. It was warm enuf to have the windows open and we cood hear it. i sat out in the school yard til 10 oclock to hear it and father came out and walked me home. Beany was mad becaus i cared more for the band than for getting rid of the warts.

April 6. dident wright anything last nite, was too scart. i never was so scart in all my life before. me and Beany came awful near getting in jale. we dident know where to hook the pork. I went to our cellar but father was down there making viniger all the evening, then we went to Beanys cellar but Mr. Watson was sitting on the cellar door.

Beany told his father that a man was looking for him to see about a horse and Mr. Watson started down to the club stable. then Beany hooked the pork and rubbed it over his warts and then i rubbed it over my warts and we said arum erum orum irum urum and nurum three times jest as Pewt said, turn round twice and i plugged the pork right threw a gaslite.

jest then the gasman came along. he yelled at us and jumped out of his wagon and went for us. we ran down threw the school yard as fast as we cood. there is a hollow in the corner of the school yard by Bill Morrises back yard and there is a little hole in the bottom of the fence where the fellers crawl threw when the football goes into his garden. we skinned threw that hole jest in time. the gasman tried to crawl threw but he coodent, then he clim the high fence but while he was doing that we ran across the carrige factory yard and down by the old brewery up Bow Street and home. i went to bed pretty lively and so did Beany. gosh but we was scart.

April 7. One of Beanys warts has gone.

April 8. my warts have not gone.

April 9. my warts have not gone.

April 10. Clowdy but no rane. my warts have not gone.

April 11. i have got 2 more warts. i gess i hadent ought to have broke that gaslite.

April 12. i have got another.

April 13. me and Potter Gorham and Chick Chickering went out after toads today. i got 14.

*"Papa has the mind of an author exactly,
    some of the simplest things he can't understand."*

Susy Clemens
[1872-1896]

She was 13 and her world-renowned papa 50 when she undertook to write the "biography" which, in its entirety, appears below. Why it ended where it did, neither Susy nor her father ever explained. But he did describe this slim, pigtailed little girl as "the busiest bee in the household hive." What with her homework, health exercises and manifold recreations, our guess is that more pressing matters forced Susy Clemens to leave the definitive biography of Mark Twain to hands less well occupied than her own.

265

She didn't tell him what she was doing upstairs in the privacy of her room after bedtime. Written a little each night, the biography takes on some characteristics of a diary. Since we can't resist including it anyhow, we may as well give this as our reason; and we think it does meet one requirement—it reveals more about the author than she may have suspected.

Whatever it was, it succeeded. When Susy's mother discovered it, sneaked it out and showed it to her husband, he was deeply touched—and so impressed that he began "posing", saying things deliberately for quotation.

Years later he said of Susy's "biography," "I have had no compliment, no praise, no tribute from any source that was so precious to me as this one was and still is."

We are a very happy family. We consist of Papa, Mamma, Jean, Clara and me. It is papa I am writing about, and I shall have no trouble in not knowing what to say about him, as he is a <u>very</u> striking character.

Papa's appearance has been described many times, but very incorrectly. He has beautiful gray hair, not any too thick or any too long, but just right; a Roman nose which greatly improves the beauty of his features; kind blue eyes and a small mustache. He has a wonderfully shaped head and profile. He has a very good figure—in short, he is an extrodinarily fine looking man. All his features are perfect exept that he hasn't extrodinary teeth. His complexion is very fair, and he doesn't ware a beard. He is a very good man and a very funny one. He has got a temper, but we all of us have in this family. He is the loveliest man I ever saw or ever hope to see—and oh, so absentminded.

Papa's favorite game is billiards, and when he is tired and wishes to rest himself he stays up all night and plays billiards, it seems to rest his head. He smokes a great deal almost incessantly. He has the mind of an author exactly, some of the simplest things he can't understand. Our burglar alarm is often out of order, and papa had been obliged to take the mahogany room off from the alarm altogether for a time, because the burglar alarm had been in the habit of ringing even when the mahogany-room window was closed. At length he thought that perhaps the burglar alarm might be in order, and he decided to try and see; accordingly he put it on and then went down and opened the window; consequently the alarm bell rang, it would even if the alarm had been in order. Papa went despairingly upstairs and said to mamma, "Livy the mahogany room won't go on. I have just opened the window to see."

"Why, Youth," mamma replied. "If you've opened the window, why of course the alarm will ring!"

"That's what I've opened it for, why I just went down to see if it would ring!"

Mamma tried to explain to papa that when he wanted to go and see whether the alarm would ring while the window was closed he <u>mustn't</u> go and open the window—but in vain, papa couldn't understand, and got very impatient with mamma for trying to make him believe an impossible thing true.

Commenting on this, papa admitted Susy was right—he couldn't understand things—but he insisted that bur-

267

glar alarm "led a gay and careless life and had no princi-
ples."

Papa has a peculiar gait we like, it seems just to suit him, but most people do not; he always walks up and down the room while thinking and between each coarse at meals.

Papa is very fond of animals particularly of cats, we had a dear little gray kitten once that he named "Lazy" (papa always wears gray to match his hair and eyes) and he would carry him around on his shoulder, it was a mighty pretty sight! the gray cat sound asleep against papa's gray coat and hair. The names that he has give our different cats are really remarkably funny, they are named Stray Kit, Abner, Motley, Fraeulein, Lazy, Buffalo Bill, Soapy Sall, Cleveland, Sour Mash, and Pestilence and Famine.

Papa uses very strong language, but I have an idea not nearly so strong as when he first married mamma. A lady acquaintance of his is rather apt to interupt what one is saying, and papa told mamma he thought he should say to the lady's husband "I am glad your wife wasn't present when the Deity said Let there be light."

Papa said the other day, "I am a mugwump and a mugwump is pure from the marrow out." (Papa knows that I am writing this biography of him, and he said this for it.) He doesn't like to go to church at all, why I never understood, until just now, he told us the other day that he couldn't bear to hear anyone talk but himself, but that he could listen to himself talk for hours without getting tired, of course he said this in joke, but I've no dought it was founded on truth.

One of papa's latest books is "The Prince and the Pauper" and it is unquestionably the best book he has ever written, some people want him to keep to his old style, some gentleman wrote him, "I enjoyed Huckleberry Finn immensely and am glad to see that you have returned to your old style." That enoyed me, that enoyed me greatly, because it trobles me to have so few people know papa, I mean realy know him, they think of Mark Twain as a humorist joking at everything; "And with a mop of reddish brown hair which sorely needs the barbar brush, a roman nose, short stubby mustache, a sad careworn face, with maney crows' feet" etc. That is the way people picture papa, I have wanted papa to write a book that would reveal something of his kind sympathetic nature, and "The Prince and the Pauper" partly does it. The book is full of lovely charming ideas, and oh the language! It is <u>perfect.</u> I think that one of the most touching scenes in it is where the pauper is riding on horseback with his nobles in the "recognition procession" and he sees his mother oh and then what followed! How she runs to his side, when she sees him throw up his hand palm outward, and is rudely pushed off by one of the King's officers, and then how the little pauper's consceince trobles him when he remembers the shameful words that were falling from his lips when she was turned from his side "I know you not woman" and how his grandeurs were stricken valueless and his pride consumed to ashes. It is a wonderfully beautiful and touching little scene, and papa has described it so wonderfully. I never saw a man with so much variety of feeling as papa has; now the "Prince and the Pauper" is full of touching places, but there is always a streak of humor in them somewhere. Papa very seldom writes a passage without some humor in it somewhere and I don't think he ever will.

Clara and I are sure that papa played the trick on Grandma about the whipping that is related in "The Adventures of Tom Sawyer": "Hand me that switch." The switch hovered in the air, the peril was desperate— "My, look behind you Aunt!" The old lady whirled around and snatched her skirts out of danger. The lad fled on the instant, scrambling up the high board fence and disappeared over it.

We know papa played "Hookey" all the time. And how readily would papa pretend to be dying so as not to have to go to school! Grandma wouldn't make papa go to school, so she let him go into a printing office to learn the trade. He did so, and gradually picked up enough education to enable him to do about as well as those who were more studious in early life.

"Got up, washed, went to bed."

Samuel Langhorne Clemens
[1835-1910]

In his book The Innocents Abroad *Mark Twain recalls "the journal I opened with the New Year once when I was a boy." Here it is—complete:*

Monday. Got up, washed, went to bed.

Tuesday. Got up, washed, went to bed.

Wednesday. Got up, washed, went to bed.

Thursday. Got up, washed, went to bed.

Friday. Got up, washed, went to bed.

Next Friday. Got up, washed, went to bed.

Friday fortnight. Got up, washed, went to bed.

Following month. Got up, washed, went to bed.

"I stopped then," he adds, "discouraged. Startling events appeared to be too rare in my career to render a diary necessary. I still reflect with pride, however, that even at that early age I washed when I got up."

271

"I let him catch me on purpose."

"Gretchen Lainer"

Eleven-year-old Gretchen could never have dreamed her "secret diary" would some day be published as a book and many times reprinted, and that psychologists, psychiatrists, college professors and thousands of students in many lands would pore over it and write papers about it.

Gretchen lived in Vienna and spent summer vacations in the mountains of the Tyrol. It was on one of these trips, a few years before World War One, that she started her diary.

The manuscript fell into the hands of a co-worker of Sigmund Freud and was passed along to him. Freud called the diary "a gem" and urged that it be published. "Gretchen Lainer" was not the child's real name. Her identity remains, to this day, a secret.

July 15. My best friend Helen and I have agreed to keep diaries from now on. My older sister Dora keeps a diary too, but she gets furious with me if I so much as ask about it. She doesn't approve of my keeping a diary—says "little children" (meaning me and Helen) shouldn't do it because they will write such silly stuff. "Little children!"—and we're only two years younger than she! Well, I'm sure there won't be anything sillier in my diary than what I've seen in hers.

July 25. Had a big fight with Dora this morning. She accused me of snooping around in her things. But whose fault is that? She leaves things lying around, like diaries and letters, where they get in people's way and then blames me! As if I care about her old things! That letter she wrote yesterday to her friend Erika and left on the table where it didn't belong—I hardly read one sentence before she came in. Just "He's as handsome as a Greek god." I didn't even find out who "he" is. I bet it's Krail Rudi, though. Dora plays tennis with him every chance she gets—and carries on like anything with him too. But "handsome"—well, there's no explaining some people's taste.

July 26. I'm glad Mother advised me to bring along my doll's suitcase on this trip. I know eleven is much too old to be playing with dolls. But making clothes, even for a doll, isn't really playing, because it teaches you how to sew, and it's quite a thrill when you finish something. That is, it would have been if Dora hadn't come in just then and said, "Well, what do you know! The child is playing dolls!" "The child"!—what a nerve! But I got even. When she sat beside me I stitched like mad and gave her a good long scratch on the hand with my needle. Then I said, "Sorry—I didn't realize you were so close." Of course she'll go tattling to Mama. Let her.

July 27. Mama says I've got to stop eating raspberries and gooseberries all day, the way I do here, because it takes away my appetite for dinner. Isn't that just the way? Dr. Klein says fruit is good for you. Then when you eat a lot of it, all of a sudden it isn't good for you. My friend Helen always says, anything you like very much, you're sure to be told you can't have. She gets mad at her mother and then her mother says, "All these sacrifices we make for our children, and look at the thanks we get!" I'd like to know what sacrifices parents make. I think it's the children who make the sacrifices. When I want to eat gooseberries and Mama doesn't want me to and says I'm not allowed, who's making the sacrifice?

July 29. The Warth family came today. I spent the whole day with them. Robert Warth is a head taller than I, and fifteen, I think.

July 30. Today is my birthday. Papa gave me a beautiful parasol and a paintbox, and Mama a big album for picture postcards—holds 800—and a book of stories, and Dora gave me a box of very fine writing paper. How wonderful birthdays are! How sweet everybody is! Even Dora.

July 31. My birthday party was such fun! Playing Truth or Consequence, we laughed till our sides ached. Somehow I was always getting put with Robert Warth. And the things we were told we had to do together!—kiss, hug, bathe, get lost in the woods. Oh, not really, of course; only on paper. (Please don't ever think I would really do such things!) When a toast to me was proposed,

Robert wanted to drink it in real wine but Dora wouldn't let him. Said it wouldn't be proper. Actually, she was jealous. She always has to be the big cheese. Well, yesterday—for once in my life—I was the big cheese!

Today we went out in the country with the Warths. Found a lot of strawberries, and when Robert picked the best ones just for me, Dora's nose was out of joint. The truth is, I would rather have picked my own berries. But when a person picks berries for another person because the person loves the other person—that's how Robert explained it—well, what can a person do? I did pick some, which I gave to Mama and Papa.

We stopped in a village for tea. Instead of sitting next to Robert, I had to sit with his sister Erna. She's kind of stupid. Mama says she's anemic. Sounds awfully romantic—except that I don't know what it means exactly. Dora is always saying she's anemic—which is a lie—and every time she does, Papa says, "Nonsense, girl—you're strong as an ox!" Makes her so mad.

After tea we played a game called Place for the King. Robert caught me, and by the rules of the game I had to give him a kiss. Erna said it didn't count because I had let him catch me on purpose. Dora wasn't playing with us, and I didn't want her to know about it because if she found out I'd never hear the end of it. I gave Erna some candy to keep her quiet.

August 2. My brother Oswald arrived here today. Very dashing—mustache and everything. Smokes cigarettes too.

August 3. I am not allowed to go swimming because I got chilled a few days ago. When the others go, Robert stays with me. We were here all alone and he told me all sorts of things. Robert says he is never going to smoke. He doesn't think it's "a thing for gentlemen to do." But what about Papa? He smokes, and nobody can say <u>he</u> isn't a gentleman. Robert says he's never going to grow a beard either. But Papa has a beard. He's always had one. I can't imagine him being without one. Well, I know one thing—<u>I'll</u> never marry a man without a beard.

August 7. A terrible family quarrel over Dora. Oswald told Papa he saw her flirting with men at the tennis court. Oswald said she was doing it so outrageously, he couldn't stand to watch it. Papa just about hit the ceiling. He was so furious, he said we can't play tennis anymore. But I don't see why <u>I</u> can't. If Dora wants to make love to boys when she plays tennis, what has that got to do with me and <u>my</u> playing tennis? One person in the family is guilty and another person gets punished. But that's parents for you.

August 12. Robert told me today about a secret society he belongs to in his school. It is called TAM because those letters are the initials of Latin words that mean Silence or Death. When they take you in, they tattoo the letters on your chest, and also a heart, and the name of a girl. Robert said if he had known me when he went into it, he would have had the name Gretchen tattooed on him instead of the one he has. But he can't do that now because it's against the rule of the society to have two names. I asked him what name he has on him but he said he couldn't tell. That's against the rule too. I'll tell Oswald to take a look the next time they go swimming.

I had to promise Robert I would never tell anyone about the society. But I couldn't sleep all night thinking about it. I wonder if they have one in the high school I'll be going to. I wonder if Dora is in one. I wonder if she has somebody's name tattooed on her chest. I wouldn't want to promise Robert I'd have his name tattooed on me!

August 15. Yesterday Robert told me there are some secret societies where the boys do terrible things. But he wouldn't say what the things were. I wish I knew! I wish I knew whether Oswald is in one, and whether Papa ever was. If I could only find out! But I can't ask them. They would want to know how I learned about them and I'd have to tell and that would be breaking my promise to Robert.

September 3. Something terrible has happened. I'll never speak to Robert as long as I live. I don't know how it happened, but he started to tickle me—I won't say where—when I was sitting in the swing. I gave him a good hard kick—in the teeth.

September 6. We are going home tomorrow. I saw Robert a couple of times but looked away.

September 22. Vienna. School began today.

September 10 [the following year] A gypsy woman told our fortunes yesterday from our hands. Dora is going to get into trouble and be happy afterwards. But me!—I shall be very happy—a great romance, marriage and a big fortune—but not until I am twice as old as I am now! Since I am now twelve, this means I won't be married until I'm 24—practically an old woman. How silly!

October 4. Yesterday Resi [a young servant girl in the Lainer household] told me something perfectly awful.

Oswald can't go back to school. He's in some sort of
trouble—I don't know what, it may be something he
does in the bathroom; anyway, that's the only thing I can
think of because when we were in the country he always
stayed in there so long. Or maybe it's got something to do
with that club he's in. Anyway, Father is furious with
him and Mother has been crying her eyes out and when
we're together at dinner nobody says a word.

Yesterday Dora and I heard Father yelling at him,
"You young devil!"—then something we didn't catch,
and then, "I sent you to school to study books, not girls
and married women!" Then Dora whispered to me, "Ah!
Now I understand!" I said, "Then tell me—he's as much
my brother as yours." But she said, "You wouldn't
understand. It's not a thing for children to hear." Imagine!—for her to hear, yes, but not for me, and she isn't
three years older than I. So grown-up!—but I notice
when she thinks nobody's looking she'll swoop down on
the jam and stuff her mouth so full she can't talk. Whenever I catch her at it I make it a point to ask her a
question. Makes her so mad.

October 9. Now I know! I know all about it. Oswald's
trouble has to do with how babies happen. He isn't married, of course. When you're not married it's a sin to do it
but when you are married you've got to do it. It hurts
something fierce, but you do it anyway because you've got
to. Well, not for me, thanks. I'll take care of that—I just
won't get married. But how lucky I've found out in time!
And still, I don't know all about it, and I wish I did. I
wish I knew exactly how. Helen admits she doesn't know
that herself. It takes nine months for the baby to come,

and then you might die. Helen's known since last summer, but it was so awful she didn't want to tell me. And that liar Dora has known for ages and kept it to herself. But I don't understand something Robert said when he tried to tickle me while I was sitting in the swing. He said, "What are you so excited about, you silly little fool? You won't get a baby just from that." I've got to find out more. I'll talk to Helen again at school tomorrow. Good heavens, how curious I am!

October 19. If I could only find out what Oswald really did. I'm sure it was something with a girl. But we can't imagine what Father meant about "married women." Well, I feel sorry for Oswald. I know how I'd feel if everything came out about that thing with Robert and me.

October 20. We've been talking a lot with Bertha Franke. She claims she's had experience. But she can't tell us until she knows us better.

October 21. I can't believe what Bertha Franke said about husband and wife. She said it has to happen every night. If not, they don't get a baby—even if they miss a single night. That's why they have their beds close together. People call them "marriage beds." And the pain is so dreadful a person can hardly stand it. All the same you've got to go through with it because your husband can make you do it. But I'd like to know how!

October 27. I'm doing badly in my school work. Yesterday I got an Unsatisfactory in history and today I couldn't get a single problem right in arithmetic.

November 2. I certainly don't know everything yet.

Helen knows more. We went into the drawing room and pretended to be going over our history lesson, and talked more about IT. Mali, our new maid, came in, and she told us something particularly revolting. All Jews, Mali said, have to undergo a dangerous operation when they are little babies. It hurts terribly. They do it because it helps them to have more children. But only on little boys. We asked Mali whether IT hurts too, as much as we've heard it does, and she laughed and said, "Well, it can't be as bad as all that. If it were, everybody wouldn't be doing it, would they?"

November 8. I saw a gorgeous young woman figure-skating today. She was so graceful I tagged after her, and when she went into the locker room she left a lovely trace of perfume. I wonder if she is going to be married, and whether she would be willing if she knew about IT. I wish I were as beautiful as she, but I am dark and she's a blonde. I must go skating again tomorrow.

November 9. I'm so disappointed. She didn't go skating today. I wonder if she's ill.

November 10. She didn't show up today either. I waited two hours for her.

November 11. At last! How beautiful she was, too.

November 12. We got acquainted! I was near the gate. Suddenly I heard someone laughing behind me, and I knew instantly. She said, "Shall we skate together?" I said, "Oh, please, if I may," and we crossed arms and off we went. My heart was pounding, and I couldn't think of a thing to say. When we came back to the gate a man was waiting there for her. She bowed to me and said, "Till next time." "When?" I asked, "tomorrow?" "Maybe," she called back.

November 13. Dora says her name is Anastasia Klastochek. I don't believe it. Eugenie, maybe, or Seraphina, or Laura. But Anastasia? Oh, no! Why are people given such horrible names? Dora doesn't think she's especially pretty. But Dora never thinks anyone pretty except herself.

November 14. I've learned her locker number—36. A lovely number!

November ·22. Bertha Franke and I have been talking about IT. She says that's why people get married—only because of IT. I didn't believe her. Lots of people marry and don't have children. Bertha said it's true all the same, and then she told me a lot more. But I can't write it down—it's just too awful. Anyhow I don't need to—I won't forget! Sitting on Mother's bed today, I suddenly realized how close it was to Father's. But not because of IT any more, I guess. After all, they have their family now. I guess they just left the bedroom arrangement the way it's always been.

November 25. I can't go skating every day. But how I do love my Gold Fairy. That's what I call her, because I can't bear her real name.

December 22. Aunt Dora came to visit us. Father says she's a beauty. She's dark, like me. I'd still rather be a blonde—a blonde with violet eyes! Will I grow up to be a beauty? Oh, I hope so!

December 23. I'm wondering whether to send a Christmas card to the Gold Fairy. I would if I didn't have to address it to such an ugly name.

December 24. Oswald came home yesterday. Everybody remarks how well he looks. I can't see it. I think he's quite pale. How could he be anything else, with what he has on his mind? I wish I could tell him I understand how he feels. But he doesn't want sympathy.

February 20. I met the Gold Fairy today. She asked why I don't come out skating more often. She looked absolutely stunning, in a rust suit trimmed with fur—sable, I think—and a wide brown beaver hat with ribbons. My guess is she'll marry the man who comes out with her—always the same one.

March 10. Helen keeps saying now she wishes we hadn't learned anything about IT. She thinks about IT when she ought to be doing her lessons. So do I. A person dreams about things at night after talking too much about them in the afternoon. Still, I guess it's better to know.

July 24. Oswald has to find something wrong with every girl he knows. He calls Dora a "green frog" because she always looks pale and has cold hands. About me, he says one can't say anything at all yet—"She's nothing but an embryo." Thank goodness I learned in natural history what an embryo is—a little frog.

August 10. Oswald made fun of Helen's and my friendship. We gave him what for, but he just laughed and said, "Girl friends! That's fine. But friendships of men grow closer with the years, and friendships of you girls—just let a new boy friend come along and they go poof!" What nerve! Helen and I are going to stick together until we

282

get married, and we've decided that's got to be on the same day for both. She'll probably get engaged before I do, but she'll have to wait for me before she gets married. That's only her duty as a friend.

September 25. School began again five days ago. All the girls are madly in love with Professor Wilke, the natural history teacher. Helen and I walked behind him today all the way home. He's a very handsome man, tall, and with a red beard that looks like flame when the sun hits it. The Sun God, Helen and I call him, or S.G., but nobody knows what we're talking about.

November 28. Mother came to school today and saw him. He was an angel. "I am very pleased with your daughter. She is very quick and clever."

December 5. I saw the Gold Fairy today. She is very pretty, but I must admit, not as beautiful as I thought her last year.

December 9. This afternoon Helen was rushed to the hospital and operated on for appendicitis. The operation was successful, but the doctors said if it had been two hours later they couldn't have saved her life.

December 14. This afternoon I visited Helen at the hospital. She looked so pale when I came in, I couldn't help it—I started to cry. Then we both cried. I brought her some flowers and told her Professor Wilke asks me about her every time I see him. People in sickbeds always look different—like strangers. I told Helen this and she said, "You and I can never be strangers, not even in death." Then I burst out in tears again and both our mothers said I would have to leave, because it was too much for Helen.

December 20. Hurrah! Helen can go home in time for Christmas. I've decided to give her a chaise longue. I don't have enough money, but Father said he would make up the difference. There's just nobody like my Dad! We're going together to buy it tomorrow.

December 21. I paid five crowns and Father thirty-seven.

March 29. Today a very terrible thing happened to Dora and me. I don't see how I can put it down, but I've got to. Dora was very sweet about it and explained to me that two years ago the same kind of thing happened when she and Mother were riding in a railway carriage. There was only one other person in the car, a man standing farther down where Mother couldn't see him but Dora could. Then he opened his coat and—I can't write it but it was the same thing the man did today at the door of our house. Dora couldn't sleep for a month. I remember that time, but I didn't know what the reason was then. Dora never told anyone except her friend Erika, and Erika said the same thing happened to her. Dora says it happens at least once to every girl. Men who do it are abnormal. I don't know what that means, but I didn't show my ignorance. Maybe Helen will know.

I didn't really look today, of course, but I guess Dora must have, because she shivered and said, "And that's what a woman has to accept from a man! THAT was why Mother was ill, and why she had to have five children." Then I foolishly asked, "But how from THAT? A person doesn't get children from THAT!" "Of course," Dora said. "I thought you knew that already. I guess what you and Helen know isn't really very much." And then she explained a little about it.

Well, if that's the way it is, then it's better not to marry. A person can fall in love—a person has to fall in love—but then a person can just break off the engagement. That is certainly what I will do. Then nobody can say I've never had a man in love with me.

Going home from school I told Helen. She doesn't know what "abnormal" means either. I mean, as far as THAT is concerned. From now on we'll use "abnormal" to mean something dreadful. Nobody will understand us, but we'll understand each other, all right! Then Helen told me about a drunken man who was walking through the streets like THAT and was arrested. She says no one can ever forget seeing THAT. She knows, too, it's from THAT that one gets children. She explained the whole thing, and now I can understand how THAT must make a person sick! Helen says THAT is the original sin, the one Adam and Eve really committed.

Oh, dear, since yesterday I've been so upset! I always seem to be seeing THAT. I really didn't look at all—at least I don't think I did—but I must have seen it all the same.

March 30. All of a sudden in the middle of the history lesson today it popped into my head again—what Dora said about Father making Mother ill. I just can't believe it. Because of Father, I'm sorry I know about it. Maybe it really <u>doesn't</u> happen the way Dora and Helen say it does. They still may be mistaken!

April 7. Mother commented that while we were visiting the Richters yesterday, I seemed to be so frightfully stupid. Why had Helen and I kept looking towards each other? It was very rude, Mother said. If she had only

285

known what we were thinking when Frau Richter said
the weather yesterday was quite abnormal!

June 1. Another experience today! Now I know it's true
that when two people are really in love they have to take
off all their clothes—every stitch! I never really believed
that, and I'm sure Dora didn't either, but—well, we both
know now! We saw it with our own eyes.

Resi came into our room and said, "Fraulein Dora,
please come with me a minute, I want you to see something!" When I heard that tone of voice, I went too. Resi
took us into her room, and from behind a curtain we
could peep into the mezzanine, where a young married
couple live. Resi says people suspect they aren't married,
but they live there anyway.

She was lying completely naked on the bed without
any covers over her. He was kneeling at the bedside,
naked too, and he was kissing her—but all over, everywhere! Dora began to feel sick. But then he stood up
and—but I just can't write it. But no fear of my ever
forgetting it. So THAT'S the way of it. I never could
have believed it if I hadn't seen it. Dora went white as a
sheet and started shaking so that Resi got scared. I nearly
cried out with horror, but I couldn't help laughing at the
same time. I was afraid he would stifle her—he was so
big and she so small. And Resi agrees, he was certainly
much too big for her and that he nearly tears her. I don't
know how he could tear her but it was easy to see that he
might crush her.

Dora was so horrified she had to sit down and she
looked as if she was going to faint, so Resi ran for a glass
of water. I'm certain now, Dora hadn't imagined it was

286

anything like that. I'm sure I hadn't. Still, I don't know why anyone should tremble, or faint. There wasn't any reason to be frightened so long as you knew it couldn't ever happen to you—that you could just refuse to get married.

But suddenly Dora got sick in earnest. We had to help her back to our room, and thank heaven we got her there before anyone could notice. When Mother came in, she sent for the doctor at once. He said Dora was "over-worked." Then he looked at me. "You don't look good for much either. What makes you so hollow-eyed?" I said I was scared about Dora. "Fiddlesticks! A little fright like this doesn't make black rings around the eyes."

So it must be true—a person can look sickly from just thinking about THAT!

June 3. Father took Helen and me to Kahlenberg. We enjoyed it immensely. After dinner we went out to pick flowers, Helen and I, and I told her what had happened on Friday. She was shocked, she couldn't utter a word. She says she'll never marry either. It's just unthinkable. Oh, yes—something else the Doctor told Father last Friday. He said, "No girl ought to study, it doesn't pay. This everlasting education is poisonous for young girls in the years of development."

If he'd only known the kind of education we've been getting!

"It is impossible not to love him."

Margaret Emily Shore

[*1819-1839*]

Emily's pet lark was a zany little character as full of mischief and whimsy as Emily herself was prim and proper in all her pursuits. Perhaps that is why they found each other so interesting.

In the English village of Casterton the Reverend Thomas Shore supported his wife and five children by tutoring young gentlemen who expected to enter Oxford. For thirteen-year-old Emily life was a busy round—the Greek and Latin and other lessons papa was teaching her; herself serving as teacher to the younger children; needlework and household chores; reading to mama; and writing, writing, writing: her diary, 2,000 pages of it in a small hand by the time she was twenty; her poems; and solemn book-length manuscripts, unpublished, on art, nature, and history from the time she was eleven years old (A History of the Jews *by Emily Shore, price one shilling, etc. etc.)*

288

*No wonder a little lark—even one in a cage—came not
amiss!*

*Much of Emily's diary was too prolix and pedantic to
be of public interest. But not when she wrote about those
dear to her—papa, mama, the little ones, and especially
the lark. Then the big words, the stilted, showy sentences
were forgotten—most of them—and the story welled up
from a tender heart so appealingly that half a century after
her untimely death a publisher found it irresistible.*

*When papa decided to buy the lark that Mackworth had
been begging for, Emily was deeply against it. Larks were
wild things. They needed space and height. It was cruel
to cage them. But from the moment she met this little fellow, she surrendered, and a few days later, when Mackworth lost interest, it was "my lark" from that time on.*

January 28, 1833. Poor mama has had a night of intense
suffering. Her pain was in some degree allayed by lauda-
num, but was succeeded by great sickness and debility.

After breakfast papa called together and spoke to us at
some length. He said that though we had never been told
so in plain terms before, he now deemed it proper to inform us that mama's life was very uncertain and would
probably not last long.

It is hardly necessary to add that papa's words made a
deep impression on us and that he left us in tears. Indeed,
I cannot think what we would do without mama; it seems
to me that if she died I should never be happy again.

At ten o'clock Mr. Magrath and Mr. Lear [the village
doctors] came; and at twelve I went upstairs to see mama.
She was more free from pain but extremely weak and

scarcely able to whisper; she looked pale and ill. I kissed her and then left the room and finished hearing the children's lessons, about which I was before employed.

January 29. Mama is rather better today. I sat with her in the evening while papa was making his usual weekly examination of the children's progress in Greek, which I teach them.

January 31. In the afternoon there was a fall of snow, and we began to speculate what we should do if every flake was a piece of gold money. To be sure, this shower of money would break all the windows, destroy the plants, and patter furiously down the chimney; but then, we should get ten thousand times more money than would be sufficient to pay for the repairing of the damage a hundred times over.

We then began to settle what we should do with all this money. We should in the first place purchase the whole estate of Woodbury and rebuild the house on a magnificent scale. Then we should have a splendid garden, filled with all the choicest flowers in the world. And we would have a noble library, and printing-presses for us children, to print all the productions of our pens. In short, there would be no end to the magnificence of our possessions and mode of living. I should also like to have a tame elephant.

April 8. Mr. Taylor [one of her father's pupils] who is always very good-tempered to us, walked in the garden capping verses with me, and after a hard-fought game of perhaps half an hour, he conquered me with a line ending in X, which rarely begins a word in English. I had, it is true, found one, but soon after he gave me another, which was the rhyme of his first one, and I was vanquished. The couplet was:

Taking special care to fix
The hour of parting, half-past six

However, when I came indoors, I was sure that there was in "Paradise Lost" some line beginning with Xerxes, and Arabella found one, which I shall have in store the next time I cap verses with this terrific Mr. Taylor.

May 7. I took a short walk on the Great Casterton road, and had the pleasure not only of hearing the nightingale a long time, but also of seeing him all the while, only a few yards from me. He is a small bird of a soft brown plumage with a whitish ash-coloured breast and throat. He flitted from bush to bush and sometimes hid himself. After a long pause he began again with a long, slow, loud note, something like "tweet, tweet." I never saw a nightingale before. This was about five o'clock in the morning. His song is rich and varied, but the blackbird's is, in my opinion, sweeter.

There are two beautiful swans. One is sitting on six eggs in an open nest which she has made on the other side of the river. Her husband takes care that nobody shall disturb her; he sails majestically up and down the water, watching, and will dart along as quick as lightning if he sees anyone approaching, and he will make a great splashing too. The way to keep him off is to push him gently away with a broom or garden brush. Aunt Jane went into the boat to fill her watering-pot, and he immediately attacked her. He hit the brush and tore up the grass in a rage. When he flies at anyone he will bruise them black and blue; the strokes of his wings are like those of sticks.

May 9. After luncheon Aunt Mary took me across the river in the boat to look for some flowers on the other side. She pushed the boat across while I held the broom. The swan was attending on his wife, but he immediately saw or heard us, for he splashed down upon us, spreading his wings terrifically. He was a moment too late, for we had landed when he reached the boat.

May 18. In the afternoon a lark, which Mackworth has long wished to buy, arrived. It seems to be full grown, and is almost twice as big as a sparrow, of a very elegant shape, and with a beautiful head. The colour is a mottled brown; the breast is whitish, with a cast of yellow. There are a few hairs at the origin of the beak, and he has a crest, which he commonly keeps lowered. He is very tame, and eats daisies out of the hand; he never seems frightened, but I pity him very much for being a captive.

May 20. Mackworth's lark is a very amusing bird. It is let out of its cage every day. The goldfinch, when let out at the same time, is unbearably impudent to him; he trots up to him and eats his hempseed and drinks his water and pecks at his turf, which he is always provided with. The lark does not like this; he opens his mouth and screams, and sometimes drives off the goldfinch, who, however, comes again with the utmost assurance and impertinence, and has once or twice fought with and conquered the lark.

These scenes are very amusing. Once, when Goldy was quite intolerable, the lark attacked him; but being unluckily worsted, resolved on retaliation, ran off to the intruder's cage, and began greedily eating his canary seed. The gold-finch looked on very peaceably, being himself engaged in theft. I always take the part of the lark; it is quite droll to see him beaten by a bird as small again as himself.

June 8. The lark has now a confirmed hatred for the gold-finch, and screams if he even sees its cage. At the same time, he is more tame and gentle to us; he always walks under the table after breakfast to pick up the crumbs we have dropped, and eats out of our hand, especially when he is in his cage. When anyone approaches he opens his beak very wide for a fly; if none is brought he looks sadly disappointed, for he loves flies. I suspect he does not like Mackworth, which is not wonderful considering the teasing and frightening he has received from that quarter; for when Mackworth attempted to give him a fly, he flew at, pecked him, and pursued him for two or three yards. He also attacked me, and tugged furiously at my finger; but as soon as Mackworth was out of the room he became quiet and ate gently out of my hand. He then walked into his cage, and grew very dainty; for he took a dislike to great flies and pecked us if we brought them; but he eats little ones readily enough. Nor would he (except once) be cheated by being presented with a bit of a large fly as a little fly.

June 13. I have discovered why the lark sometimes attacks me so violently. It is because I wear a different frock from what he has been accustomed to see me in. This shows a great deal of observation and intelligence.

June 14. When I had done the work of planting my mulleins I came indoors and brought some flies to the lark;

but he, instead of eating them, flew at me in wrath and bit me very hard. At length it occurred to me that this might be the consequence of my hands being dirty from gardening. I accordingly went up and washed them. When I came down the lark was all gentleness and quietly ate my flies.

June 28. The lark is a most engaging and interesting little bird, though he has quite got over his ill temper and never pecks; but he still will not eat from my hand if I have got on a different frock.

July 6. My poor little lark is very ill today. He will scarcely either move, eat, or drink, but sits shivering and panting. I suspect the cause is that I gave him a sowthistle yesterday. I very much fear that he will die. If he does we shall miss him very much, for he is a universal pet. By the advice of the "Boy's Own Book" and Mrs. Keal, I gave him a little saffron and licorice in his water, besides three fat spiders which he ate greedily.

July 8. All of us continue to watch with great anxiety the condition of our favorite little lark. All yesterday he continued dull, and pretty much so today. But at six o'clock a decided improvement took place. His appetite had been before returning, but he now began to lift his head and look about him, and he even began to plume, peck and shake himself. Still he had no strength to stand actually up, and whenever he wished to move, toddled along with the help of his wings, though only for a moment. He drinks readily, and once tried to clean his beak, so that I have great hopes of him. Two or three times he crowed.

July 9. The lark continues much the same. While I was cleaning out his cage I put him on the table beside mama, and there he remained some time after, while I was shelling and bruising his hempseed; for Richard, when he went to Potton today, applied to Mr. Telibut, his former master, about him. By his advice, I feed him with a mess of the yolk of an egg, boiled very hard and chopped quite fine, mixed with bread crumbled, and bruised hempseed. He is also to drink toast-and-water the first day, plain water the next, and on the third plain water and saffron. Mr. Telibut attributes his illness to sowthistle.

While I was preparing his food the lark toddled up to observe my proceedings, and shortly after he walked on further still and tumbled himself down into my lap. There he sat quietly for almost half an hour, and greedily ate his food when given him. He retains his rancorous hatred of the goldfinch, for he screamed even when he flew over his cage.

July 11. My lark, though still ill and weak, continues to show his instinct, for he bit Mackworth's finger, which had a bandage on, and tried to pull off some goldbeater's skin from my thumb. He also has tried to fly a little.

July 15. I am delighted to view the improvement in my lark's health. He is quite brisk and lively, and can crow, scream, and bask in the sun as before. He cannot yet, however, fly a long way, nor does he sing, but he will certainly recover. He has now been ill nine days.

July 18. Tuesday evening witnessed the first of those tea-parties under the shade of the ash which had been anticipated ever since December. We indeed spend our whole days in this hot weather out of doors as soon as the morning dew is off.

On all these occasions the lark in his cage is brought out
and sits with us underneath the ash and is most beautifully
interesting and intelligent. He evidently likes company
very much better than solitude, and is constantly chirping
and crowing to bring people about him, still continuing his
love for flies. When people put their mouths to his cage
he kisses them; that is, he lays his beak on their lips, and
even puts it into their mouths.

We had a consultation yesterday as to the safety of al-
lowing him a little run under the ash. It was urged that he
knew us so well that if he did escape, he would certainly
return; that he never flies far in a room at least, but goes
walking about, and here he would be engaged by picking
up insects; that he would conceive himself to be bounded
here as in a room, etc. But the danger of his escaping forever, and the disappointment that would ensue, prevailed.

July 22. The lark grows tamer and tamer every day; he
runs up to people, follows them about the room; he has
even learnt to sit on people's hands and there eat flies. His
manners are so interesting, engaging, and void of fear that
it is impossible not to love him.

July 23. My lark is quite a companion to me now in my
room. He jumps on my hand, walks about the table and on
my desk, examines my pencils, netting and work, and is
as familiar as possible. Today Richard was writing a letter;
the lark placed himself on the paper, and every time the
pen came down he pecked it and curiously examined the
mark it made.

July 25. He has a great deal of curiosity. If anything drops
from the table he hops up to examine it and pulls about

everything he sees. He has also a particular regard for a paint-brush of mine, which he makes a plaything of, tosses about, carries with him, pecks and bites.

July 29. A most sad misfortune has happened. The day before being very hot, we as usual spent it under the weeping ash, and, as is customary with us, took the lark with us in his cage. We allowed him to come out on our knees to eat little crumbs of bread, and as he always popped back again, we apprehended little danger. At length he came out with no object but to ascertain the extent of the weeping ash, and then walked beyond it to the gravel walk.

This looked rather alarming. Papa went in for flies, and I for a piece of bread, to entice him back again. When I returned I held out a crumb to him, expecting him to eat it. Instead of that, he spread his wings and took a prodigious flight over the trees and across the yard. A hue and cry was instantly raised. But everybody expected him back again, and for at least an hour the children good-naturedly employed themselves, under a boiling sun, in toiling over the garden with his cage and looking for him. We spied him several times flying and singing, extremely happy, the first flight he has taken since he was born!

I hope he will not get into dangers abroad. He is very much missed by everybody, but I fear he will not return. I hung his cage out my window to attract him back, and sat up till ten o'clock to watch for him; but alas!—he never came, and I must make up my mind to bear the loss. It is the more disappointing because his tameness was daily increasing. My only consolation is that he will be happier at liberty than in a cage.

A few years later, on July 7, 1839, Emily Shore died at the age of 20. Here are the last entries in her diary:

May 18. On the fourth of April I broke a blood vessel, and am now dying of consumption, in great suffering, and may not live many weeks. God be merciful to me, a sinner. God be praised for giving me such excellent parents. They are more than any wishes could desire or than any words can sufficiently praise. Their presence is like sunshine to my illness.

May 22. My portrait has been taken; they say excellent.

May 27. I feel weaker every morning, and I suppose am beginning to sink; still I can at times take up my pen. I have had my long black hair cut off. Dear papa wears a chain from it. Mama will have one too . . .

On the next page were a few more lines. But the hand, once as clear as print, was now illegible.

Acknowledgments

Barrett, Richard. From unpublished manuscript owned by the Berg Collection of the New York Public Library. Reprinted by special permission.

Clemens, Susy. From *Autobiography of Mark Twain* edited by Charles Neider. Copyright 1917 by the Mark Twain Company. Copyright C 1959 by Charles Neider. Reprinted by permission of Harper & Row, publishers.

Cummings, Bruce Frederick. From *A Last Diary* by Bruce Frederick Cummings, copyright 1920 by Chatto & Windus, Ltd., publishers, reprinted by permission of the publishers.

"Dirk van der Heide." From *My Sister and I* by Dirk van der Heide, copyright 1941 by Harcourt Brace & Company. Reprinted by permission of the owner of all rights, Stanley Young.

Garfield, Mary. From *Mollie Garfield in the White House* by Ruth S. B. Feis, copyright 1963 by Rand McNally & Company, publishers, reprinted by permission of the publishers.

Morris, Walter. From *American in Search of a Way* by Walter Morris, copyright 1942 by the Macmillan Company, publishers. Reprinted by permission of the author.

O'Brien, Margaret. From *My Diary* by Margaret O'Brien. Copyright 1948 by Margaret O'Brien. Published by J. B. Lippincott Company. Reprinted by permission.

Olcott, Euphemia Mason. From unpublished manuscript owned by the New-York Historical Society. Printed by special permission.

Owen, Maggie. From *The Book of Maggie Owen* by Maggie Owen Wadelton, copyright 1941 by the Bobbs Merrill Company, Inc., reprinted by permission of the publishers.

Paxson, Mary Scarborough. From *Mary Paxson Her Book*, published in 1931 by Doubleday & Company, Inc.

Roosevelt, Theodore. Reprinted with the permission of Charles Scribner's Sons from *Theodore Roosevelt's Diaries of Boyhood and Youth*. Copyright 1928 by Charles Scribner's Sons; renewal copyright C 1956.

Spencer, Harriet. From *Lady Bessborough and Her Family Circle* by the (Ninth) Earl of Bessborough in collaboration with A. Aspinwall, copyright 1940. Reprinted by permission of John Murray, publisher, with the consent of the Right Honourable (Tenth) Earl of Bessborough.

Thorne, Samuel. From *The Journal of a Boy's Trip on Horseback* by Samuel Thorne, copyright 1936. Reprinted by permission of Samuel Thorne, grandson of the diarist, who edited the journal, for which his father, the late Samuel Thorne, wrote the foreword.

Tolstoy, Tatyana. From *The Tolstoy Home/Diaries of Tatyana Tolstoy*, copyright 1950 by the Harvill Press Ltd. Reprinted by permission of the publishers.

Whiteley, Opal. From "The Story of Opal Whiteley" published serially by *The Atlantic Monthly*, 1920. Reprinted by permission of *The Atlantic Monthly*.

Bibliography

ALCOTT, Louisa May
   Louisa May Alcott: Her Life, Letters and Journals, Ednah D.
   Cheney, editor (Boston, 1889)
BARRETT, Richard
   Unpublished manuscript, Berg Collection, New York Public
   Library
BASHKIRTSEFF, Marie
   The Journal of a Young Artist (New York, 1889)
BELL, Marilyn
   Unpublished manuscript in possession of the author
BISSELL, Howard T.
   Unpublished manuscript in possession of the author
CLEMENS, Samuel Langhorne
   The Innocents Abroad, Mark Twain (Hartford, 1870) p. 637
CLEMENS, Susy
   Autobiography of Mark Twain, Charles Neider, editor (New
   York, 1959)
CUCA, Marian
   The Diary of Marian Cuca, privately printed (New York,
   1956)

301

CUMMINGS, Bruce Frederick
A Last Diary by W.N.P. Barbellion (pseudonym) (London, 1920)

DIRK VAN DER HEIDE (Pseudonym)
My Sister and I / The Diary of a Dutch Boy Refugee (New York, 1941)

EDWARDS, Esther
Esther Burr's Journal, Jeremiah Eames Rankin, editor (Washington, 1903)

FLEMING, Marjorie
Marjorie Fleming / The Story of Pet Marjorie Together with Her Journals and Letters, Lachlan MacBean (London, 1904)

GARFIELD, Mary
Mollie Garfield in the White House, Ruth S. B. Feis (New York, 1963)

GRETCHEN LAINER (Pseudonym)
Tagebuch Eines Halbwüchsigen Mädchens, Hermine von Hug-Helmuth, editor (Leipzig, 1921)

HAVENS, Catherine Elizabeth
Diary of a Little Girl in Old New York (New York, first edition undated)

HAWTHORNE, Nathaniel
Hawthorne's First Diary, Samuel T. Pickard (Boston, 1897)

HESTER, Sallie
"Sallie Hester: The Diary of a Pioneer Girl," *San Francisco Argonaut*, Vol. 97 (1925) Sept. 19, p. 3; Sept. 25, pp. 3-4; Sept. 26, p. 3; Oct. 3, p. 3; Oct. 10, p. 3; Oct. 17, pp. 3-4; Oct. 24, pp. 3-4

JERNEGAN, Laura
"A Child's Diary on a Whaling Voyage," Marcus Wilson Jernegan, editor, *New England Quarterly*, vol. 2 (January, 1929) pp. 130-139

KOSMODEMYANSKAYA, Zoya
The Story of Zoya and Shura, L. Kosmodemyanskaya (Moscow, 1945)
McNEELY, Sylvia
Diry (New York, 1931)
MORRIS, Walter
American in Search of a Way (New York, 1942)
MUSSER, Benjamin
Diary of a Twelve-Year-Old (Caldwell, Idaho, 1932)
NIN, Anaïs
Diary, *Birth*, Tuli Kupferberg and Sylvia Topp, editors, Issue no. 2 (New York, Summer, 1959) pp. 6-10
O'BRIEN, Margaret
My Diary (Philadelphia, 1948)
OLCOTT, Euphemia Mason
Unpublished manuscript owned by New-York Historical Society, New York City
OWEN, Maggie
The Book of Maggie Owen, Maggie Owen Wadelton (New York, 1941)
PAXSON, Mary Scarborough
Mary Paxson, Her Book (New York, 1931)
RICHARDS, Caroline Cowles
Village Life in America (New York, 1908)
ROBBEN, Susan
Unpublished manuscript in possession of the author
ROOSEVELT, Theodore
Theodore Roosevelt's Diaries of Boyhood and Youth, Mrs. Douglas Robinson, editor (New York, 1928)
SHORE, Margaret Emily
The Journal of Emily Shore (London, 1891)
SHUTE, Henry Augustus
The Real Diary of a Real Boy (Boston, 1902)

SPENCER, Harriet

Lady Bessborough and Her Family Circle, The (Ninth) Earl of Bessborough in collaboration with A. Aspinwall (London, 1940) pp. 18-30

THORNE, Samuel

Journal of a Boy's Trip on Horseback, Samuel Thorne and Samuel Thorne, Jr., editors, privately printed (New York, 1936)

TISHY (Pseudonym)

Diary, *Birth*, Tuli Kupferberg and Sylvia Topp, editors, Issue no. 2 (New York, Summer, 1959) pp. 34-36

TOLSTOY, Tatyana

The Tolstoy Home / Diaries of Tatyana Tolstoy (London, 1950) pp. 1-10

WHITELEY, Opal

"The Story of Opal", *Atlantic Monthly*, vol. 125 (March, 1920) pp. 289-298; (April) pp. 445-455; (May) pp. 639-650; (June) pp. 772-782; vol. 126 (July) pp. 56-65; (August) pp. 201-213

WINSLOW, Anna Green

Diary of Anna Green Winslow, Alice Morse Earle, editor (Boston, 1894)

WORTIS, Emily

Unpublished manuscript in possession of the author

Index of Diarists